CR

THAT MAN IN OUR LIVES

A NOVEL

XU XI

for Bill McGuire

the man in my life

Cover Art "Burning Up" by Eugenia Loli
Interior design by Tiarra Gadsden
Exterior design by C&R Press

Library of Congress Cataloging-in-Publication Data

ISBN: 978-1-936196-53-1
LCCN: 2016930894

C&R Press
Conscious & Responsible
www.crpress.org

CONTENTS

THAT MAN IN OUR LIVES

PRELUDE TO . . .

Let's say it's the 21st century (2005 or maybe 2006) and we're partaking of tea and sympathy when Bino says I'm in love with Gordie. What Bino Realuyo actually says to me is this: *girl, you're too much in love with Gordie.* I blanch—there's white somewhere inside all this yellow, this Meyer lemon yellow. We're floating round the vicinity of the Asian American Writer's Workshop on West 32nd off Sixth in Manhattan's Korea-town. Later though, alone at the blank page, I can't help thinking perhaps he's right, because Bino doesn't lie or undermine. After all, he and I have not trod the tried and true path, the one that allows us the delusion of having somewhat arrived, the one that makes us think we're headed in the right direction. We're always on the edge of things, silently shrieking, *precipice, precipice,* as if the edge is edgier, the edge more in tune with souls in doubt. Tottering around memories of Manila and Hong Kong as we dance to the rhythms of margarita and tripe, two-for-one martinis, the clubs in Chelsea where the gay world plays, and monstrous sushi in our New York City habitats.

When you arrive in America, China becomes merely a thing of the past. Of foreign bodily feeling. Of the blood and guts and gore of centuries. Of peasant heroes you long to revere but cannot because of famine, delusion and other transgressions, leaving you with only monkey kings and whirling white snakes to worship. Of megacities— Hong Kong, Shanghai, even Guangzhou—that gleam with superior mimicry. Slave to all those imperialist fuck-me's that they can't help succumbing to (even you succumb, which Bino knows) because the gleam off that Main River (watch how it swells beyond a stream) is too shiny, too brightly liquid, too irresistible even for us formerly colonized beings who should know better. So you arrive in America because to arrive is to shed the longing for self in favor of the self America confers. Can choose to confer.

Gordie was America, oh so beautiful Americana, all that was *so easy to love, to idolize, all others above* . . . as reverential as this hymn of Cole Porter's. Arrivals. Beauty. Cultural pop. Desires adopted and shed at will in transnational, multicultural mingling, the rednecks be damned to their neck of the woods, away from the cities and coasts. As long as there's leisure, lots of leisure, we play hard because don't we, doesn't everyone, "work" just hard enough—however work is defined and manifest—to earn that play? The penultimate passport. The possibility of the presidency for your new world birthright, even if that is a myth, *but oh what a glorious myth!* Even perhaps a little fame. Money, and in Gordie's case, lots of money, unearned, so that its taint belongs to the previous generation, not him. Not us. What better than to be an American child of wealth and privilege, as all upwardly dreaming parents hope to attain for their offspring, if not for themselves (perverting the cliché that *it skips a generation*)? Right school, right job, right society and if the gods deign to bless you, fame from a financially rewarded/rewardable talent—golfing, modeling, rocket science, *whatever*—it doesn't matter *what* ever, ever, ever it be as long as you attain the lifestyles of the richly famous.

Gordie had all this without even trying, plus the privilege, freedom, and generosity to love the world, China especially. Now for what more should this Hong Kong-China "goil" ask?

I don't mean to make him sound shallow. Even if he isn't all that deep, I'll tell you no lie about the way he was, the way he used to be. He embraced that other America as well, the one the world could love if infected at just the right moment of naïveté, youth, and the desire to inhabit that foreign body, that American self. Music, for instance. Jazz especially. Laughter. Unbridled optimism. Gotta love that *never-say-die* attitude. Hollywood and TV land's power of persistence—go west, east, north, south, or ford streams, climb mountains, stake out the world, conquer the internet—the sheen deflects what corruption lurks beneath. Does corrupt rot lurk? Gordie wouldn't know. These are not questions to ask of one so young, of a nation that has not yet, like China, witnessed four thousand years of history, annoyingly, horrifically, futilely repeated.

So about being in love with Gordie, maybe I am. Gordie got under my skin somehow, stuck himself there and wouldn't go away. Bino tells me this because he can read the signs of sweet delusion, because he, too, sings of friends and lives in poetry and words and more words. Friends do this for each other, warn them, I mean, when life fumbles into fiction, when love sends you off course into that other world. That giant universe. Where that American dreamscape collides with the America of arrival.

What can I say? Bugs Bunny's to blame. Gordie is all about Bugs etcetera, this friend, this 朋友 *peng you* who imitates cartoon voices, who charms his way into your life over and over again, even when you think you're done with him, who does this to you on many continents, in cities from here to eternity and then some. What can you say? You didn't mean for it to happen, to let this man talk his life into your heart, the way he did to Larry Woo and Harold Haight and their extended families and the friends in their lives.

With me, though, he had ulterior motives. *If you asked me, I could write a book.* Whenever I said I'd had enough he would croon a tune, speak low, hum Duke Ellington's "Prelude to a Kiss" till I gave in and promised something, anything, just to shut up his sexy baritone. Gordie's voice. His voice always took me way back to when that foreign bodily feeling first became real. Back when listening to Jim Morrison's siren call—tried to *run / tried to hide / break on through to the other side*—sent me to where my self could be lost forever. An intoxicatingly sensual foreign, urgently propelling me faraway from where I might never return. Gordie's voice was like that, a seductive whisper—*arrival, arrival, arrival.* A one-way ticket to . . . was it always his America? So I shut out the voice that lured me towards such sweet forgetting. Because you know you must return. Must break back through. Must never lose that you of remembering.

But, since the world simply shouldn't forget, *herrrrreeeee's* Gordie.

MARCH 2003

The flight delay from JFK into Tokyo meant that Gordon Marc Ashberry (born Gordon Haddon Ashberry) missed his Hong Kong connection and spent the night, without luggage, at a hotel near Narita, courtesy of Northwest. His travel companion Larry Woo was billeted at a different hotel as a result of alphabetical logic. In the morning, Larry Woo boarded Japan Airlines flight 731 for Hong Kong. He looked out for his long-time friend, the man he met some forty years earlier on board a flight from Hong Kong when Larry was still an eager "foreign student," leaving home for the first time for college in New York. As boarding ended, he listened, concerned, to the announcement that departure would be delayed due to a no-show, because that passenger's baggage had to be offloaded. Procedure in the best of times, but post 9-11, the travel world took fewer chances. Larry flagged the purser, and suggested the airline page Gordie one last time because his friend must be around. "Perhaps he didn't wake up in time," the purser remarked, although she made no attempt either to stop the offload or issue an announcement. Larry sat back, trapped, unable to decide whether or not to disembark. In all the years of their friendship, he had never known Gordie *not* to wake up, Gordie, the man who never slept.

Gordon Ashberry meant to board JL 731. The check-in counter was frantic when he arrived, because some dignitary had lost either his passport or wallet, or so Gordie ascertained from the Putonghua conversations among that Chinese party. Japanese agents were bowing; Chinese faces looked perplexed. Sino-Japanese relations were at their usual impasse, their minimally shared language notwithstanding.

It was, as Chairman Mao might have said, a moment to be seized.

Gordie had been prepared for the past year and a half. In the men's room, he chose a stall at the far end, away from the entrance, to delay discovery. There, he removed from his calfskin travel wallet the driver's license, social security and credit cards of one Marshall Hayden, as well as a U.S. passport that listed his occupation as a jazz singer (baritone) with a work visa for Japan. The passport and wallet of Gordon Marc Ashberry he left in the stall. From his carry on, he pulled out a pair of black Levi's and a gray sweater (never his colors *anytime*), took off his dark olive Armani suit, and effected the change. Shoes! He had not considered shoes, but then he remembered sneakers in a locker from his last trip, two months prior, too-bulky sneakers he had stuck away without further thought. Fortuitous. The locker had not expired and, in what he later considered his most brilliant move, he locked his leather shoes and overcoat in there. For a second, he regretted the coat, a camel cashmere, one he had owned for at least twenty years, purchased at the Peninsula Hotel's shopping arcade in Kowloon. True to form, he did not think either too long or too hard, and folded the coat neatly for airport employees and detectives to puzzle over in the months to come.

Just before heading to the Northwest customer services desk, he discreetly tucked the carry-on containing his suit and shirt between a row of seats. Then, Marshall "Mars" Hayden presented his credit card and identification to purchase a round-trip ticket for Tokyo to Detroit. "It's a family emergency," he explained, his boyish features poignant. "My mother's cancer took a turn for the worse. They say she won't make it. I've had to cancel all my performances." The Japanese woman behind the counter was sympathetic, but mostly, she was charmed by this green-eyed *gaijin* with the Reds baseball cap and sexy smile, who spoke halting Japanese and said he sang jazz (*Kool! She would tell all her jazz club friends, how jealous they'd be!*), this man who was so upset that he at first gave her his U.S. driver's license (State of Ohio) instead of a passport. She glanced at his age, forty-two, *but he looks so much younger.* A willing vagina does many things, not the least of which was that she charged him the cheaper medical emergency fare which, technically, she shouldn't have without proof, but what use was being thirty-something and a "supervisor" if you couldn't occasionally *act* that way? "You're a sweetheart," Gordie-Mars exclaimed, blowing her an air kiss. She blushed pink as a dyed turnip on a sushi platter, and giggled like the schoolgirl she still, at heart, was.

D.O.B. on Gordon M. Ashberry's New York State driver's license was 1948, as the detective noted in his report the next morning. The police did not talk to the Northwest customer services supervisor because there wasn't any reason to. Had they done so, she would have recalled those magical green eyes, which might have tipped them off. She might not have remembered the dirty blond hair peeking out of the baseball cap, but she would have remembered the eyes. Eye color in Marshall Hayden's passport was declared to be gray, and the photograph showed his hair a dark auburn hue. Gordie had hesitated a second as he jammed the cap on his head in the men's room; he had forgotten his kit with the hair dye and gray contacts. So it was a gamble, one of his last.

By the time his calfskin wallet had become "evidence," as had the carry-on (although these two items remained unconnected for months afterwards, almost a year, because Larry Woo could not recall what Gordie was wearing, other than, *oh, I don't know, what he always wears*) Marshall Hayden was long gone.

And that was how Gordon Marc Ashberry disappeared, became invisible, vamoosed once and for all down his rabbit hole, where he could croon like a lounge lizard and mimic Bugs, forever, in peace.

I

FOUR YEARS LATER

To get rich is glorious
Deng Xiaoping

1

In the sky over the harbor, a helicopter hangs. Its blades chop, slice, shear the air, as it hovers, insistently loud, as if the city needs more noise, an even louder soundtrack to its story. Perhaps the pilot, too, is tentative—his brain fried like Pete's—and waits, like some lost bird, for a sign from the severe clear blue.

Hong Kong is hot and Pete Gordon Haight is muddled. Noon on this Saturday in July, 70% relative humidity, is almost "severe clear." In pilot speak, such clarity can be blinding. Pete knows; his godfather, G, taught him that years ago, the first time he took Pete up in the Cessna over Block Island Sound and beyond, east towards the Atlantic. He had been eleven, his heart jumping out of his chest as he peered through his glasses at the disappearing isle below, where his father waited nervously and his mother glowed with pride. *Hey G*, Pete said, *it's like the world's vanishing.* Yeah, Gordie replied, it is P, it is.

But today, he is trying not to think about Gordon Ashberry for a change, and concentrates instead on Tiara Fung, his sweetie, his *fiancée* who is never, ever muddled, who always knows why she does what she does and will make sure he knows as well.

"So," she is saying, "you do like Tempest, don't you? I thought about it a long time."

He holds back, avoids any witticism that will sting. "It's okay, I guess. But what's wrong with Tiara? I liked that name." And, he does not add, he is finally used to calling her that in bed and will not blurt out some wrong name at the worst possible moment, the way he once did back in New Haven when he yelled, "Carmen!" *There's no Carmen, I promise,* he pleaded afterwards, desperate for her to believe he was faithful, which he was. It took months of coaxing before she would trust him again, during which time she did what all doubting girlfriends do: withheld sex just often enough to hurt. In his defense, she had toyed with Carmen as a name and previously went by her Chinese name Suet-fa. What Pete hadn't confessed, however, was that it had all been Bizet's fault. His damn aria was the cell phone ring tone of his hot Taiwanese language tutor—*what* was *her name?*— the phone that went off at all the wrong moments in class, the moments when Pete was imagining those parts of him against all those untouchable parts of her anatomy.

"Tempest is memorable," she says.

"Strange you mean."

"Not so strange."

She follows his eyes up towards the blue, feigning a deep interest in the helicopter that still hangs. They are under the covered walkway outside the Ocean Terminal in Kowloon, sheltered from the glare, their hips against the railing along the pier.

"Hey." He leans in close and slides his finger along her bared midriff. "Tempest Fung Suet-fa is the most gorgeous woman in all of Kowloon." His teeth part her hair and his lips touch the back of her neck.

"Only Kowloon?" She continues gazing upwards.

But he can feel her smile.

Mrs. Fung does not know quite what to make of this polite, perpetually disheveled young man. He seems so unsuitable as a future husband for their youngest child and only girl, their late-in-life baby, although Mr. Fung roundly dismisses her fears. She concedes to his intelligence (a degree from *Yale-O*), and nice features (not perhaps the best-looking Westerner, skinny and small, even shorter than their sons, although of course, their daughter is average height so they're well-matched) because he has an open expression and a thoughtful demeanor. Also, he does speak passable Cantonese, but surprisingly good Mandarin, his accent much better than their own. Classy, like the Beijing elite. A reasonably good family, although his parents are divorced, regrettably. His father is a tax and estates lawyer who used to work for the investment bank Merryweather Lind right here in their Hong Kong office, and he struck her as a nice man, honest and conservative. So maybe Peter will eventually land a proper job, instead of his current state, at twenty-seven, still in school for what Suet-fa says is graduate research in some "Asian studies"—*incomprehensible*—not like business studies, in which both their two sons have degrees and are now well-paid, the eldest running an international ad agency in Shanghai and the second boy at home, a senior VP for a major American bank.

Pete has been staying in their home for a little over a week now since his arrival. Their relatively new home, a private flat in a brand-new building out near the Gold Coast into which they moved five years ago, the purchase and mortgage arranged and paid for by their two sons. It's the first time the Fung family has not lived in public housing. Mr. Fung was reluctant to leave the old neighborhood— *Shek Kip Mei was the first public housing built by the Hong Kong government so it's historical*, he is fond of reminding them—but the estate was old and had to be vacated for preservation and, besides, Mr. Fung is no longer the son of squatters—uneducated immigrants from China— the man who must hoard relentlessly in anticipation of the next disaster, like the Shek Kip Mei fire of 1953 that destroyed his original home, a hut on the hillside, who had to leave school at thirteen to work his parents' butcher stall at the wet market, whose only dreams in life were for the generation to come.

At dinner, Pete eats little from the array of dishes. He tried when he first arrived to explain his vegetarian dietary preference but gave up. Isobel, his mother, who is staunchly vegetarian, had said, *surely it won't be a problem aren't they Buddhist, they're vegetarian, right?* What Mom doesn't understand, even though he's tried to tell her, is that Buddhism here is just life, like her own Catholicism, and not shrouded in the spiritual purity she ascribes to it, and besides, Mr. Fung used to be a butcher after all.

Mrs. Fung frowns at her daughter. *Why doesn't she serve her fiancé*, her eyes demand, but Suet-fa ignores her, as usual.

Mr. Fung declares, "Those two helicopters, bang! Right in mid-air. Imagine that."

"Phoenix, wasn't it? News choppers?" Tempest asks Pete in English.

Her second brother interrupts in Cantonese. "*Wei*, the 'humans' don't understand."

"Shut your mouth!"

Pete catches the 'humans' reference and winces. He is glad that his stay is almost over and that he can move into his own place next week. The Fungs are more than hospitable, especially Mrs. Fung who is once again heaping more food into his bowl than he can possibly eat. But his presence makes things a little tense in their eight hundred square foot, three-bedroom flat, and bunking down in his sleeping bag on the living room floor each night has taken a toll. When he first arrived he headed towards Tiara's—Tempest's—room but she gave him that *what are you, insane?* look and he quickly detoured. The brother did offer—*you can have my room?*—in a voice that said *you fuckin' well better not* and the sofa wouldn't have contained Tempest, never mind him. After the first four days, the brother softened up enough to call him a "Western human," raising his status from that of merely a "ghost guy."

Mr. Fung addresses him in a mix of Cantonese and Mandarin, something he regularly does, because he knows Pete still can't hear Cantonese properly. "Why is it American journalists go so crazy chasing some stupid story?"

Before he can respond, Tempest says. "Come on, Hong Kong journalists are just as bad, aren't they?"

"Am I talking to you?" Her father demands in his deliberate manner. "Besides, local stations don't fly so many helicopters." He looks at Pete expectantly.

Pete clears his throat, stalls for time. "For the pursuit of happiness?"

All the Fungs laugh, even the brother.

Mrs. Fung is relieved. This bantering between husband and kids gives dinner an edge she doesn't always like. By now she ought to be used to this, and in a way, it is a good thing that Peter—*Pete, Pete,* Suet-fa insists, but, honestly, young women are so fussy and the boy answers to Peter anyway—gets to experience their family's ways. Just as well, too, since her daughter is the most argumentative of all her children. Mrs. Fung sucks on a fish bone until it glistens. Instant recall: how she misses her oldest boy, the one who best loved her steamed fish, the one who knows more about food than even his father. He approved of Peter, liked him immediately. Her second son on the other hand, well, he always takes time to warm to anyone. When Suet-fa sent photos back from the U.S. of Peter's home in New

Jersey, taken before the divorce was final and the father still lived there, he had shrugged aside her comment that the Haights must be rich. *Middle class*, he said, *upper middle.* She believed him because he is the smart one, the Stanford MBA who makes shocking amounts of money but contributes much of what he earns to the family, who paid for most of his sister's university education and spends frugally on himself. The worry is that he is too frugal for any wife, which is why, at thirty-seven, he is still unmarried and lives with them, and she is still waiting for grandchildren. As for the oldest boy, well, it's that media and advertising world as her husband says . . . but about all that, her brain simply tunes out, simply will never, ever understand why her son is gay.

Meanwhile, husband and daughter are making loud noises about the meaning of the news. Peter eats so little that she still fears he doesn't like her cooking. *Pete's got no problem*, her husband constantly assures. *If he really wants to marry our daughter, he will adapt to her environment and background.* Her husband is right but still she worries, because Peter stutters when he speaks—Suet-fa says it's nothing, that he's always had a slight stammer but Mrs. Fung thinks there must be something wrong—and he always seems to wait for her daughter to decide about every little thing. What kind of man does that? Furthermore, he's chosen such a strange name for himself—Ha Pak-fu—when everyone can see that the last thing he is, is tiger-like, although, secretly, she suspects he is more tiger-like than he lets on, which is another reason to worry for Suet-fa.

As far as Mrs. Fung is concerned, that's all the news she cares about.

Pete stares at the cornucopia that is tonight's dinner. Steamed fish, beef and green peppers with black bean sauce, sweet sour spare ribs and summer's favorite vegetable dish, water spinach with preserved tofu. Fresh pineapple, peeled and sliced into the thinnest of rings, garnish the pork. Earlier, Tiara-Tempest warned, *you must eat a little of everything tonight otherwise Ma will be offended, she's making this huge meal especially for you.*

Mrs. Fung addresses him, cutting across the conversation clatter between Tempest and her dad. "Right taste for you?"

"Very right." He spits out a fish bone on the table, adding to the pile.

"Here, have more sweet sour."

She spoons the orange sauce over his rice. Tempest works hard to suppress a giggle as Pete raises an accusatory eyebrow at her from across the table. Mr. Fung chomps loudly away, talking noisily about the news reports earlier. *Like predatory birds,* he describes the helicopters. The world is going to hell in some insane hand basket, Pete thinks, as he swallows the sticky sauce and rice, smiling all the while at his future mother-in-law. Tempest is apoplectic. Her lover, she knows, despises sweet and sour.

2

It was not so long ago that life for Pete was crystal clear. Half a year, no, slightly more, the season of Thanksgiving dinners with his family. His father had conceded to Wednesday night at a restaurant so that Mom could do the full-on dinner for the day because his brother and wife would be there, back east from L.A. where Harold Jr., *a.k.a.* Dunderdick II (but only to Pete of course, courtesy of Aunt Patti who christened her brother, their father, the honorable first), now lived with his wife, pregnant with their first child. His brother! Barely thirty and almost a father, imagine.

And there it was, late Tuesday afternoon in New Haven where the campus had already begun to empty. Tiara was freaking over what to wear to the city and no matter how often he said she looked great in everything, she countered with *you're just saying or shut up, please*, neither of which made sense. Pete remained calm. As she tore around their apartment, packing, unpacking, repacking, he watched this typhoon girlfriend negotiate an uncertain path of destruction. It reminded him of his high school days back in Hong Kong when the government issued a signal 3 warning and everyone wondered, will it or won't it intensify, will we or won't we have school tomorrow?

He tried another tack. "Pity Dad didn't want to do Aunt Patti's. That would be some meal what with both my cousins and uncle home this year. She's a fabulous cook."

Tiara glared at him. "You are insane. Like it's not enough that you give me less than a week's notice that we're doing this whole family

Thanksgiving thing, now you want me to meet even *more* family."

"You've met pretty much everyone there. Aunt Patti and her husband Richard, and my uncle John. They were all there that first Thanksgiving you came to, remember?"

"But not your cousins and their wives, well wife of the older one, or Laura."

"Only because she and the Pater man weren't shacking up yet."

"Don't talk about your father like that!"

"Why the hell not?"

"It's not respectful."

He dropped it then, not wanting to start yet another Sino-American conflict. Tiara, he knew, would have been completely at ease with his crazy Kahn cousins and the girls they brought home—well, wife now, for Brandon (what was her name again? Tiara would know, of course, since she had his entire family tree memorized)—but there was no telling her that, not now, not while she couldn't decide between the rose-grey cashmere and silk thing, and whatever the other outfit was. What she didn't know was how little all these appearances mattered to the Kahns, and how his father relaxed around his siblings, especially Patti. How that would have been the easiest family dinner to get through. Never mind, another year. Meanwhile, what Pete wondered was *will she or won't she* and for a minute panicked at the thought of what he would do if she said no. He fingered the ring box in his pocket. Tiara was doing yet another outfit and mirror thing. Now was as good a time as any.

Laura Polk Silverstein spotted it first. From across the table, she glanced at Pete and then at Tiara. "Congratulations in order?"

Harold was frowning at the menu. When he'd agreed to an Italian place for a pre-Thanksgiving Thanksgiving dinner, he hadn't expected Laura to pick something quite so, well, not *nouveau* exactly, but, well, peculiar. He looked up. "What for?"

Her lips smiled-quivered. She laid a hand on his arm and gestured elegantly towards Tiara's hand, on which sparkled a discreet diamond. "Your future daughter-in-law."

The shock on his face was palpable. Pete gripped his fiancée's right hand under the table, willing calm. He was afraid she might start crying, which wouldn't do. "Hey Dad," he said. "One of us had to quit shacking up, right?"

Laura was doing the silent guffaw. Tiara was on her way to a mini stroke. *Speak Dad, quick*, he prayed. *Do it right.*

Harold's thick, dark eyebrows valleyed, connected. He did his two-breath thing, and Pete hoped his father wouldn't start with the word spacing thing, a sign of more than mere discontent. But then his lips twitched, he looked directly at Tiara, and then he rose, went round the table to give her a hug and say *welcome to the family*, and Tiara melted into his father's arms. Pete caught Laura's gaze—those magnificent eyes; who didn't love goddess Laura?—and was finally, now, for the first time in days, truly at ease.

Afterwards, Tiara assailed him. "Why didn't you tell me she was *the* Laura Silverstein. I mean, I've read everything of hers, and everything she recommends on her website booklist."

They were back in the guest room at his mother and Trevor's apartment, overlooking Central Park. "You liked her didn't you?"

"Of course! She's absolutely amazing. Your father's so lucky to be with her. But why didn't you tell me?"

"I said she was this writer."

"You kept saying Polk."

"That's her name. It's what she prefers. She just kept Silverstein after the divorce because of her books. Anyway, you were a hit with her, too. We guys couldn't get a word in edgewise or any-wise."

"Oh, you."

It startled him to see that she was blushing, pleased. There was something so unspeakably charming about her, about this larger-than-life woman who had agreed to be his wife. She unzipped her dress (she went with the rose-grey cashmere and silk), and it softened on her body like butter on a hot griddle. In her pale grey bra and matching thong, she was obscene.

Afterwards, Tiara slept peacefully. Pete lay beside her awhile, running the back of his hand lightly down her side. The tiny waist, cinched as if laced into a whalebone corset of another era. Her physique was counter intuitive, at least for a Chinese girl. *A perfect Monroe hourglass, what a hottie!* His bad Aunt Patti had whispered to him the first time they met. He thought briefly of Colette Woo whom Tiara had yet to meet. Other than the excessive height, Colette—or rather, *Co-Late*, as he'd known her since they were kids—was the slender Chinese beauty, the heavenly spirit figure that graced classical scrolls. His hand stopped at Tiara's waist, and he turned it, elbow out, and cupped the curve of her waistline. *A Scarlett O'Hara waistline*, G's voice from a long time ago. Pete might have been thirteen, maybe fourteen when they were all in Hong Kong, before his mother Isobel and Harold Jr. left them and headed back home to the States. G was at their place, the first one out near the American Club—drinks and dinner probably—and Mom was reaching for something right in G's line of sight and that was when he said, under his breath but just so Pete could hear, *A Scarlett O'Hara waistline your Dad went so goddamned wild for that. Apeshit.*

He got out of bed, his legs buckling slightly from the earlier, orgasmic exertion, and wandered out to the kitchen for water. His mother was up, leaning against the kitchen counter, sipping a glass of clear effervescence. She and her husband hadn't been home when he and Tiara got back, which surprised Pete, but Trevor was big on the social circuit. Tiara had yet to meet him properly, because all they'd managed earlier were brief introductions as both couples passed each other on their way out to their respective evenings.

"Hey. You guys have a good time tonight?" Isobel asked.

"Pretty fair. Food was good."

"How was he?"

"Fine. Looks fit. I think he spends a lot of time at the gym." His mother's thickening waistline bothered him. She tugged at the belt of her kimono when he said that.

"That's good. Was he okay with your engagement?"

"Couldn't be better."

His mother glanced vaguely around the kitchen. Her eyes rested briefly on the refrigerator door. She placed her glass on the counter. "I'm beat. Switch the light off would you when you're done?"

" 'kay Mom. G'night."

Isobel sidled out, and Pete wondered at her furtive manner. She hadn't kissed him. In fact, she hadn't been much like herself, the hundred-and-one questions, *so-tell-me-the-latest*, checking-behind-his-ears Mom. He complimented her earlier that evening, because she did look nice in her Vivienne Tam (*Tiara recognized, whispered, so he said that hoping to impress Mom*), but she barely responded. Although, truthfully, when he recalled it now, he thought the colors of her cocktail dress too rich, the shape too much, and even her makeup more fierce than he was accustomed to. Trevor, of course, was his usual glib self. *Glib.* The thought arrested Pete. Okay, he didn't think much of the guy but if Mom was in love with him who was he to say, but *glib*, this was a first, thinking of Trevor Silverstein this way (*not, thank god, Laura's ex, but her ex brother-in-law which contracted his already too-small world into a clear plastic bag, large enough to suffocate a careless child*).

He picked up his mother's glass and sipped. Sprite. Since when had she begun drinking that crap? His mother drank water, sipped seltzer at most, drank moderately of wine and other spirits, always worried about her waistline. He opened the refrigerator and checked the freezer. Six, count them, *six* pints of Ben & Jerry's ice cream, not even frozen yogurt. Was Mom bingeing or something? He would have to talk to his brother about this. Tomorrow. Another trial.

The turkey was overdone. Not outrageously so, but enough so that his brother turned down seconds. Dunderdick II always took seconds, and Pete, feeling sorry for Mom, held out his plate for more, as did his new sister-in-law, at whom he shot a grateful glance. Tiara looked a question at him but he shrugged it off.

On Trevor's plate, his turkey sat uneaten.

His mother's husband raised a wineglass. "A toast," he said. "To this wonderful family gathering. And to Tiara and Pete, especially." His eyes held Tiara for a minute too long until she blushed. "Congratulations and welcome to the ranks of newlyweds," because he and Isobel were themselves married less than a year.

Harold Jr., red-faced, married a year and paternally poised, added. "Hear, hear."

After-dinner drinks came with coffee, but Pete was feeling bloated, and he turned down a second pour of single malt. *Wow Laphroaig 25*, his brother had exclaimed at the first round, and Trevor had made some inane remark about this Bourbon blended with whisky from sherry casks as being a *marriage made in heaven*. Now, Harold Jr. was going for his third. Tiara was having a good time, a little giddy he suspected from three wines at dinner and her second Frangelica, a first tasting for her of that thickly-sweet, nutty liquor. She and his sister-in-law were laughing at something Trevor was saying. Funny, that, how all the girls always surrounded Trevor. He was some kind of magnet.

His mother was in the bathroom.

"Hey, do you think something's wrong with Mom?" Pete asked his brother.

"Wrong, what? She looks fine to me."

"Like she's gained weight, hasn't she? Looks a little peaked?"

"You're imagining things." Harold Jr. cuffed him lightly on the cheek. "You worry too much, kid. You always have," and then went to join Trevor and the girls.

Tiara was still giddy when the party turned in for the night. She was overdoing the come on, taking his hand and rubbing it against her breasts, plunging it down her neckline, pushing her crotch against his. His fiancée, Pete knew, was a hopeless drunk. Oh she'd get horny and start up but never finish, falling asleep before he could come, sometimes even before he could unzip his cock. He disentangled her from him, helped her off with her clothes, and tucked her in. His mother had put his old, baby-blue bedspread with the one-legged tinder box soldier pattern in their room, and Pete felt strangely protective as he leaned over Tiara. Her eyes were already fluttering shut. He gently kissed her lips which were slightly parted, sensually bee-stung and sweet. She sucked on his upper lip, a tremor, and then she was asleep.

Tonight though, he couldn't sleep. His mother's face at dinner had a vacant glaze, one which cracked into smiles that struck him as fake. Dunderdick II didn't seem to notice a thing, busy as he was yukking it up with Trevor. What did his brother see in the man anyway? Okay, so he had a job in the L.A. office of Trevor's firm, but with his law degree from Austin, he could have gone anywhere and it wasn't as if Trevor had to pull strings or anything with the partners. Also, the older his brother got, the less he looked like Dad, for whom he used to be a dead ringer.

He needed to take a leak and slid out from under the covers, surprised by the timorous nudge of a starting erection. Tiara was sprawled across the bed, the sheet tangled between her legs, naked; he hadn't been able to pull a T-shirt or anything over her limp weight. Her ass was invitingly bare. He resisted the urge to wake her.

In the hallway, a light. Two figures engaged in agitated conversation, propped against the archway to the living room.

Trevor and his sister-in-law.

"Hey," Pete murmured.

Trevor craned his neck towards the ceiling, away from Pete's gaze. His sister-in-law gave a cursory, two-fingered wave. For an instance, Pete thought they started at the sight of him, and the wisp of a notion—*guilty?*—but of what indiscretion he could not say, and by morning he had dismissed all memory of that instance.

Later, much later, when Thanksgiving was well and truly over and his engagement no longer the first topic of conversation, Pete found himself calling his mother more often than usual, sometimes as much as weekly or twice-weekly. She seemed glad to hear from him, but her voice was bland and non-committal, not Mom at all. Who was there to tell? Tiara was back in Hong Kong, impatient for him to get there; his brother was busy making babies and money in L.A.; and the Pater man, the one reliable adult in his life, was in love with a goddess and talking about moving to, *get this*, Rhode Island to shack up with her. Mid February in New Haven, alone, sucked.

The Chinese pig year dawned cold and even Tiara's long-distance phone sex did not cheer him as much as it normally did. Sometimes, he thought about calling Colette, but it wasn't as if she knew his family all that well. But she was his lifeline to G, the man he really wanted to tell, the one who had always been around in his life until one day he wasn't. G would have listened; G would have told some story of his parents from before he was born; G would have reassured him about the unremitting advent of change. And then he might have burst into some corny old tune, or rolled a joint, or taken him flying. Something. The point was, he would have just been G, crazy, unpredictable, the way he always was.

3

They board the MTR. The familiar interior of the subway car excites Pete. He really is back in Hong Kong, he finally knows, and that jagged, unpredictable rush flares up inside. Rampage. That's what this city does, sends a rampage through him. It was what G used to say about the effect of this place. Tempest points to a vacant corner seat by the door. He sits on the chilled metal surface and leans against the clear plastic divider between him and the standing passengers.

Fatigue overpowers. He did not sleep much more than an hour the night before, too wound up by the move. "I feel it now," he says.

"Want to go back?"

"No, I'll be okay. It's a long enough ride. I'll recover."

"Close your eyes," she says. "Rest a bit."

Obediently, he shuts his eyes against the constant light, the glare that prevails 24-7.

In the half-dark, he senses Tempest's hand close to his face and gropes in the air, meaning to kiss it. But he misses, having reached upwards towards his hair which he assumes she is going to smooth. Very gently, she begins to rub his chin. He almost pulls his head away, it feels so weird. How did she learn how to do this? How for that matter has she become like this, somewhere between girlfriend and boss lady but always dominating in a way he hasn't always recognized, since their reunion here after their longest separation?

But her touch is soothing, comforting in a way he's never known. Then, she positions her thumb at the base of his chin, and massages the point just above his Adam's apple in a slow, circular motion. All the fatigue leaves him as energy flows around his head, reviving him. Before he knows it, they have arrived at Sai Wan Ho station at the far eastern end of the island. When he opens his eyes his fiancée is smiling.

Tonight is the first night they will sleep together in his new home. It has been a horny, difficult two weeks, trying to be discreet at Tempest's home, and uncontrollable arousal in public places is just not his thing; also she has been strangely prudish, refusing to go to a love motel, something she never had a problem with before. Yesterday, Pete worried briefly about the Fungs, because there was a long and hurried conversation in Cantonese he couldn't follow properly between Tempest and her parents. He caught the term "sincere" several times and was sure Tempest had been crying in her room that evening, because her eyes looked swollen at dinner. She denied it with a startling vehemence, said, *pollution*, and that some eye drops would relieve them.

This evening, though, now that he's moved in, showered and fresh, out on the town for dinner and a movie at the Film Archives with his best girl, nothing seems amiss. After five years with Tempest—still not used to that name—he knows better than to press her about what might be wrong. Don't ask, won't tell is the measure of their relationship. She'll tell when she's ready. She always does.

In the middle of the movie, a long, drawn out Chinese melodrama from the 1960's that Pete has trouble following but which has Tempest in thrall, his cell vibrates. Short vibe, signaling a text. Shielding the screen with his palm, he reads the message from Colette Woo. Stopping in Hong Kong next week, with her mother, on their way to Taiwan where Mrs. Woo is originally from. Can they meet, she wants to know, he texts back immediately, *when*? And they have a date.

Afterwards, Tempest is pissed about Colette's visit.

"I've told you," Pete pleads. "She's just a long time family friend. There's never been anything between us."

"If that's true why do you two text and email all the time?"

He rolls his eyes. "I've told you, we talk about G. We're both committed to finding him."

"Oh, him again?"

Was she being deliberately dim? He inhaled, counted to five.

"Look, I know you never got to meet him, but besides family, he's the most important person in the world to me. I mean, he is the reason I'm here."

"I thought *I* was the reason . . ." but her voice is subsumed by the roar of a passing plane.

They are dining demi-*al fresco* along the quay at Sai Wan Ho, because it's too hot to really eat outdoors. The air-conditioned blast is noisy but does the trick. It's Wednesday and Pete wants to enjoy these last few days off from any kind of regularly scheduled activity except sex. Next Monday, his intensive Cantonese classes begin, a daily grind of getting tones right; he does want this added fluency to complement his Mandarin, but also needs to justify the Light Fellowship from Yale. Come September he starts work at Lingnan University as a tutor at the English department. All Tempest's doing, of course, although she denies it. He is sure she cajoled Professor Ingham, her former thesis advisor, into sponsoring his Fulbright application ("contemporary Chinese writing in English" is his purported field, something in which Ingham is apparently an expert). Not that he minds her efforts on his behalf, is in fact grateful for this combined financial support from the Fulbright on top of the Light. Between that and what he'll earn as a tutor, which includes a small room at the hostel, it is almost enough to live decently here, without invading his trust fund, the money he wants for a down payment on a home eventually.

Tonight, though, Tempest is acting up. She's sent her wine back, as well as her steak which was too rare, and earlier found the escargot too greasy. Pete has no problem with the food. The movie dragged on till 9:30 and he is so hungry even *goong jai mien*, instant "doll" noodles with its surfeit of MSG, would taste just fine. More for me, he said, when she declared the escargot inedible which only pissed her off further.

Contrasted with his earlier trip at spring break—the first half with Mom and the second with Dad so that they could meet the Fungs—these past two weeks have felt like disaster waiting to happen. Of course, parental visitations meant a suite at the Intercontinental with Mom and his own room at the Conrad with Dad (who had the corporate discount) and invitations on board launches and to private clubs for drinks and dinners, all of which meant Tempest could look like a million dollars every day, and be admired and ogled by his parents' expat crowd who lived here but knew few locals, especially not someone like his girl, so perfectly packaged, educated and enticing. He caught those dirty old glimpses, perving disguised by breeding. It also meant privacy and sexual relief, even if she went home each night. The Fungs seemed won over by Isobel who, Pete had to admit, was pretty charming as mothers went (being without Trevor helped), and Dad was just the Pater man, solid, reliable, pragmatic, financially prudent, all his best qualities on display to enchant the Chinese soul. He even managed to utter *hou gou hing yihng sik neih*, atonally off key enough to make everyone laugh. But the gesture did not go unappreciated.

Meanwhile, Tempest is saying, "And why did you have to arrange to meet her when I'll be at work? Are you embarrassed to introduce me to your family friends or what?"

"Don't be absurd. I didn't know about your schedule change," although privately he wonders what kid would agree to tutoring on a Saturday evening?

"Maybe because you don't listen when I talk?"

"Look, I'll call her and reschedule if you want, but she's doing a really quick visit and her mother has them fully booked with her dad's family, and she flies out Sunday afternoon."

"Oh forget it!"

Later they will fight all night, the worst fight ever since they fell in love, the first great war of their relationship when hitherto it had been merely skirmishes and battles, and then much later, will reconcile, make love, and the heat of a summer's dawn will drench them in waves of sweat because they didn't even stop to turn on the air conditioner. They will swear never to argue again and all the misunderstandings of the past two weeks will have been aired and in the moment, they will mean every single word they say.

Right now, though, Pete twirls pasta around a fork and thinks perhaps Tempest is right, perhaps the food does suck, in which case why the hell are they eating in this restaurant? And why the hell is he in this town where it's too hot, too difficult, too noisy, too everything when all he really wants, right now, is to see G? Already the person he was has begun to fade and Pete wonders, does he still look the same, what would he think of all the changes in our family and the Woo's, would he like Tempest / Tiara / Suet-fa, (he think-imitates his father's word spacing, like a poem)? All he wants is one right minute of his time—catching G was always about right time, right touchdown in between his journeys—one right phone call if that is all he can have to implore: *Come back. Don't leave us. Please?*

Colette Woo is still the babaliciousiest grrrrlllllll Pete's ever laid eyes on, bar none. They do the cheek thing. In her three-inch heels she is over six feet, taller than Pete, and leans forward to match his height, five-eight-and-a-half (*nine*, he tells everyone).

"You look great," he says. She does too, in her short, hip hugging shocking pink and green skirt with that skinny midriff bared. He sees the tattoo, a deliberate scrawl, graphically pleasing, just below her waist. If he dared, he would trace his thumb over it.

"Thanks. So," she drawls, "how does it feel to be back?"

"Complicated."

They walk west, away from the escalator on Staunton towards a bar in SOHO that Colette knows. It's some Italian wine promotion so the pour on Pinot Grigio is large and cheap, exactly what suits.

He takes a long sip of the cold, dry crispness. "How's your Dad?"

"More white hairs. His second book on *South Park* is out. The reviews were pretty good."

It still amuses Pete, the idea that the otherwise serious and staid Dr. Larry Woo spends his life analyzing cartoons. "And your mom?"

"Same. Still trying to marry me off now that Violette's all settled." She means her older sister, the finance professional, the responsible one.

Pete smiles. "Shouldn't be a problem for you, should it?" And gets a scowl in response.

They're on their second drink before the talk turns to G.

"Maybe he doesn't want to be around us anymore," she says.

"Seriously?"

"I mean, why would he just disappear and not say a word to anyone?"

That's when Pete tells her about the detective's report he commissioned, and she listens, her lips set in a hard, sad line. He hasn't mentioned it to a soul for two years, wanting to forget even the possibility of what he'd been told.

"I don't believe it," she declares. "So what've you done since you've arrived here?"

"Give a guy a minute? I mean, I've literally just arrived."

"You've had a week." She checks her watch face, squints at the date.

"More. That's mondo time," and she proceeds to tell him about all the contacts she's made since her arrival three days ago, the people she doesn't really know but has heard of who knew Gordon Ashberry. Pete's mind reels at the familiar names, the ones G goes on about when he's kicked back with a little weed, pulled out the scotch and begun rambling, sometimes all night long. (His Dad would flip if he knew the times he spent with G, especially in the eighteen months or so before he disappeared, often with Colette as well). G's people, Colette says and goes through the list she's compiled: Uncle Jimmy Kho and his daughter Rose who date back to his childhood; Skip Moy a jazz guitarist and sound man; Fa Loong Szeto, his half-sister Gail's mother although she was killed in an accident, remember, Pete says; Rick Hammond, an American journalist formerly with *The Asian Wall Street Journal*, now with some other financial media; Lau Kin-wai, a writer and art critic who owns a couple of *si fohng choi* places—home-style restaurants—and a jazz club; Albert Ho, a wealthy man-about-town; Tang Kwok-po, the CEO of a telecommunications concern and his half-sister's classmate from Harvard; the street artist known as the "King of Kowloon" and a host of others, and these are just the ones in Hong Kong, never mind Macau, Singapore, Bangkok, Jakarta, Taipei, Tokyo, Seoul, Shanghai *et al.* It has sometimes seemed to Pete that his godfather knows everyone west of the Pacific on both sides of the equator.

"Unlike some people," and here Colette glares pointedly at him, "I don't even speak Cantonese. Or know the city."

He pretend-smirks, but knows Colette's Mandarin fluency—virtually mother tongue—does make a difference. "So what did you find out?"

"Some of them are dead, the most recent being Rose Kho. Breast cancer I think her aunt, or some relative of hers I spoke to, said. Oh and that calligraphy graffiti artist, the "King of Kowloon"? He's gone too. It was all over the local media just before we flew out. Most of the others hadn't seen him in years."

"But how did you track all these people. It's not like you know them, or do you?"

She shrugs. "Google, face book, local news archives, even the phone book. You can find pretty much anyone these days if you try hard enough."

Except G. "But what did you tell them?"

"The truth, more or less. Said I was a family friend visiting Hong Kong and that Ashberry told me to look them up. They all send him their regards."

"So they don't know?"

"Guess not."

"Right." He holds up his glass to the bartender and indicates another round.

"Are we getting drunk or something?"

"Why the fuck not?"

"I guess."

In Colette's presence—what has it been, a little over five months since they last met?—he is once again overwhelmed by the whole package that is this older girl he's had a crush on since encountering her at age eleven. That makes her, *shit*, thirty-one now, and she is still the most intense, intelligent, outrageous, and unbelievably amazing woman he knows anywhere on the planet, virtual or otherwise. Her long hair, hacked different lengths, colored pink and green to match her skirt, emits the scent of oranges. Two rings, gun metal rough, pierced through her left eyebrow, and the music whenever she clinks the tongue piercing against her upper teeth. Tinker Bell, resonant as a Buddhist gong. When he stops to consider, she isn't his type at all. Lean and long, hardly any boobs, yet he wonders if it isn't her absolute un-attainability that compels him, as well as her boy-face identity, "Co-Late," on the game website she set up at seventeen, one that's since been in the pages of *The Wall Street Journal* as a successful virtual space that consistently guarantees advertisers the 13 to 31 male audience (middle to upper middle with the most amazing cross-cultural demographic) plus a surprisingly high percentage of females aged 15 to 25 (20% of the customer base, she claims). Even his father is impressed, especially now amidst talk of venture capital and the possibility of an IPO. Co-Late Inc., on the NASDAQ. Imagine. *Consistently late for life*, she told him way back when, a *rage game for losers, like you and me, kid*. Pete has his character (Dragon Boy Fly) on her site, and plays, has played since its inception, and made more money than he's lost over the years.

Yet now, all she is, is just Colette, daughter of the last person he knows to have seen G, the woman he can get drunk with if he wants who will never carp, unlike Tempest. Some five months earlier, her

text that afternoon as the lunar moon smiled on the pig—*Sino chi?*—
like code, and the cloud lifted off his misery, and that night he joined
the Woo's at dinner, a feast for the new year, a salve to the homesick
longing for a world that was and wasn't home, the one his family
would never in a trillion years really understand, no matter how
sincerely they tried. Tempest's world, the Woos' world, and G's.

Three bars later, he is slumped against her on a long bench
somewhere. Like siblings, he thinks, out on a date. He feels the droop
of imbibing; she, on the other hand, seems unfazed, but then she
always could pack it away. "Hey," he says. "You had a bad crush on
him, didn't you?"

She stretches, and her arms trace a wild arc. " 'course I did. What
girl..."

"...wouldn't be in love with Bugs?" He finishes and they both laugh.

"Hey yourself," she says, and her tone implies *since we're being
confessional now,* "when you lived here, did he ever take you, well, you
know?"

His mind snaps to, and it takes a minute or so to comprehend,
and then he stares at her, feels the frisson of horror—not mock
either—and his father's voice *the Chinese are different I don't care what
anyone says* because he knows she means, can only mean, a whore
house. He is 99.99% certain that neither his father nor Colette's dad
would ever have darkened a doorway of said establishment, but G,
well, G wasn't like his two closest male friends, was he?

"So?" She stares right back. "Did he?"

He glances up at the mural above the bar, nudes in a tableau of
Greek mythology that feels peculiarly out of place. "I was kinda young."

"That never stopped him." And then, because he doesn't speak,
she says. "He bought me a gigolo once."

"What?!?"

"It was kinda weird."

"How old were you?"

"Twenty-four."

"The year you started your blog," he says and then hesitates,
almost afraid to ask. "Why did he do that?"

She stretches out her hands, palms down, and gazes at them
for a long while. The manicured but unpolished nails. The rings on
both hands, chunky, metallic. The long, elegant fingers, surreal but

beautiful. Almost like G's hands. "He said," she begins and stops, then forces herself to go on. "He said it was high time I got over virginity."

There is nothing more to say, Pete knows. He takes those hands of hers in his, as if his touch can bless her, as if the pain they share of the man they wish they really knew, the man they think they know, will somehow be ameliorated. He strokes both her pinkies with his thumbs, sliding his palms under hers in a slow, repetitive movement. She leans forward and kisses his lips. Her smile is wicked, drunk. "Before you get married," she says, "let's do it at least once?" He nods, even though there is no real desire, just longing, and together they stumble towards the nearest love nest, somewhere on Stanley, and some time towards dawn when he awakens from his inebriated fog, she is already gone and he isn't sure sex happened, except that his cock hurts something terrible, as if all sensation has been throttled out of it. Meanwhile voice messages have accumulated, as have texts in the inbox, and without looking he knows they are all from the same number, inquiring, demanding, *screaming* finally *where the fuck are you?* And if that detective was right, from some purgatory hiding hole, G is laughing.

4

A man cannot just vanish. Of this much Pete was sure even though he was not sure of much else. G was somewhere. Even his father, Harold the lawyer who wouldn't answer questions regarding G's assets over which he was now legal custodian, the one who cooperated the least with the cops—even Dad acknowledged that *well yes, perhaps this is rather a long time for Mr. Ashberry to be out of touch*, but, as he told Pete privately, *Gord's like that. We shouldn't worry. Not yet.*

Which was why Pete did not tell his father about the private detective, because Harold Bartholomew Haight would have blown a gasket had he known. What puzzled Pete, what he failed completely to understand, was the *laissez-faire* attitude everyone had towards his godfather's disappearance. A man could not just vanish. Pete was perhaps not sure about much, and these days, especially not about his mother, but one thing he felt positively *concrete* about was that a man did not just vanish for no good reason.

It was his second year as a grad student of Chinese Studies at Yale. The other concrete thing was that he didn't know why the hell he was still in school. This too was not something to say to Dad, unlike the news yesterday morning, that his mother and Trevor had called off their wedding *for the third time Dad would you believe it, she's not going to do it, I bet,* he had emailed his father. Meanwhile, his brother, old Dunder Dick II himself *(a.k.a.* Harold Jr.) was finishing up his JD at Austin in the spring. His brother, who didn't tell anyone he was taking the LSAT, and then scored obscenely well, surprising

Dad and vindicating Mom. What minimal respect he once had for his older brother who dared to blow off school, while he obediently aced everything, was undergoing seismic adjustments. Sibling reversal. In Pete's life, the hand basket loomed hugely, more enormous than even the brimstone world it contained.

That morning—some two years before Pete would move back to Hong Kong—was a cool one for early autumn. Private eye Frank Littlejohn delivered his report on Gordon Marc Haddon Ashberry to Pete in New Haven.

"*Nada*," Frank said. "It's all there but bottom line, couldn't find a thing. If he's dead the body's well and truly gone."

Pete scanned through the pages, did not look up. "He's not dead."

"What makes you so sure?"

"I just know he isn't."

Frank's tone softened. "Look, kid, I'm sorry but even if he's not dead, he might as well be because he's done his damnedest not to be found."

"Maybe Dad's right," he said, still staring at the report. "Maybe it is too soon to tell."

They were in a Starbucks where the latte was playing havoc with Frank's stomach. He badly wanted a cigarette.

Pete closed the report and looked up. "So how well did you know him, like when he was my age or younger? You lived in Greenline too, right?"

"As well as anyone from inland G—that's what we called the part of town I grew up in—could know a Haddon."

"But his name's . . ." Pete began.

Frank cut him off. "Not in Greenline."

Later, after Frank took off, Pete tried to imagine this retired NYPD detective as the older boy who used to bully his godfather. Absolutely did not compute. The man was ancient, even older than his dad who was approaching decrepitude. They had met on board an Amtrak to New York four months earlier and fallen into conversation, or rather, Pete never stopped talking once he realized just how connected this Littlejohn was to all that part of his life. One thing to another and Pete heard himself say, *so like what's your hourly rate could you, like, track him for me*, and despite the casual throwaway tone, Littlejohn heard his desperation and told the boy, *don't worry about the money kid let's just say I'll do it for Mark Ashberry, in memoriam*, which startled Pete who had never really thought about G having a father, his godfather not being like anyone else he knew, old or otherwise.

The village of Greenline, situated on the Connecticut coastline, sat on a divide that was Haddon's Way. Named for Mrs. Rosemarie Haddon Ashberry's great grandfather, the road separated those who were Greenline and those who merely worked for it. Littlejohn's late father had been the village police chief and was thus privileged, more than most, to cross the Way and glimpse behind the imposing facades of the mansions along the coast, including at Gordie's home.

At the New Haven station, Frank boarded the train back to the city. It was on schedule and empty. He chose a window seat. Digging around Gordie's life had been strange, and he was sad knowing that the man was most likely dead. People *didn't* disappear. They abandoned families, shucked off responsibilities, embezzled, ran off with lovers. But there would be signs, and at least a hint of a trail, beginning from before the idea to run away had formed: phone records, bank withdrawals, unusual credit card purchases, schedule lapses. His best conjecture, after talking to his buddy in the Tokyo police department, was that Gordie had run into someone and decided not to board the plane, or had been made to leave the airport. Gordie's alleged phone call to his butler was a cover, and even Reginald admitted on further questioning that he wasn't sure it was the "young master," because the line was static-laden. That didn't sound like Detroit, which was from where he supposedly called. More like international. At the Haddon estate, there was only an old fashioned phone with basic service, no caller id or anything. The phone records weren't much use. Reginald used the cheapest calling card for all overseas calls to Gordie, the kind Russian hookers in New York used and Filipino domestics in Asia favored; similarly, Gordie purchased SIM cards at each destination for his GSM cell, hence leaving no trace. And the young master, as Reginald said, almost always used cash.

Frank was six years older than Gordie and from the time he was eleven, Mark Ashberry would often take him flying. When he joined the NYPD after graduating *magna cum laude* from Connecticut State, Mark gave him a sizeable sum, saying, *rent will kill you put this down on a city apartment, son,* which he did and later sold for a capital gain that was fifteen times the purchase price. Frank had been one of the few mourners at Mark Ashberry's funeral in 1968 where Mrs. Haddon-Ashberry completely failed to recognize him, which was just her way. Gordie remembered him, even though it had been years since they'd seen each other. He was like that. The kid was just finishing up at Yale at the time.

In '78, Gordie had asked him to check out Jack Hwang, his mother's alleged lover. Frank refused to take any money and the man reciprocated with a huge Thanksgiving basket and a case of exceptionally good Chianti, *fifty five a bottle*, as Frank's wife learned. She guarded the wine with a parsimony that bordered on certifiable. But there had been nothing on Jack back in '78, just as there had been nothing on Colin Kenton, the Australian ex-business partner who swindled Gordie back in '87, any more than there was anything on Gordie now.

Although he and Gordie hadn't been close as adults, by helping him out over the Kenton business, it was clear to Frank that the man was involved with the wrong world. Something had happened to Gordie in Tokyo, and Frank's suspicion was corroborated by his Japanese detective buddy, who tracked down Gordie's acquaintance among disreputable types. The wallet in the toilet stall had to be a coincidence. Gordie probably dropped it when he went to the john and never knew his identity went missing. Alternatively, if there had been a forcible removal, his abductors might have grabbed him in the john. The fact that no ransom demand surfaced was likely proof of his demise.

What stayed with Frank however, now that the case was more-or-less closed, was just how sad much of Gordie's life seemed to be. The man had been friendly, generous, never a bad word for anyone. A socialite, harmless as a lizard. That's all. How the hell did he get mixed up with the sewer rats? Mark Ashberry's son should have had a better life. When they were boys, Frank thought the kid a sissy, and was quick to lose him. Yet he had never felt worse for Gordie than over that awful Townsend case. Mimi Townsend had been murdered in New York by her fiancé, right in his own precinct, and Frank witnessed details that made his stomach turn worse than any case of his entire career. Her killer was locked away for life with the insane, although if he ruled the world, the man would be dead. *Gordie and Mimi*, now those two could have had a sweet life together,

Frank thought, as he left New Haven that day. Mimi of the large Townsend home with their burst of crocuses in the front yard. On the right side of the Way, albeit not coastal.

That godson of Gordie's though, Pete. Nice kid. Imagine, Gordie with a godson.

But the investigation also stirred up in Frank his own Greenline years and they flooded back as Connecticut flashed past on his ride home. *Old history, wow,* the waves of childhood, his father, long deceased, coming home with "loot" from across Haddon's Way: hunks of baked ham and roasts from the parties and feasts; frozen steaks flown in from Argentina, Australia, Colorado; bottles of hard liquor, many, many bottles of wine and cases of beer; cakes, transported from New York City, specially ordered, which Frank could taste, even now. A surfeit of wealth for the other half. *Don't you remember, remember when?* A long time ago in Paradise.

"Dad." Pete said later that afternoon. "What're you doing here?"

Harold walked into his son's apartment. A pile of empty pizza boxes leaned against the garbage bin. "The place stinks."

"I would have summoned the cleaning squad if you'd given some warning." He kicked dirty underwear and socks from the night before beneath the sofa, but not before his father glimpsed them.

"Didn't you get my message?"

Pete rummaged around his desk for the uncharged cell phone and plugged it in. The screen flashed six messages, one from his father and the other five, he was sure, from Tiara. This was crashingly not the time for a visit from the parental front.

Harold knew the scent of sex. Sentiment swished briefly; his son was no longer a boy. Grabbing the towel that was draped over the back of the sofa, he chucked it at Pete. "Get cleaned up. I'll take us for beers. Dinner too if it suits your schedule. Without the girlfriend though this time if you don't mind."

A town like this would be okay, Harold decided as he drove them, ten minutes later, to his favorite *trattoria.* Last week Laura Silverstein casually remarked that she'd been asked if she might want to move to Rhode Island as the writer-in-residence at a newly formed arts center near Brown. Good money, and a light teaching load she told him, the wine flushing roses to her cheeks. *And you told them?* Trying not to sound too demanding, the idea of her possible departure from New York an unexpected jolt to his system. That she'd think about it because it wasn't for at least another year or two, she replied, adding, *I wonder if it's anything like New Haven, that might be okay, don't you think?*

Harold was in town to attend an alumni association board meeting the next day and had told Pete at least two weeks ago, emailed a reminder the day before yesterday and called in the morning just before lunchtime. Grad school had turned his son into a space cadet, something Isobel, his ex, refused to recognize. Pete wanted dinner, which surprised him, this rail of a boy who hardly ate. Harold didn't know whether to be relieved or concerned as he watched Pete wolf down a porterhouse that evening while he himself slowly digested a seafood salad.

"So," he said after Pete, to his further surprise, ordered dessert, "what do you think of Laura? If things with us got more," he stopped, unable to articulate.

Pete burped quietly, the problem of Tiara the Tempestuous temporarily dulled. He did the Groucho eyebrow thing. "Out with it Pater man, you want to shack up, don't you?"

"Something like that." Harold's eyebrows valleyed into a single dark line across his forehead.

"Have you told Mom?"

"Of course not."

"She'll be furious, you know."

"Yeah."

"Irascible," Pete concluded as his banana split appeared.

What bothered Harold that night when he dropped Pete off, besides the rumor Laura had heard about Trevor ferrying around some super model—he *should* say something to Isobel but how much obligation did he really have to the woman who abandoned him—was his son's confession that he wanted time out. *Don't do anything you'll regret,* he cautioned, *college years are the best ones of your life,* although afterwards he regretted saying that, because it wasn't true, because despite what happened with Isobel and all, raising Pete and Junior were the very best years he wouldn't have traded for anything, even now when there was Laura, who was some kind of witch or—*who would have thought it, at* my *age*—and between her atrociously healthy meals and his gym routine, Harold looked ten years younger and felt it, and from the way women flirted with him these days, he knew it as well. *If only Gord were here to see me now. If only Gord.*

Okay so . . . Pete dropped the cellphone on his desk, *Dad can handle things if I withdraw or take a leave or something.* One year, two, max, he promised Harold by the end of the meal. To go to China, he said, although what he really meant was Hong Kong where, he knew, he could appear to do some research, assuming he could get a Fulbright. No point talking details though, getting the Pater man riled up into an inquisition, until he knew what was what. He needed to figure things out, to shut Tiara up. *To decide.* He had come close, this close to spilling about Littlejohn—the Pater man forced unintended intimacies—but managed to zip it. A good thing, because he hadn't had time to read the report closely. Luckily, Dad never noticed the folder, prominently labeled "Ashberry" which he had quickly shoved under a stack of papers.

His mother, meanwhile, was being a royal, whining pain and he wished his brother would *take over, dude, she'll listen to you.*

His cell played the opening of "Boogie Woogie Bugle Boy From Company B" because Tiara had re-programmed it, again, despite all his entreaties to leave it alone, and there was her number, flashing. *The deadline*, he realized, *it's tomorrow*, the last possible withdrawal date without forfeiting tuition, and his mind raced through the permutations of scheduling life—the trumpets ascended, ascended, descended—and then recalled, *shit*, he was supposed to have met *that girl what's her name* at eight which completely slipped his mind and now it was too late because of the Pater man, *yeah, he did email to remind me he was right.* The instrumental Bugle Boy persisted. There were moments he wanted to, tried to—what's her name was just a harmless flirtation but Tiara would blow a, if she knew—but would he, dare he forfeit the sex with Tiara, even if she did go into unreasonably jealous rages, wrecking his things only to buy him pricier replacements later, sobbing regrets over her temper? Tiara who virtually lived with him even though she kept up the pretense to family and friends that she shared with two other nice (read, virginal) Chinese girls? A pretense she insisted he use with his folks?

The idea, recurrent, of a journey, one he didn't dare articulate even to Tiara, and especially not to Harold who would have blown the whole engine. To find his godfather, as he knew he must, since no one else would. He could imagine G somewhere in Asia, even in Hong Kong, which was the real motive for his desire to relocate. Meanwhile, "Bugle Boy" hadn't ceased, *how's a man supposed to think with all this noise,* not to mention the promise of Tiara in the flesh who, *admit it,* would turn him to mush again if he answered, eradicating entirely those minor lusts. Should he? Would he? What to do, what to do?

"So when do you tell your parents?" Tiara asked early the next morning.

It was almost light. Pete was still collapsed from six, count them, six! His body in shock. A recent *New York Times* article his mother sent detailed the sexual habits of young women who didn't consider oral sex, sex, which they performed in lieu of . . . and this part she circled in blue with the comment, *how things have changed.* The same piece, by a woman probably Mom's age or older, said young women failed to see how exploited they were despite their seeming independence and cool, because they thought they got what they wanted but really didn't, that part he circled in red, and marked *crap!* The way he felt right now was indisputable proof that the young woman in his bed would get exactly whatever it was she wanted.

"Pete, I'm asking a question."

"Give a guy a moment to recover. We're the weaker sex, remember?"

"Pete! This isn't the time for your jokes."

"I wasn't joking."

"You're . . . you're just toying with me!"

He could not suppress the guffaw, and turned it, unconvincingly, into a hacking cough, saying, "got to quit smoking," which only made Tiara madder. "You're mocking me," she said. "You know perfectly well you don't smoke." Her literal-ness, which he found endearing, only made him laugh harder, and he grabbed her wrist tight as she tried to push him away and pulled her down towards him. Any minute now, her face would turn red, and if he didn't do this right, they would be in the midst of another tearful argument. He folded his arms completely around her, fingered through her warm hair with its faint, green tea fragrance, and placed his mouth over her left ear.

"Darling," he whispered. "I love you. And I will come to Hong

Kong, I promise. I just need a little time to think things through so that I know how to arrange it all and convince my parents this will be okay."

He felt her body relax. "But Pete, you know my J-1 expires at the end of the year and I can't get another visa. I can't stand being without you."

"Anyway, Dad already knows I intend to go. I told him."

"When . . .?"

"Yesterday. He was here."

"And you didn't tell me? How dare you! What will he think of me, not even around to say hello?"

It was at moments like these that Pete, usually quite laid back, worried. Tiara's idea of how to deal with family was not how he did things. She had risen and stood naked in the middle of his room, and was fishing around for her underwear. That long-waisted stretch, shaped down towards a V, then rounding out. Irresistible from day one. His cock responded, and for the moment, the worry ceased until the next, undeniable assault on his way of being.

5

A drenching downpour, just as he heads out onto Garden Road. What the fuck possessed him to try to go to *church* of all places? The 10:00 am service at St. Joseph's is in full swing behind him and he isn't there, having arrived too late--the throng of Filipino women astounded him. It wasn't like this when he lived here before. He should have gone home, resumed real life. But an air conditioned room, already paid for, anonymous and quiet in the dead of Central on a Sunday morning when what he needed was a few more hours sleep, how could he resist?

Vibrating pocket. A reminder of his delicate manhood. Two Chinese characters—*morning tea?*— and too late, he remembers that the Fungs are expecting him. His whole being is bi-coastally split. In one world, parents and the Catholic Church (*you a Roman too?* G once said to him which had made him laugh); on this coast now, in the world he thinks he wants to join, the feasting family provides an excuse to inspect, prod, corral the son-in-law-to-be into suitable submission.

He ducks into the doorway of the Helena May, a genteel social club cum old-world residence for mostly foreign women, and quickly texts in English—*sorry, forgot to set alarm make excuse please*—and hits send. He can hear the argument later, her voice shrill, berating him, the *how could you why can't you don't you have any sense of responsibility?* Right now, he should be concocting some plausible story for Tempest. Right now, he should be in the confessional—*for I have sinned*—an adultery, of sorts.

Or was it?

Tempest. Tiara. Suet-fa. Coming home had turned his girl into some kind of shrew.

Pant leg vibrations again and he is tempted to switch his cell off but gives in, checks. Colette at the airport. *Tks fly by d-boy-f x x x C U!* and her signature, the tattoo scrawl.

He should go home. By early afternoon he should be showered, apologetic, sorry with a story about too much to drink which she will believe and, if not forgive, at least not suspect about him and Colette. For one panicked second, he wonders if she's already been to his place—she has a spare key after all—but thinks, no, she still trusts him on that score as well she should since he's never given her reason not to, at least not till now.

But thunder and an unremitting rain. Time that is all his own for one more day. He wants time to himself, away from Tempest and the Fungs, a moment to think about something other than the wedding. *There will be time, there will be time / To prepare a face to meet the faces that you meet.*

Church and remembrance and rain. St. Joseph's being opposite the American Consulate was why Isobel originally found it for the family back in '93. Somewhere in this town is a friend from that past— Marcel—who will not appreciate Pete's too-early-for-a-Sunday call, but who will tell him, nonetheless, *get your ass over here* tout de suite *I'll have the Bloody Mary's ready it's about time you checked in*, salaud! *Bastard.*

Marcel's flat, set back at the far end of Prince's Terrace away from the escalator, is the Hong Kong bachelor's dream pad. A short walk or taxi ride from the only weekend hangouts that matter to the global set. Top floor, one-bedroom, open kitchen, make-out couch and king-sized bed. His buddy has done well. Emerging from the shower, Pete dries off with the thick, man-sized whiteness of the hotel-style towel and slips on a pair of Marcel's shorts. His clothes, meanwhile, are tumbling around in the wash along with the rest of his friend's laundry from his trip.

"I called when I first got back," Pete says, as he sips the strong, dark roast. "Your office said you were in Paris."

Marcel hands him a plate with a hot scone, lathered with butter and raspberry jam. "Visiting the folks. Doing the head office homage. You know the drill. Got back Friday. How the hell are you, anyway?"

Pete bites into the dense, crumbling sweetness. "Better, now."

From the stove top, an aroma of melting butter. Marcel is busy whipping up four eggs. On the counter is an array of chopped tomatoes, spring onions, mushrooms, *jambon* and *fromage*. Soon, a perfectly crimped and folded omelet will slide off the pan. His buddy, Pete thinks, has grown into exactly the kind of guy that was evident in the boy. Marcel, two years older, had been exactly the kind of big brother Pete wanted.

As boys, they did not attend the same school. Pete was at American International, and Marcel, son of the French Trade Commissioner, at French International. They were neighbors though, and even when Pete and Harold moved to a smaller place in town after Isobel split with Harold Jr. and headed back to New Jersey, the two boys hung together constantly. Weekends at the American Club where Harold's firm had a membership or at the Jockey Club where the Trade Commission had theirs; later they trawled the bars at Lan Kwai Fong. After completing his bachelor's in France, Marcel returned to Hong Kong where his folks still lived and joined BNP's Asian regional office, which was where he still worked. Later, an executive MBA at Harvard meant he and Pete got to hang out together on the east coast. Marcel had known G.

He sits opposite Pete at the small dining table and divides the omelet into perfect halves. "So when's the wedding?"

Pete grimaces.

"Cold feet?"

"Not exactly. This isn't one of the better days though."

They eat. Pete wolfs down his food and takes a long sip of his Bloody Mary. The sharp tang of tabsco, horseradish and fresh lime stops him short. "Spicy," he says, fanning his tongue.

"Slow down. You'll get indigestion."

It is always like this: Marcel slows him down in private and speeds him up publicly. Marcel is the sophisticate, the one who gets the girls with his irresistible accent, who fits inside his skin. Pete is still re-sizing, unpicking a seam here, a lining there, still adjusting and adapting the inner wear which he hides under the uniform of universal youth. Yet when the laundry finally tumbles out of the dryer, he can't help but notice the smart designer labels on Marcel's jeans and T-shirts, and considers his own, predictably serviceable Lee or Levi denims, and Giordano or Old Navy T's, all of which Tempest disdains now, although back in the U.S. where love conquered all, fashion hadn't mattered one whit.

This morning though, he and Marcel are being boys again, howling over forgotten teenage pranks, recalling bodies that once fed their lusts, emptying almost half a bottle of bloodied Chopin, his friend's vodka of choice. By early afternoon, Pete's mood is markedly improved. His face feels prepared, readied again to be the fiancé, the man in love and willing to discuss wedding banquets, guest lists, church vs. city hall, there vs. here vs. two ceremonies, even though they agreed (*yes they did, of course they did the night she said yes*), that they wanted a long enough engagement so Pete could get his life in order. Job, mortgage, future. What he knows his mother expects and his father would not want him to marry without. What, he is sure, the Fungs also want.

Before he leaves that day, Marcel says. "We need to get together for dinner, all three of us. My shout. Give Tempest a hug for me."

Pete stops short. "Tempest. How did you know?"

"What do you mean?" Marcel is genuinely puzzled.

"That she changed her name. She's only just done it."

His friend frowns, thinks hard. "You know she called me, right, when she first got back, to fill me in on what you guys were doing?"

Pete nods, waits.

"She must have told me then." He pauses, his mind scrambling, RAM-remembering. "Oh yes, I know, she said she was feeling, how did she put it, 'Shakespeare-inclined' and wanted a new name. So I said the first play that came to mind, the one you and I acted in, remember? We did a bit part in that community drama group, what was its name again?"

But Pete's mind is speeding, shooting off in ten different directions, the way it used to whenever he and Marcel were out together, two guys journeying. *He suggested that stupid name and she listened to him?* Now he wonders, and did they meet during those long months when he, hornier than a toad, stayed faithful to her? He looks into his friend's eyes, but they are bland, unrevealing. He never could tell, cannot tell with Marcel because they don't talk female intimacies, except for the out-in-the-open, predatory posturing, Marcel being the kiss-but-never-tell type. Only intimacies about family, work, being The Man. About G.

Marcel is unfazed and two-cheeks Pete. "Take it easy, pal. Call me when engaged life gets too much, you know? It's like *Monsieur G* used to say. *Goils. They're always the same. Way too much for any man.*

And what would Dad have said if he had known, back then, how often G bought them rounds, drinking with him and Marcel till three or four in the morning? At strip clubs and all-Chinese joints, not just the hang of the expatriate young, confined to the party slope at the Fong. It hadn't been about the booze or even the women. It was G's access, one that fascinated two foreign teenage boys, watching this older man slot into life here as if he belonged, speaking Cantonese and Mandarin like a native. Pete discusses G endlessly with Marcel, much the way he does with Colette. Speculating, imagining, desiring to fill the hole that is G, the man who could be Yosemite Sam, Pepe le Pew, JFK, Richard Nixon, Edward G. Robinson or John Malkovich, mimicking voices and identities, just like that. Pete sometimes thinks his father doesn't know the range of articulation that is G, because all the Pater man recalls is, *Bugs Bunny, he'd answer the professor in Bugs' voice and the class would break up*, as if that was all G could do.

Pete is riding the West Rail, the long commute back to his room at the university. He has finally spoken to Tempest, who grudgingly admits she's too busy to come over till Tuesday anyway, and that her parents didn't really mind his not being there today. He is relieved. The whole episode with Colette weighs on him. *Bless me father . . . six years since my last.* This is not a sin: disloyalty to a fiancée is not adultery.

The train emerges out of the underground into the open. Pete likes the KCR which feels to him like the real train it once used to be, even if it is virtually an extension of the subway system, the MTR, into which it will soon be swallowed. He marvels at the open vistas of green, all that empty, undeveloped space along the western corridor of the New Territories, but which is, as Tempest assures him, rapidly transforming like the rest of the city. This isn't the Hong Kong he once knew. Not that he didn't see the countryside of exclusive private clubs, but until now, he never knew how much locals also lived and played amid the unfettered rural landscape, the walks along country paths and parks, the public beaches where people continued to swim despite uncontrolled algae, red tide, raw sewage, civilization's detritus. He still doesn't quite believe he lives out this way, at least an hour's train ride from the city at what is, essentially, the city's rural university.

Lingnan University, a post-modern, Sino-art-deco campus on Castle Peak Road, is the smallest and youngest institute of tertiary education, and the last choice of secondary school graduates who cannot get a place at the older, esteemed institutes, especially the University of Hong Kong. Tempest, though, is fiercely proud of her *alma mater*, one she willingly chose even though her exam scores could have easily gotten her into any local university of her choice. *Our English graduates speak just as good if not better English than the ones from HKU and aren't nearly as stuck up. Besides*, and this part always makes Pete laugh, *over on that side, they still haven't gotten past the 19th century, and Hong Kong might as well still be a colony.*

When they first met, she was in her last year of her Bachelor's and, learning that Pete was at Yale, declared she would have to go there then, wouldn't she? Pete had been dubious, wondering how she thought she could get into Yale, just like that. Even his brother hadn't, despite Harold's alumni loyalty, and their father refused to pull strings much to Isobel's chagrin, because he believed everyone deserved what they got and besides, Harold Jr. goofed off, wasted his intelligence and privilege, and it was some time before he redeemed himself.

So when Tiara-Tempest sat for her GRE's, Pete said nothing and hoped for the best.

Perfect scores, all through, *how was that even possible?* It flummoxed him, as did the scholarship she won, the accolades her professors routinely heaped on her, the distinguished publications and collaborations she managed even as a first year grad student. *You're some kind of genius*, he told her but she just smiled modestly, said, *it's nothing, no big deal. Just words and ideas, they don't mean much really.* But what he wanted to know was why she hadn't gone for a Bachelor's at a more prestigious university, Oxford or an Ivy, perhaps, since, both her brothers had gone to college abroad? That was his world, the way he understood how things needed to be. For the longest time, she was evasive, dismissing his question as if it did not bear consideration, until he gave up pressing her. Yet now, here, the far less distinguished scholar, he finally understood. This was her world. She couldn't leave family, home, the embrace of upbringing and culture. Which is why he is sobering up on a Sunday afternoon, speeding his way out to Lingnan, horrified at his disloyalty to her. *Situational ethics*, the last thing he recalls Colette saying before she slipped off her panties, and then it was all over.

By Tuesday, life is on a new track and he can't imagine ever being without Tempest. By Tuesday, he has deleted the random recall: himself at sixteen, catching sight of his father's face when G told him, *sorry, pal, but you needed to know about Trevor,* his father's recognition that Isobel, the woman he still loves, will leave him, that their separation would be permanent, and not because she didn't like living in Hong Kong. It had been late on a weekday night. Pete heard them in the living room and had come out of his room but stopped, remained in the corridor as he comprehended what G was saying. That his mother in New York was cheating on his father. Harold's face—*first chill, then stupor, then the letting go*—and the howl of agony that followed was something Pete could never forget.

Fung Wing-gaau's Interlude

Hold on, I'm wanted again, awakened from my little life just as it was rounded with sleep, luxuriating in the stuff of dreams. It's 0400 hours somewhere, and the blank page beckons because it's just that time. An interlude, it appears, is inserting its musical nose into things. Someone else demanding space.

At first I thought it was Tiara-Tempest, given the Shakespearean echo. It wasn't her, though, but her brother instead. Her much older eldest brother, the family's lost boy according to Mrs. Fung, the one Pete wishes was around more because Wing-gaau, unlike Wing-haau who lives at home, actually seems to like him.

When Wing-gaau called, out of the blue, it must have been at least five, actually six years since we'd last seen each other. He was on a prolonged business trip in Hong Kong, and wouldn't be returning to Taipei for at least two more weeks. *Of course I'll meet you for dinner,* I told him, *name the place.*

"The agency is relocating me to Shanghai," he says after we do the global, two-cheek thing of friends and friendly acquaintances. "It'll be their new regional office."

I smile. "Let's see. Your dad's mad, your mother's pragmatically reasonable, and Wing-haau shrugs at the inevitable." I don't include Tempest-Tiara-Suet-fa in the Fung family equation, I realize later, but then she is so much younger than he—twenty years—and is more like a distant cousin than his sister. Taiwan vs. China does not compute for her generation.

He laughs. "That's pretty much it."

I am arrested by, as I am each time I see him, how much he is indeed a handsome composition. In fact, all the Fungs are gorgeous southern Chinese, unconscious of their good looks and natural physicality. He's made for kung fu, with a muscular subtlety that isn't all lumpy six pack. But he's no jock, no earnest beauty mouthing rehearsed platitudes about team spirit for the camera; instead he's a vulture with sensual eyes, eyes that make him look deeper, more cultured and intriguing than he really is, the man who knows when to keep his mouth shut and just be. Think Bruce Lee crossed with Tony Leung Chiu-wai. Wing-gaau is my favorite gay Cantonese friend, the kind of man who could almost turn me into a fag hag.

Wing-gaau has led us to Kin's Kitchen, a "home cooking" Cantonese restaurant in Tin Hau, hidden on Fresh Wind Lane. That's the Chinese street name, not the English one which is unromantically, and un-readably, transliterated. We are close to Victoria Park and the harbor where sea breezes still flutter as they did once— not-so-long-ago, mid 20th century, say—before reclamation, high rises and highways. The food he assures me will be brilliant and as usual, he is not wrong, never wrong when it comes to cuisine or wine. It is just another reason a girl wants to strangle him for his "bent."

Halfway through the third course I ask. "How's your sister doing?"

He shakes his head, impatient. "Project Runway."

"You should talk," because he's nothing if not a clothes horse.

"Yes, but I don't make my boyfriend spend everything he earns dressing me up, never mind all the fancy places she insists on going to. She should watch it. It's no wonder Pete's started on his 'quest to find G' again."

My eyebrows rise involuntarily. "Oh really?" It's been at least two years since Pete moved to Hong Kong, and I was pretty sure he'd let all that go. I mean, you can't beat a dead horse forever, can you?

"Suet-fa's furious at him. Although that girl's always furious at something."

"Takes after her brother, I guess."

He gives me his slit-eyed glare. "Don't you start."

It still amuses me that the Fungs gave birth to this one. He could be the changeling, the switched-at-birth error, the foundling on the doorstep. Even though Tempest-Tiara-Suet-fa acts out her "I'm not part of this family" routine, she's such a Fung through and through. Diligent, disciplined, directed. Always gets what she wants, including Pete. The poor guy never stood a chance with her, that much is clear. Wing-gaau is strictly a go-with-the-flow man, despite his occasional temperamental outbursts.

But then something I've been dying to ask him since Tempest-Tiara-Suet-fa first got together with Pete Haight. "So does she know about you and," and here I even use air quotes, " 'G'?"

His look could wither cactus in summer. "How long have you known me? Are you insane?"

After dinner, we walk the park and talk. It's early November and the air is finally tolerable. I tell him about the rabbit holes of Norwich, which I saw in early summer. *A hillside of holes. Like nothing I've ever seen.* What I'm thinking, of course, is Paradise for Bugs and Gordie.

"So even you are occasionally surprised?"

I link my arm through his and slap his hand. "I'm not that jaded." Then. "I've missed you. Why haven't you been in touch?"

"Where's G?"

His question startles me, especially the angry tone. This is too abrupt given his long absence from my life. "What do you mean?"

"Quit hedging."

"I'm not. I know about as much as," I pause, unwilling to let him trap me. "As much as Pete does."

"That's, excuse me, bullshit."

I delink my arm, but he catches my hand, picks it up in a playful swing, and starts singing a Cantonese children's song to the melody of "London Bridge is Falling Down," about the bird that falls in the water. We don't say much to each other after that, and when we part that evening, it occurs to me that in recent years I've seen much more of Tempest (partly thanks to Pete) than him. That's even true for his brother Wing-haau whom I don't know nearly as well. Why is it we allow the important ones in our lives to get away from us and fritter time away instead on those who do not know, who cannot know, who will never know the inner workings of our hearts?

That was last year. Afterwards, he didn't text or email, didn't even send his new Shanghai contact information. I know through mutual friends that he likes it there, that he has a new boyfriend, a Shanghainese shoe designer. Wing-gaau, I catch myself whispering from time to time, where did *you* go? Or are you, like Gordie, deserting me too?

The Cantonese "London Bridge" song repeats in my head, about what must be a suicidal bird.

Yauh jek jeukjai ditlohk seui, ditlohk seui, ditlohk seui.
Yauh jek jeukjai ditlohk seui,
Bei seui jamsei. 給水浸 死.
The bird that fell in the water? It drowned.

***

The previous time we met, I was visiting Taipei. We were walking the *Meishuguan*, because I hadn't yet been to the modern art museum and Wing-gaau was the best possible person to accompany me there. Taiwan was abuzz at the time about the death of Madame Chiang Kai-shek who finally expired at 105.

Her longevity, however, was not uppermost on Wing-gaau's mind. But Gordie was. He told me he had taken him to Propaganda, Hong Kong's first, unapologetically gay bar, only the week before. Not the original bar, Wing-gaau emphasized, but the second one, hidden in a lane, the way a gay bar ought to be to feel authentic.

I considered this last assertion which seemed oddly conservative. "Did he say why he wanted to go?"

"You know the way he is. Always after the untried and new."

That did not compute because I knew perfectly well that Gordie frequented Propaganda and other gay bars in Hong Kong and elsewhere on a regular basis. I didn't respond and was about to change the subject but Wing-gaau had more to say.

"What I don't get," he said, "is that Gordie is the straightest arrow I know. I mean, even someone with the worst gaydar would be unlikely to hit on him. So why?"

We rounded a corner and came upon a curious installation, watery calligraphy in a light box structure that was reminiscent of Escher. "Look at that. Isn't that something?" I exclaimed and began to walk around it.

"Derivative. Don't change the subject. What's up with Gordie?"

"What's up doc?"

"You're being evasive."

"No I'm not. I don't have any idea why."

"I don't believe you."

When I think about Wing-gaau now, I wonder if that moment was the turning point for us, when he started to ease me out of his life. Even when we think we know another's heart, we rarely can be completely sure. Perhaps it was important to him that the man he once had a crush on ought to be gay, or that he did not fully believe Gordie was straight. I didn't believe then, or now, that Wing-gaau *didn't* know Gordie incited desire in numerous gay men.

Besides "gay" and "straight" are silly labels. Aren't we all a bit of both? Don't we all find those of the opposite and our own gender attractive? And who ever said our lives with others is ever only just about sex? Not I, that's for sure.

But I digress. When I think about that moment now, it makes me shudder that I was so insensitive in what I next said to him, pretending it was just a joke.

"Oh you know Gordie. It's all about Bugs who was, if not gay, transvestite wouldn't you say?" I was thinking of all those Bugs-in-drag moments, batting lashes at Elmer Fudd so that he'd tumble, stumble or otherwise fumble.

So maybe it is my fault that Wing-gaau no longer calls. When he didn't send his new Shanghai contact, as much as I hated to admit it, I knew he was dropping me off his radar forever.

***

A long time ago, long before the hand basket loomed, Wing-gaau and I exchanged a very long, very passionate kiss. Just a kiss, nothing else. Surprisingly, no alcohol was involved, although there was much tea.

To put this in the right context, I must explain about Taiwan tea.

Under certain circumstances there are few hours in life more agreeable than the hour dedicated to the ceremony known as afternoon tea. There are circumstances in which, whether you partake of the tea or not—some people of course never do—the situation is in itself delightful.

Henry James knew less about tea than he thought, despite this magnificent pair of sentences, this almost-couplet, so Chinese. His ladies knew even less, despite the oft times delightful situations in which they found themselves. Wing-gaau and I were in just such a delightful situation that late spring afternoon in a tea house. The only missing romantic trope was an August moon.

1995. He had just moved to Taipei a couple of months earlier, right after lunar new year. More significantly, he had also just come out, finally, to his family. We, meaning all his closest friends, had known for some time, but it meant a lot to us that he had done this. He was thirty-five, I a few years older.

He had asked me to visit, to stay with him, in fact, in his studio apartment. His was a high bed, an old Chinese style one with wood planks covered with a bamboo mat instead of a mattress, and he had insisted I sleep there while he bunked on the floor in his sleeping bag. "You're my *ga je*," he insisted when I arrived, because he called me "elder sister" and had since we first met. "It's my duty as your *di di* to surrender all comforts to you." I demurred but there was no getting around his insistence.

We went to a tea house. It was in a quiet alley hidden behind a main drag right in the middle of the city. If you closed your eyes and let your mind wander, you could shut out the sounds of scooters and car horns tangling in the streets of Taipei. The dust and exhaust and exhaustion vanished as we ascended the stairs and seated ourselves on the floor by the window.

He repeated himself in disbelief. "You've really never done this?"

"Never."

"Then let me be your first."

It is not only the ritual of brewing and steeping, the patient wait for perfect tea. Nor is it the ceremonial arc of the pour, from a long spout, that the seasoned hand deftly manipulates. Reclining on cushions on the floor, next to each other, all this contributes to the romance of course, but it is the conversation between friends— no, not just friends, we were intimates then—between two people who trust each other with secrets and more, with the most painful revelations of their lives. I already had an inkling that something was wrong with Gordie by then and said as much to Wing-gaau. He listened, understood, even held my hand as I tried not to cry.

"He's been with me for so long," I said. "I can't stand watching this strange decline. I don't understand it."

"Perhaps it's just a phase?"

"I don't think so."

He delicately, diplomatically steered us to another course, about names, his and his brother's. "Forever Fung and Filial Fung." He had switched to English to declare this before resuming the conversation in our usual Cantonese. "My parents may not have been the most literate, but at least they had an unintentional sense of humor."

His tactic worked and I started to laugh, which made me feel better. "Didn't you ever have an English name?" Many in his business, advertising, did.

"Back in school, Teacher Cheung gave me one for English class. It was dumb and I dumped it as soon as I graduated from secondary. In the States, I just used my Chinese name." He winked at me. "All my lovers thought it was cute."

We sat and drank as the afternoon light slanted across our space. Before we knew it, three hours had passed. He was telling me a story about some client which was making me laugh so hard I almost peed myself. In the charged, rambunctious moment of communion, we fell into each other, he put out both hands to steady me—one landed on my left shoulder, the other on my waist—and then his arms circled around and he clasped his hands for a moment against my back, like a lover's embrace, and then he said, "I've never kissed a woman."

I hadn't pulled away, had in fact leaned a little closer. "Not even in school?"

"I didn't date girls. Ever. They terrified me even when I was little."

He was looking at me with those eyes, not demanding, not insisting, not anything. Just looking. My position was awkward. He had leaned back against the corner, one arm propped on the window sill and I, in the aisle position, was half leaning on the pillow against the wall behind my back, half tilted towards him, my leg stretched out under the table against his.

"In fact, you were the first girl I asked out."

He was joking, naturally, because when we met he told me he was gay right off the bat and then said, *but I'd still like to take you out,* which was how our friendship began.

From some layered mist, Gordie's face and his merged. Could a girl in her right mind resist? I leaned forward and held his face in both hands, he did not pull back, we kissed but did not otherwise feel each other up for at least a minute and a half, if not two. I'm a good kisser, I'm told, but he was brilliant.

The thing about tea, it's a diuretic. When we surfaced, we raced each other to the one and only unisex john.

6

When Pete's uncle John calls the last week of August, to say he'll be in town in a couple of days and let's grab drinks and dinner, Tempest is ecstatic. Of all his relatives, she is most comfortable with John, who used to live and work in Hong Kong, who is now resident in Singapore running his firm's practice there. John only dates Asian women.

Sunday night is nice for meeting up in Central, Tempest says, because the weekend avalanche is over. Pete is not so sure as they negotiate a path through the Filipino villages and dialects—staked out in their respective street corners or intersections, stretches of pedestrian bridges, archways beneath overpasses, doorways of silent office buildings where security does not hold sufficient sway to chase them away—marking territory on their day off, reminding this Chinese world that they are their own tribe, unchangeable, replete with their own foods, languages, ways of being, erupting once a week in a necessary relief from indentured servitude. He feels like an intruder, disturbing humanity's borrowed space.

Tempest, though, does not seem to notice, is comfortable in this overwhelming outdoor gathering, and smiles occasionally, waves at some of the women, tosses out a line of Tagalog in greeting. His fiancée is like no other woman he knows.

John is at the Four Seasons, the six-star tower floating above what was once water. His invitation is to one of the most expensive French restaurants in the mall next door. Pete hates eating in malls. He misses the street level restaurants of New York or New Haven, the human dimension spaces of what has begun to feel like a very distant past. All this glitz and glamour his uncle is so comfortable in, that Tempest seems increasingly at home in, feels foreign.

"You look fabulous," John says to Tempest after he hugs her. "And I love Tempest. Great name."

Pete takes in his uncle's Armani shirt and slacks, the Bally loafers. His father's younger brother is nothing if not a clothes horse, so unlike Aunt Patti and Dad.

"And you," he hugs Pete. "When are you getting a real job?"

"You mean like you John? Pimping for the Asian mafia?"

"Such hostility. It must be all that liberal university thinking you're immersed in."

John is always just John, more like an older cousin than an uncle. He has spent most of his professional life in Asia, but pretends not to speak a single Asian language (even though he is fluent in three), never eats Asian food by choice, and only holidays in Europe or back home in the U.S.. Which is why, G once told Pete, Asian women love John, because he releases them out of their world. At forty-six, however, John is still a bachelor and likely to remain one, to the dismay of his long string of girlfriends.

John is asking Tempest about her work at the business research institute where she monitors and summarizes economic news for reports to the finance sector. This job of hers baffles Pete. The long hours, okay but not great pay, the complete abandonment of her academic path in literature, in which he once believed she would get a PhD and become a scholar and professor. Instead she picks up private tutoring to make extra cash.

"You should be at an investment bank, like J.P. Morgan," John is saying. "You'll go much further there. And have you thought about an MBA?"

Tempest nods. "Absolutely. UST would be good."

"That it would." John agrees.

Pete is stunned. *Since when . . .* ? The University of Science & Technology, Hong Kong's top MBA program, is a far cry from Yale's English department, or Lingnan's. But he doesn't want to question her in front of John. Besides, his uncle is already ordering glasses of champagne—*just as an aperitif*—and Tempest's delighted murmur, accompanied by a quick squeeze of his thigh, distracts him.

"Hey," John says a few minutes later, holding aloft his glass of bubbly, "to wedded bliss, right?"

Tempest's face breaks into such an enormous smile and Pete

thinks, *John is winning hearts and minds for the Haights.*

The work of ordering a fancy French dinner clatters around their conversation and Pete wonders what his uncle wants. They don't often meet, a couple of times when Pete first met Tiara and flew out to Hong Kong every chance he got, when John still lived here. But with the family, he seldom saw John after his parents' divorce and family gatherings were bifurcated, re-invented, except at the odd Thanksgiving dinner at Aunt Patti's.

"So Pete, besides marrying this gorgeous lady, what *are* you doing with your life here?"

At least John never calls him "kid." "Did Dad ask you to find out?"

"Something like that." He grins, and gives Pete what he thinks of as the evil Haight look, the one John and Aunt Patti share, the one his father doesn't.

"I came to find Gordon." He hears himself say this, unable to stop himself. The champagne has gone to his head; he drank it too fast on an empty stomach. He can feel Tempest groaning mentally beside him.

"You serious?"

"He can't just disappear."

"I see."

John goes quiet. The escargots appear and they turn their attention to the *maitre d'* and his spiel. Tempest, Pete notes, does not complain about too much grease, even though the critters are swimming in melted butter. Tempest, he realizes, is in ecstasy at having arrived.

Later as they give thanks and say their goodbyes, Pete thinks he will live to regret this dinner. John pulls him aside, becomes avuncular for a second. "Look Pete, I don't know how to say this because I like Gordon and all. You know he's nothing like your Dad though, right, even though they're best buddies?" He glances away at the long, white corridor, the one that leads back to his hotel. "Don't take this wrong, okay? But you really shouldn't waste your time over this. Get on with your life. You've got a terrific lady there."

Tempest is strangely calm that night as they ride the train back. She even suggests going to his place, and when he wonders aloud, *won't it be too late when you get home,* she places her hand on the back of his neck, tugs him gently towards her and kisses him on the lips. "I'll stay the night," she says. "My parents will just have to get used to it."

It's like before, the ease, her playful manner, the kind of foreplay he thought had ended. She is not intoxicated, despite the champagne and wine and the multi-course cuisine. It's the six-star booze and grub, Pete decides, because he is sated but not bloated, buzzed but not drunk. There is a pleasant, unhurried tenor to their lovemaking, and when they come together, it is the communion of skins. *The communion of sinners.*

They stay awake afterwards for over an hour. Long silences, broken by the occasional embrace. She sits up, thoughtful. "Do you have a picture of him?"

"Who?"

"G, of course. That man in your life?"

It's the first time she's expressed any real interest and it dawns on him that he's never had a proper photo of his godfather, despite all the years of family gatherings with his parents, at Aunt Patti's, even at the Elf Boot as G called his palatial manor home in Greenline, or out on Block Island at the Haddon summer home to which they sometimes went along with the Woos. When Littlejohn had asked for a recent photo, Pete ransacked through his boxes of prints and was surprised to find nothing. G was half in several shots, but there was no frontal shot, not even a good profile. How could that be, he wondered at the time. Now, he tells Tempest about the photo of his confirmation, when G first became his godfather, and how that photo got messed up because the camera fell into a fountain and destroyed all record of himself in that silly white monkey suit, thank god. He retells the story of G, about his giving away his wealth, about the book and his own unwitting part in it, the essay he wrote after G told him his plan. His words that Chinese journalist found and turned into a public fiasco. He never forgave himself for posting that stupid piece on the internet—*so naïve, thinking the web his own private space*—even though G said it wasn't his fault.

For the first time, Tempest listens, and he knows she is finally hearing him, acknowledging the importance of G in his life, not because she isn't as important, but because G is like a part of him, logged into his DNA, and to pretend otherwise would be false, would be worse than beginning his life with her based on a lie, worse than even an indiscretion with another woman—Colette is the first and last—something about which he will remain forever silent.

7

If not for G, he would never have met his wife-to-be.

It was summertime, almost exactly five years ago, right after he'd graduated from college. The present he wanted, which neither parent would give him, was a holiday in Hong Kong and his godfather, without even being prompted, handed him a first class ticket, five-star hotel expenses covered for a three-week stay, and a spending allowance. Harold frowned, Isobel wavered; she initially wanted Pete to return the gift but gave in when she saw how over the moon he was. A godfather had some obligations, she reasoned, even though reason told otherwise. Besides, by then his parents were already splitting the nucleus that once was family and their authority diminished, allowing Pete to ignore them.

Marcel met him at the airport from where they rode the limo back together to the Peninsula Hotel. "You," he said, "are the luckiest geek on earth. Even my parents never got to stay at the Pen!" Marcel was just beginning his career at BNP then.

"He gave me two thousand to blow. That's how he put it."

"Hong Kong dollars?"

"No, jerkoff. Real dollars."

"Hey. I get paid in local currency. It's real."

"Never mind that. You going to help me blow this?"

Pete was on a high from the flight and the two of them hit the party zone an hour later. By one the next morning, Lan Kwai Fong was still ablaze. He picked up his seventh vodka shot for the night, raised it to his lips between two fingers when Tiara walked in, alone, and scanned the room, obviously looking for someone.

Marcel followed his eyes. "Whoa."

Pete tossed back his drink in one gulp. "I saw her first," and made his way towards the siren's shore.

She had walked into the bar that night, alone, against all better instincts, because she had to know if Cara, her best friend, was there with Alan Ho, her boyfriend. Her almost ex-boyfriend. They weren't, and her first sense of relief was quickly surpassed by shame, that she should be so suspicious and unfair, especially since she was on her way to breaking up with Alan. When Pete stumbled towards her, his foot caught on a bar stool and he staggered a little before straightening up, she was alarmed, afraid he was drunk and about to throw up. Not on her new shoes! She stepped aside, but his body did a funny curve as it followed her movement until he stopped abruptly, said, "You're Mary's friend, aren't you," echoing what G once taught him as the least threatening pick up line to use, *because everyone has a friend named Mary.*

He was holding an empty shot glass, which he then stared at, blinked, looked around distractedly before motioning the glass in Marcel's direction, "Care to join us for a drink?"

She glanced at Marcel – not bad – and then stepped back, away from Pete. "I don't know anyone named Mary, and even if I did, she doesn't know you."

Marcel was heading in their direction and she flashed him the briefest of smiles.

"Hey," he said when he arrived. "My friend here being rude?"

Pete glared at him. "Don't pay attention to Pepe Le Pew here," and then, catching himself, "oh sorry, you probably don't know who . . ."

"You lie, and you condescend. Two strikes."

Marcel burst out laughing. "Three and maybe I'm in?"

"So," she said, looking from Marcel to Pete and back again. "I guess my friends aren't here tonight."

"Yes they are," said Pete, and signaled a waitress for three more shots.

Later, when he recalled that night, it was her hair, a thick and abundant coal black crown around her face, that his eyes were drawn to. Cleavage, yes, but that came next as he told Marcel, because you don't perv on boobs in public, however irresistible. Definitely the hair, and lips, because Tiara-Tempest's features were all about that mouth, naturally bee stung without botox. Juicy, they were, and how the first time he kissed her, he couldn't get enough of those lips.

Four weeks later, Pete confessed to Tiara that he had never succeeded with a girl in a bar like he did the night they met.

"Never? What made you try so hard?"

"You know why. Marcel of course. There was no way I was going to let you go with him. Why did you give me your number and not him?"

"Probably to shut you up. You were babbling."

They were in bed in the bedroom at Marcel's flat, late on a Sunday morning. By now, Pete was overstaying his welcome, although Marcel kept saying it was okay, no problem, and cheerfully bunked on the couch. The problem was, he had postponed telling Tiara that he really had to leave and now, with his departure only two days away, he was still postponing.

"I'll shut you up." He slid his teeth across her upper lip.

A rap on the door. "Guys, I'm out of here."

"Okay," they chorused.

"Oh and Pete, there's a message on the voicemail from Northwest. About your flight Tuesday."

Pete blanched.

She waited till the front door shut before turning on him. "You better have a good explanation!"

"Suet-fa, *ni jidao wo . . .*"

"Don't you pull that Putonghua love call crap. Were you just going to leave and not tell me?"

"Of course not. But you know I have to get back in time for fall semester."

"You said you weren't sure about grad school, that you might get a job here, like Marcel, that . . ." And she burst into tears.

She was sitting cross legged, naked on the bed, sobbing. Pete was trying hard not to freak, because he had never been in the presence of a naked, sobbing woman before, especially not when he was naked himself, and doing his utmost to calm the erection that was forcing forth its unseemly head. He knelt beside her, jamming his thighs firmly together.

"Of course I was going to tell you. I want you to come see me in the

States. To meet my family." He blurted out the last part, surprising himself with the truth of that emotion.

She calmed, stared at him, silent for a long two minutes, almost enough time for an egg to be served. "And how do you suppose I'll get a visa?" It was Alan all over again, heading off to medical school in Iowa of all places—she actually had to look at a map to find it—saying she could come visit. Her ex boyfriend was a returned ABC, one who had spent the better part of his life in the U.S., and as Hong Kong as he eventually became, he still didn't get how visas weren't exactly plucked from trees by non-Americans. This was worse, though. Here she was incurring parental wrath by staying out overnight on weekends—if they knew he was a *gwailo!*— and coming home late almost every night. But Pete made her insatiable, embarrassingly so, and she couldn't bear the idea of living without his touch. Perhaps this was just about sex, but why then was she so obsessed with him, with the whole package that was him? She was such a fool, destined for humiliation! And she turned her face away from him and began to cry again.

Pete suddenly knew there was only one thing to say. He re-positioned himself into the correct kneeling posture, took both her hands in his. "Marry me?"

She stopped crying and stared at him, horrified. "But . . ."

"It doesn't have to be right now."

"You're crazy!"

It was her smile, an uncertain quiver between ecstasy and shame, that did it. Pete flew back to the U.S. with his entire life mapped out, or at least, the next three or four years, more or less. He was going to tell G, planned to visit and thank him for the life-altering trip. He was becoming G, the man who fell head over heels in love and proposed marriage over and over again, the difference being, Pete knew, or at least at the moment he thought he knew, that he would stay in love forever. Perhaps that was how G used to feel too, Pete thinks now that life has proven the fidelity of his emotions to Tempest. The school term begins, he tutors, home seems more and more like where he is right now and not over there. When Mom calls because it's a holiday, he forgets for a moment about Labor Day, thinking, *it's too early for Mid Autumn festival, isn't it?* Even when Tiara finally confirms that she's decided about doing her MBA at UST, *and that if he loves her this time he can stay in her country instead of making her squat in his*, he acquiesces, figures he can work something out, even consults John who is only too pleased to get his nephew started somewhere in his Asian network, pleased that his brother Harold's favorite son is no longer a space cadet, is becoming responsible and readied for marriage.

The world feels less like a hand basket these days as the future solidifies, what with Tempest calmer, secure in the knowledge that Pete loves her, will not leave her at the altar so to speak, the thing that most mortifies her and has done ever since he told her about G doing that to his first fiancée, the Chinese woman, Shih her name was she thinks. She's never confided this fear to Pete, refuses to give it voice because he won't understand, will dismiss it and then she'll feel like such a fool. As the year draws to an end along with Pete's story, Pete occasionally feels a guilty shudder when he remembers G. Not because he's resigning himself to G's absence, even though he is, but because, as he tells Colette, *he wanted to disappear the choice was his.* Yet the one nagging thing that he doesn't share with anyone, not even Colette, is that he never did go see G, or thank him for the gift of meeting Tempest, and then G was gone, just like that. What he doesn't know how to say is that he let G go long before the actual disappearance because he (and for that matter everyone else, Pete believes) didn't bother to really know him, to know who he was, too enamored as he and they all were of what G did to them, for them, because of them. That ignorance is the real sin he should confess but in the crush of living, the thought is too ephemeral to stay put, and besides, absolution is well beyond its use-by date, along with remorse and penance, lost somewhere in that hell of forgetting.

II

LARRY WOO: BIG BROTHER

Nixon: *Let us join hands, make peace for once.*
            History is our mother, we
            Best do her honor in this way.

Mao: *History is a dirty sow:*
            If we by chance escape her maw
            She overlies us.

Nixon: *That's true, sure,*
            And yet we still must seize the hour
            And seize the day.

from ***Nixon in China*** Act I Scene 2
music by **John Adams** · libretto by **Alice Goodman**
premiered Houston, Texas October 22, 1987

Earlier, before March 2003

"It's *not* my fault."

The computer says this whenever Larry Woo sends off an erroneous command. A woman's voice, or something like a woman's. *It's not*, pause, *my fault.* The pause is important, emphasizing negation. Americans are emphatic about what they're not.

Larry Woo is an American. He wasn't always one, but while in grad school, his girlfriend with the green card swore allegiance and dropped bombs, not hints, about marriage. As Anita Li was the only woman with a doctorate he could imagine spending his life with in America, things worked out. Plus she was pregnant and they did want children. However she, and consequently their two girls, are more comfortable than he in their American skins. Anita's family immigrated—aged sixteen when she arrived—while Larry's will never leave Hong Kong. The Li's are from Taiwan. They are, or were, Kuomingtang loyalists, connected to Chiang Kai-Shek & Co., more than Larry would like.

These conversations with the computer are necessary because he is trying to write a book about what Hui Guo (*a.k.a.* Gordie) did. Mainly to set the record straight. These are the things you do for a friend. Besides, a university press is interested, strictly from a cultural studies standpoint, and, as a pop-culture sociologist, he has some insights.

"You should be writing about Sino-American relations," Anita had said when he told her of the press' interest. "China is the most compelling growing concern."

What his wife said in Chinese was "our two nations' relations" although of course he knew perfectly well what she meant. "You write it. You're the political scientist."

"Who said anything about politics? I'm talking *relations*. You know all about those."

His last paper, delivered at a university in Taipei a month earlier, was titled "Cross Straits Relations: A Chinese-American Perspective." The university president was Anita's childhood friend, and his wife, now on "permanent domestic sabbatical," basically wanted to take Colette, their younger daughter, for an ancestral home visit which is how he got roped into being a speaker, all expenses for self and spouse paid. His wife is nothing if not pragmatic.

He shot back. "Like I really know so much about that?"

"And you know so much about philanthropy?" She persisted.

"I know Hui Guo, and that stupid book by Zhang Lianhe makes me so mad I could, oh, I don't know."

"*Wei*, calm down. You know she's just an opportunist. Not necessary to 'explode a bomb.' Think of your stomach."

His ulcer acted up, tap danced, took a bow. He placed an arm around Anita's shoulder and kissed her cheek. "As usual, you're right."

Now, it dawns on him that Hui Guo *is* Sino-American, which is not the same as being Chinese-American, which is what Larry is, or not, depending on your perspective.

From Larry Woo's Computer Files:
Notes for book 1.1 (May 7, 2001)

I first met Lianhe in Hong Kong's Mandarin Hotel lobby on a warm-ish April day. She was with an American man. I would encounter her often with American men—photographers, journalists, critics, sinologists, the occasional writer. She seemed to need their company.

At the time we met, back in '96, I was the visiting Lingnan scholar at Baptist University, a useful way of being filial to aging parents without sacrificing my position at NYU, and Anita *loved* affording domestic help. Lianhe claimed to be twenty-four, in transit to New York where, she claimed, she had been accepted at NYU and Columbia as a grad student in journalism. It was a long transit. For the next year and a half, I would catch sight of her around Hong Kong, where she maintained an equally long "internship," variously at *Time, The Asian Wall Street Journal* and CNBC. It was not clear to me what she actually did, although she was on payroll at least at CNBC. My primary school friend who is head of Accounting there confirmed this. When she finally arrived in New York, she was still twenty-four.

I am getting ahead of myself. It's too soon to introduce Lianhe, who is after all less important than Gordon Ashberry—Gordie—my protagonist. Son of Mark and Rosemarie Ashberry of Greenline, Connecticut. Rosemarie, née Haddon. The Haddons were landed gentry while the Ashberrys, well, the Ashberrys merely made money, from buttons (Berry Buttons™, now defunct), and smart property and stock investments.

But this story begins in 1998 when Mark and Rosemarie are dead and Gordie is fifty. A man at fifty is many things, but invisible he's not, not if he is as wealthy and good looking and as continually eligible a bachelor as Gordon Ashberry. Gordie, who'd rather be invisible.

Protagonist. *Is* he a protagonist or merely the subject of my research? Am I writing a defense, an accusation, or, as my editor believes, about "a cultural phenomena that has repercussions for the new century"?

Perhaps I should ask Anita's friend Laura Silverstein for advice. She teaches at that low-res MFA writing program and says I tell good stories. Only how do you tell of a man who is plagued by *Honey Money*, the book by Minnie Chang, *a.k.a.* Zhang Lianhe (Impermanent Press, North Park, Vermont, Spring 2000). Okay, Lianhe's a little bitch, but that is a catchy title for a book. You have to hand it to those Mainlanders, *especially* the Beijing babes like her. They're smarter than we "civilized" Chinese like to admit, being the new barbarians that they are. But *Minnie?*

***

Several hours later, Larry looks up from his computer. Anita is standing in the doorway of his office, waiting.

"Maybe it should be a biography," he says.

His wife makes a sound like a duck being strangled. "You *really* think Gordie will let you *fong wen* him after everything that's happened?"

He contemplates the idea of "interviewing" his friend. "But this is different. He can trust me."

"Oh, so he *knows* you're writing this book."

"This is early draft stage. Too soon to tell him."

"Then get Laura to read it. She'll do it if I ask."

"I'd be embarrassed. I mean, she's a *real* writer. I'm just an academic."

"Oh, then this isn't a *real* book?"

"Don't know what it is. It's not like anything I've ever written."

"Which is why you get a real writer to give an opinion. Do you know how many people would kill to have *Laura Silverstein*'s opinion?"

He makes a face like a lone sheep, separated from its flock. "Not exactly."

"My point, exactly," she concludes, in English.

They have gotten into the habit of finishing conversations in English. Larry has long supposed this inevitable. It was part of the process to ensure their daughters' native fluency, without his and Anita's accents, and over the years, the family's language slid into a new tongue. Anita complains that his Mandarin sounds Anglo now; previously, she said it was too Cantonese. Not *Guo Yu*, he counters, whenever she uses the Taiwanese term, meaning "nation's language," and names Putonghua, meaning "common tongue" or China's official *pinyin* term for national Chinese, replacing the Englishman's "Mandarin." It's mean of him, but he can't resist the dig, because she never deigned to learn *his* Chinese, and because even though she claims to be objective about politics, as befits a social scientist, Anita can't help bristling at the idea of what China is, of what China has become, shunting Taiwan aside.

Sino-*Chinese* relations, that's what he'd rather write about. If you're from the Mainland, Beijing or even Shanghai these days, you're Sino, the fact of Chinese-ness being a given. All the rest, Hong Kong, Taiwan, American- and other hyphenations, or, as his two daughters are so fond of saying in unison, *Daaaaadddd, wha da?* are merely Chinese.

From Larry Woo's Computer Files: Notes for Book 1.2 (sometime in June, 2001, but after June 4 and those Tiananmen memories that haunt the collective consciousness of some Chinese)

I met Gordie on board a Pan Am flight in the summer of '66. It was my first time on a plane and I was scared. Not that I'd admit this to my parents, since it had taken the entire three years at Chinese U while finishing my B.A. to convince them to let me go study in the States. Luckily, they respected Frank Carter, my American professor who helped me get a fellowship at NYU.

I was staring out the window, trying to wave to my family who had monopolized one corner of Kai Tak's raised outdoor lookout, trying to fight the nausea and trepidation, when Gordie crashed into the seat next to mine. He was complaining to the air hostess, an older woman with a beehive so stiffly sprayed you could balance an egg on its crest.

"But Dad flies for Pacific American. I *always* ride up front."

"Perhaps on Pacific," she smiled. "Not with us." Her tone was condescending and final. It was one of the few times I ever witnessed Gordie failing to charm a woman.

"Goddammit," he muttered as she walked away.

We stared at each other. What with my unease, the newness of everything, I blurted out what, in retrospect, was a pretty odd question. "Are you American?"

"Why?" he snapped.

"Because I need to make some American friends."

He looked at me like I was nuts, but something made me barrel right on. "Do you live in New York?"

"Sometimes."

"And do you listen to jazz?"

He cracked a smile and my stomach began to settle. "Yeah," he said. "Do you?"

That was how our friendship began. He was eighteen, headed to Yale as a freshman and I was twenty one, a virgin, and a jazz head. You understand, of course, how weird this made me back home, the jazz part I mean. My family didn't understand that, anymore than they understood my desire to major in American Studies, having completed a BA in a mish mash of languages and modern Chinese history. My oldest brother entered government after reading philosophy at Hong Kong U (he was the smart one), my second brother helped run the family fish business, and my sister became a primary school music teacher. With three respectable siblings, one weird child my parents could almost tolerate. Besides, being the baby, as my sister says even now, I get away with suicide, if not murder.

Of course, we did not talk of this during the flight, but of everything else under the stars.

About an hour before landing—we hadn't slept at all, having talked continuously about all the jazz and life that mattered—Gordie showed me his newly coined Chinese name, and said he was going to major in Chinese.

"Kinda strange, isn't it?" I said.

"You sound like my mother. She thinks I'm crazy to study Chinese."

"Not that, I meant your name. *Ya Gao-daan* is synthetically phonetic in Mandarin, but sounds terrible in Cantonese."

"My dad's buddy, Jimmy Kho, gave it to me. He speaks better Cantonese than Mandarin, I think. But I'm not sure."

I frowned. "I don't mean to insult your father's friend, but frankly, *Aa Go-tan*, the Cantonese pronunciation, sounds Japanese. Besides, the characters mean Mr. High Beach. That's absurd."

Gordie laughed. "So can you give me another name? I gotta have a Chinese name, right?"

I ruminated a moment. Then, I wrote two characters. 灰果

"*Hui Guo*," he repeated after me. "What do they mean?"

"The first character is 'ash' although it can also mean the color gray. So that's appropriate because it's the first syllable of your name, and your eyes are gray."

"Hazel," Gordie corrected, "according to Mother. That's almost like a gray, but they're green, according to my license."

"Okay, that works more or less. So *hui* or *fui* in Cantonese. Then, *guo* or *gwo* means fruit, but is also like the genus for berry, I think. But the *sound* is like the first syllable of your Christian name. It's also almost a homonym for 'nation' which elevates its possibilities."

Being young, I was impressed by my own brilliance and pleased that Gordie seemed taken by what I said, because he listened attentively. This was long before anyone was forced to listen to me, before I taught and lectured sleepy undergrads.

I continued. "That fulfills both criteria of a properly constructed name for a foreigner. It resembles the sound of your origins, yet also has a relevant Chinese identity and meaning. The art of naming in Chinese is a balance of beauty and meaning."

He nodded slowly. "But that's only two characters. I thought Chinese names were always three, like the one Uncle Jimmy gave me."

"No, many use two, and some even have four. We're negotiable."

"Ash Fruit," Gordie said. "I like that."

Laura Silverstein looks up from skimming Larry's print out. She is fast, having flipped through thirty manuscript pages before the tea can go cold. "This is a good start."

"I don't know," he replies. "It sounds too much like a novel or something."

She smiles. "Is that so bad?"

Laura writes slim novels about family intimacies that are critically acclaimed as "elegant." Anita and the girls rave about her books, and she is the reason his younger daughter wants to write. Larry doesn't read novels as a rule. It's a failing, he knows, especially in a home full of intelligent women and their friends.

"I feel like I should write a factual account of who he is."

She flicks her thumb slowly across the edge of her mouth, knuckles pressed against her chin. It's the same habit he has whenever he's thinking and he decides it means Laura and he must be connected, a reason he probably finally succumbed to seeking her advice. Over the course of several conversations, he's talked far more than he's written. This is the first time he's shown her anything.

Finally. "Larry, why are you really writing this?"

"Because." He stops and looks at her hair. It is an intense mass, honey chestnut, long, thick curls. Her pale complexion reminds him of Gordie's. "Because I miss him. He's become almost like a recluse. Even Harold barely gets in to see him and he's the best friend." The almost best man, he recalls, startled by a brief twinge of jealousy over this remembrance of life past. Very brief.

"You invest a great deal of yourself in him, don't you?"

He considers the way she phrases the question. "It's like family, like the care you take of family, assuming you're lucky enough to have one. There are very few people you meet in life like that. Know what I mean?"

"Yes," she says. And then. "Facts alone won't do the trick, I'm afraid."

A little later, but still well before March, 2003

"What about Stella Shih?" Anita asks in English. "I'm sure she'd talk about Gordie."

"What's she got to do with my book?" Larry demands. They haven't seen Stella in a while now that Anita's less interested in the world of politics that once so engaged her.

"Husband," she says in disgust, in Chinese, "sometimes your brilliance astounds me," and disappears to go shopping.

Since retiring from professional life, Anita shops. It's as if she's entered a new world where time and money can be spent on frivolities. Larry, surprisingly, quite likes this. His wife always was a serious academic and, later in her career, a competent and dedicated administrator. As the former director of the Institute of Sino-Pacific Studies, she haunted conferences and networks with a zeal that was viral. Publicly, he brags of her achievements which far overshadow his own, but these days, when she shows him a cleverly wrought brooch, or an elegant scarf, or a book about house plants—bought for herself and not their daughters—the delight in her voice almost moves him to tears.

The shopping is partly his fault, he's sure. He was always the less serious one, ready to put aside work for a party, dinner at a new restaurant, a visit to friends or relatives. The *frivolous* one, Anita accused when overworked or stretched to her limits. His dissertation had been on jazz in cartoons, a subject his parents never believed was real, convinced for years he was teasing. Although Anita never said anything, he's always suspected even she found his studies somewhat less than admirable. Yet, as he reminds her now, *he* has no desire to retire, while she couldn't wait to quit work. Not that he minds, because their sex life has improved since her retirement, almost frighteningly so because his wife's passions feel like a regression to their early, post-virginal sex. Anita says it's the advantage of menopause; she complains, often, that Americans focus far too much on the *disadvantages* of aging, although both their daughters and Larry hope she'll find another topic of conversation soon. If there's anything remotely American about Larry, it's his belief that work *must* be play, because it's certainly not Chinese, well, not the kind of Chinese he and Anita were raised to be.

But Stella! An intellectual heavyweight, despite her slight frame. An advisor to senators and presidents on U.S.-Sino relations who, surprisingly, speaks in favor of the People's Republic despite her Kuomingtang family heritage—military—an even weightier and more burdensome one than Anita's. Stella pursued the path Anita could have but didn't. Anita's no lightweight, hardly, but her professional involvement always was secondary, one notch below the big girls and boys, engrossed as she was in motherhood (she says this often for all to hear) and even with being a wife, which, naturally, she will not say except in private to Larry, because that confers a right to call him *lao kung*, "old man," the Chinese slang for husband, uttered in that paradox of disgust and love.

From Larry Woo's Computer Files: Notes for Book 1.3 September 10, 2001, before a date became history and life was more or less normal in the collective consciousness of most Americans

Gordie got engaged to Stella when he was twenty. The day he announced this to me, by phone, I told him he was way too young. She was his Chinese tutor and one of Anita's close friends.

He protested. "Why? It's not like we're going to get married right away."

"Oh, so she's *not* pregnant."

"Good grief, of course not. *Ah Go,* she's *Chinese,* What on earth made you think that?"

Gordie called me "big brother," about which I had mixed feelings. It was flattering, but it also meant I wasn't a buddy, the way Harold was. Back then, the age difference was not apparent to me. What I couldn't admit to him, and in retrospect I'm not entirely sure why, was that Anita and I were as rabid in our passions then as the butterfly lovers of Chinese mythology.

I cast around for further objections. "Your mother will never approve."

"My father does," he said, triumphantly.

"She's *met* them."

He was offended. "Of course. What's the matter with you today?"

That morning, Anita's period was late, again. We used condoms religiously because she refused to take the pill, claiming she couldn't swallow tablets.

"And you've met her parents?"

"Not yet." He hesitated and added quickly, "but they'll be here for the wedding. So when will you and Anita announce . . . ?"

"Don't change the subject. You can't fool *Ah Go.* Hui Guo, why are you doing this?"

"You're as bad as Harold! Why won't anyone believe I love her?" And he hung up on me. Gordie didn't slam phones, or anything, not even back then when he showed his temper and impatience more readily. It was a quality that was endearing.

This was all our fault, mine and Anita's I mean. Well, mine really. Gordie wanted to meet Chinese girls, to practice speaking he said, so I invited him along to the NYU Chinese student parties. Gordie was a hit, naturally, because he was tall and good looking, but mostly because as the Taiwan girls said, he had *lei mou*, or as the Hong Kong girls said, because he was *see mun*. Back in the sixties, there were no China chicks. What girls never understood was that anyone speaking a foreign tongue *always* sounds polite because the formal language is all they ever learn.

During my first year in the U.S., *life* was a constant party. In spring, there was this Hong Kong chick who was attracted to me—*porcelain*, Anita says—even though I wasn't interested in her. Anita insists otherwise and recounts my bad taste to our daughters, saying I chased the porcelain miss. I eventually stopped contradicting her. All I know is by that summer, I was "going out" with Anita and Stella, who was Anita's grad school classmate, and Gordie would "conveniently" show up to make a fourth. I had *no idea* anything was happening with those two for real, since she was older than him by at least three or four years, a big deal when you're that young. I assumed it was all for show, the standard Chinese girlfriend chaperone routine, and that Gordie was playing along.

I know this sounds terribly convoluted in American, especially for the sixties when rampant lusts and conscientious freedoms were *de rigueur*. But we were trying to do the proper Chinese thing, which meant not "acting like Americans" as far as our families were concerned, until we couldn't take virginity any longer and succumbed. As for Gordie being with Stella, well, that was *only* because he needed language tutoring. *Guess Who's Coming to Dinner* was not about people like us.

Anita calls me convoluted in any culture because she thought them perfectly matched. Anita seduced me, after all, even though she never admits it, approaching sexual relations with the same determination she brings to the study of political chaos. Says they're the same thing, because power comes to those who either claim or inherit it. But Anita doesn't claim power. What she does is get rid of the opposition so that power is no longer an issue. I, on the other hand, inherited power, being 1) male 2) the youngest child 3) an immigrant by marriage and 4) Chinese, in that order. This, you understand, is the world according to Anita which is pretty much the one that rules in this version of my life.

In retrospect, she might have been right about convolution, although in my defense, Gordie's mis-match when it came to Stella was the one subject about which Harold and I concurred, and were, as it turned out, entirely correct.

***

"So what happened?" Laura asks after reading.

"He did the worst possible thing. Left her at the altar, literally, well, at the garden party. They were doing religious cum civil at his Greenline home. Her whole family was there, flown in like a diplomatic contingent from Taiwan. His mother threw this huge affair—the father was already deceased—invited all her society hoity-toits. It was *disastrous*. Harold beat him up something awful when he found him, which was harder than you might imagine given Gordie's inebriation. I had to drag them apart, with help from some of our *kung fu* friends. Me, the guy who's still rubbing sand out of his eyes. Harold was a wrestler then, unbelievably strong, and Gordie has always been fit, a long-distance swimmer and runner. My glasses got smashed in the fracas."

"I didn't think Mrs. Ashberry would have approved."

"She didn't, neither did the Shihs who were relieved, actually, and brought Stella home to Taipei for a month or so. But you know how things go. Some things in life you don't back out of, no matter what."

"So what was his reason?"

"Reason?! Gordie doesn't have *reasons*. He just does life." His vehemence, unintended, startles him. He grimaces. Laura notes his discomfort.

"Then why do you like him so much? He doesn't seem like a likeable guy."

"You're wrong there. He's not just likeable, he's loveable."

"Why?"

"Doesn't *everyone* love Bugs?"

Laura laughs. Her voice has a light, silvery quality which is at odds with the rest of her. Her intensity is such that Larry expects her to intone rather than speak. He thinks her quite marvelous. His wife says he's developing a crush on her, which he denies. But he wishes Anita never said that, because whenever Laura laughs now, he hears "I've Got A Crush On You," Art Tatum's lush and multi-layered version, and this embarrasses him.

"What's this Bugs thing about anyway?" And then, without waiting for an answer, she says, "I thought Gordie was always a ladies' man."

"He was, and is."

"Then what I don't get is why you think he couldn't have been in love with Stella. She's intelligent and gorgeous, a real catch."

"Because he only has passions. Being in love is more than a moment's crisis. That's why the whole thing with Stella was so entirely wrong."

She looks puzzled. "Because?"

"Because Gordie *can't* possibly marry."

"So he exists only to be your friend, to entertain you? Is that why you're writing this?"

Her question arrests him. His first instinct is to protest but then he backs up, thinks about the query from her point of view as his reader. An unexpected sense of shame overcomes him. "I've never thought of him that way but I suppose . . . well, we've always gotten along and yes, he's tremendously entertaining. Anita and the girls adore him."

"And if he had married, had a family of his own?"

"He'd be a terrible father! He's so irresponsible."

"What kind of husband would he be?"

"Wouldn't be able to sustain the love."

She pauses. Her eyes go sad. "Not all marriages are premised on love."

He recalls, too late, that Laura's ex-husband left her for one of his students. Larry kicks himself mentally and remains silent.

"It's okay," Laura says, reading his mind. "We get over these things." But there is a glistening of the cornea she doesn't pretend to hide.

Larry wants to reach over and embrace her, but in that desire, he experiences a jolt, not an urgent flash or punch, but a strange jerky sensation, like the recognition that you've shifted into the wrong gear. He is surprised by the slow but unmistakable release of his mental safety belt, an unbuckling while the engine is still roaring down the highway. It is as if he is opening the driver's door at 65 mph and stepping out to his doom. There it is, the realization, the dawning, the uncontrollable grief that has overtaken him for his missing friend. No, not friend. Gordie isn't just a friend, or blood brother in that schoolboy-in-the-playground *swear it* manner, accompanied by bravado rituals. Gordie is, and here he is at a loss for the right word, as if his brain has drawn the shutters on memory, on some teasing refrain once sung in the privacy of his mind about himself and Gordie, that cartoon-being. That man.

Laura glances at him, concerned. "Are you alright? You suddenly don't look very well."

"Oh, I'm." He stops. The notion of speech confounds him.

"Can I get you something? A glass of water maybe?"

"No," he says, slowly, as he turns to face her directly. "I'm okay. What you said just now, that 'we get over these things.' We should, shouldn't we? But that's my problem, isn't it? I can't get over Gordie."

Earlier for Larry before the year has ended but his computer files are crashing, slowly at first, and then with a vehemence that no machine should exhibit, and these are the last surviving notes for Book 1.#&!%

When Gordie began seeing Anna, I thought he would finally settle down. It was right around the same time his mother and Jack Hwang became friendly. Anna was right for him, the way Stella wasn't. Harold didn't think so but he never got to meet Anna. Harold and I both were his big brothers, although Harold only by a few weeks, but that was the one time I was the better brother. Besides, I was the only one Gordie called *dai gor*.

I saw Anna first. She sang at a club in Harlem, where a musician friend of mine brought me. I told Gordie about her and he came along one night, semi-reluctantly as I recall, because he was still in hiding over what he'd done to Stella and avoided the life that mattered. Actually, most people didn't think he was in hiding, so to speak, because he carried on like the party animal he was, only worse. Four years, *more*, blowing off life. There's something monstrous about a young man who doesn't have to earn a living and isn't driven by passions to other enterprise. He flew to Asia a lot, mostly to Hong Kong, even visited my family. What else he did there I'm not sure and he seldom said. Back in New York, he went to parties, gave parties, bought fancy cars and flew his late father's Cessna now and then. Took Pete Haight and Colette up in it a couple of times, out to his family's summer home on Block Island, while the rest of us drove and took the ferry. He didn't really like to fly though. He just could.

What I've never understood is why Stella forgave him and

continued to be a friend. I asked her once, years later, the year she won that Presidential award—Carter was in office then—why she did. *Look at my life,* she said, *I wouldn't have achieved nearly as much with him, would I? Besides, he's never been unwilling to open a door or provide the right introductions when I've needed it, long after everything was over.* Stella never married. Anita thinks she's still a virgin although I can't see how that's possible.

But I was writing about Gordie and Anna.

She was on stage when we walked in, sounding like a cross between Lady Day and Betty Carter, and looking better than Diana Ross who, as far as I was and am still concerned, has it light years over that super model the kids all think is so hot. A body's nothing without that which graces the world, and grace derives from a worthwhile enterprise, and not merely physical beauty or fashion.

We maneuvered our way to the edge of the bar closest to the stage. Gordie closed his eyes and listened, the way he does when the music's more than just about show.

She was singing "My Romance."

I love that song. It's one of those that makes me wish Rodgers never had to drop Hart as a lyricist in favor of Hammerstein. The melody's luscious. Of course, I'm no musicologist or anything, but that progression, from a F sharp minor 7 to a B7 flatted 9 (in the B flat Real Book version) on "hide-a-way" always makes me tremble. Gordie was never as much moved the way I am by Bill Evans' live recording of the song, although he loves the lyrics. Anita, Stella, Harold, Isobel, none of them really like jazz, not the way Gordie and I do, so when we were young, before responsibilities piled up, it was usually just the two of us at the clubs, listening, listening. Here are the words:

My Romance doesn't have to have a moon in the sky,
My Romance doesn't need a blue lagoon standing by;
No month of May, no twinkling stars, no hide-a-way, no soft guitars.
My Romance doesn't need a castle rising in Spain,
Nor a dance to a constantly surprising refrain.
Wide awake I can make my most fantastic dreams come true;
My Romance doesn't need a thing but you.

During the instrumental solo, Anna stepped aside, the "stage" being level with the audience in the tiny bar and club. I was practically touching shoulders with her. When she began again she turned and sang to me—being a typical Hong Kong guy, I was just short enough for her to gaze down at, especially because she always wore four-inch spikes—all the way to "soft guitars" before returning to center stage. At the end of the number, the band took their break.

"Bad timing," I said, meaning our arrival close to the break.

"That's where you're wrong." His eyes followed Anna. "I'm going to talk to her."

He returned a few minutes later, looking like a kid who just lost his favorite toy. "She won't have a drink with me."

"Hui Guo, she's working. Come on, have a drink. She might talk to you later."

We stayed through her last set, after which she disappeared too quickly for Gordie to catch her.

Laura weighs her words carefully before speaking. By now, she has read over three hundred manuscript pages, *twice*, both the original and revision, and feels Anita's husband is abusing her as reader. "Larry, are you writing about Gordie or yourself?"

Larry blinks. "Didn't you like these last chapters?"

"It's not a question of what I like or don't like. What are *you* trying to write?" Because he doesn't answer, she continues. "Why all these pages of, what should I call them, *lectures* maybe, on jazz standards, and composers, and renditions?" because the riff on "My Romance" is one of perhaps a dozen songs he analyzes, many of them in painstaking detail, entirely lost on a lay person.

He looks away from her. Lately, Laura's presence is like a shock of static electricity, a familiar sensation that's nonetheless unexpected. When did she become erotic to him, so that he kept writing, even when he himself knew it was all wrong, was going nowhere, just because it meant regular contact, because she seemed fascinated by Gordie? Forcing aside inappropriate lusts, he replies, "Gordie's very big on jazz. I've always thought he would have been happier as a singer."

"Was that why he was so in love with Anna?"

"In part. She was a true artist, and willing to surrender everything to her career. All she cared about was the music. It broke his heart when she just up and left one day, took off to Europe where she still is and has done well for herself. I have some of her recordings here. Would you like to listen?"

Laura shakes her head—she isn't particularly fond of jazz—but what she really wants is to extricate herself from this predicament. She likes Larry, admires his effort and dedication to his friend but feels he would do better to stick to writing an objective, academic study of the phenomena that is Gordie. But he has been deaf to her increasingly forceful editorial suggestions. She takes her leave, cursing the long friendship that made it difficult to say no in the first instance, but resolved at last to speak to Anita and end things.

Afterwards, Larry knows it's time for him to call it quits, this thing for Laura. Anita suspects, he's sure, but lust in the heart need not be articulated. He's not the president and has no impetus to make public apologies for inappropriate thoughts. Naturally, he wouldn't ever jeopardize their marriage by something as absurd as an affair, and Anita knows him well enough to know that. What *would* matter to Anita, which is why he really must quit writing this thing for Laura, is the disclosure of private lives in these pages. That has been wrong of him and he knows it, all this disclosure about Gordie of course, and Stella and Harold *et al*, but more to the point, *about her and him*. As close a friend as Laura is of his wife's, some of what she's now knows about them would upset Anita if she only knew—which she won't—because she has not and never will read this manuscript that he hasn't offered to show her. At least he hopes she won't. He's pretty sure that Laura will treat the material with professional discretion. As she herself said, when they first talked and he was hesitant about showing pages, *even a novelist shouldn't reveal her sources.*

Besides, the press is impatient. It's been over half a year and he hasn't delivered a draft of any kind, not even a detailed outline. It's time to write what he should and cease and desist this nostalgia for the days of Gordie and Anna. Because that's what it is, a sentimental rewrite of history. His friendship with Gordie is not like that anymore, hasn't been like that in years. Oh, they're still friends, for life for sure, but life forks when you don't want it to and by the time you're ready to tread alternate paths, it's usually too late.

What he *can* do is see Hui Guo, or try to. To pull him out of hiding because this time, he's really hiding, worse than post-Stella and pre-Anna. His friend's life is measured in love spaces, like long and intense jazz solos during which the singer is silent, instrumental choruses of improvised passion, and risk, that can succeed or fail or totter in between.

What he also needs to do is pay more attention to Anita and his daughters.

Days, weeks pass and before he knows it, a new year and resolutions.

On the first morning of January, 2002, Larry reaches for the phone, to punch in the numbers he knows by heart, to wait through the rings until that familiar voice responds, to ask—*Hui Guo, ni jai naar li?*—meaning, "where are you" but which Gordie will understand to mean, and where, my friend, is your spirit, why are you hiding, why won't you stay here with me, with all of us? He knows that things have really changed since the time of Anna, that time has more than passed, because once, it would have been unthinkable to ring his friend on new year's morning. Not now though, not anymore. Not for—and he's startled by the accuracy of his observation—not for at least a decade, if not longer.

A few days later, Anita announces that Violette, their eldest, is getting married. Their daughter is thirty three and Anita thinks it's about time.

Larry looks up from his computer. "To whom?"

She cups her hands over her mouth like a horn. "Wake up, Nutley, you're sleeping again," she says.

Lately, his wife misquotes cartoons. "Oh, you mean, what's his name."

"Ryan, it's Ryan. And Colette," meaning their younger girl. "Colette's been accepted at Vermont's creative writing program, beginning this summer. Laura's recommendation didn't hurt."

"Really?"

"Husband," Anita switches to Chinese, *"you're* the one who named her."

Larry's youthful linguistic flirtations extended to French and Norwegian. "There's a lot of fish in Norway," he'd told Anita when they first met and she expressed disbelief at this peculiar range of language acquisition. "It's the least I could do for my family's fish enterprise." Mercifully, as their daughters often note, their father refrained from potentially more outlandish cultural reconstruction at the moment of their births.

"So," he says, "what does all this mean?"

"Wedding dinner. At the Fortune Luck. It's been arranged for March 16." She waits as he absorbs this. "It's a Saturday."

He blinks. "I thought he was Korean?"

"That was two boyfriends ago. This one's half Chinese." She pauses, waiting for his brain to catch up with the present. "You know, the half Norwegian one. You *liked* this one. He listens to that Jan Grabarek whose CD's you have?"

He conjures up a picture of future grandchildren, black-haired, blue-eyed too-tall Asiatic girls and too-small Caucasian boys, and forces the image to vanish. "Have we met the parents?"

"We have. Now remember to congratulate both girls when they come over for dinner tonight," and she leaves him to shop for the freshest fish she can find. A *problem* this book of his, because she's never known him to be quite this distracted.

It has been a long summer and an even longer fall, Anita thinks, as she boards the Lexington line to transfer to the 6 train for Chinatown. 9-11 is the least of their worries now that almost everyone they know is safe, and this new year hasn't come soon enough for her. The Woos live in Prospect Heights, within walking distance of Grand Army Plaza where almost all lines converge. They bought their condo exactly 20 years ago, when Brooklyn was still cheap for an academic couple, because Manhattan was mired in youth, real estate exuberance and too much crime. Colette was five and had to change kindergartens, a traumatic time for her temperamental younger child. How hard *lao kung* resisted, because it would crimp his jazz nights out with Hui Guo, but he came round in the end for the good of family. If there was one thing she didn't like about that friendship, it is the way both men carry on for hours over jazz, a subject that bores and excludes pretty much everyone else. Oh, once in awhile, who doesn't like a night out to hear live music or to listen to a new CD. But daily? Well, not the going out part, not anymore, but certainly, *lao kung* plays jazz non-stop while he works which was why a larger space that Brooklyn afforded had been crucial if she wasn't going to go insane.

The trains are not yet back to normal, and she has to stop a moment to determine how to get to the 6 line for Canal. Uptown beyond the normal point and then reverse to head back down. *What a pain*, and catches herself, recalling Colette who, at twenty-four, is as sensitive as a sixteen-year old, who admonishes Anita's insensitivity at the plight of 9-11 victims. She has seen her daughter crying over the photos in the *New York Times*, all strangers because Colette has lost no one, and she still lives at home where she spends her life in front of a screen, since she is unable to settle into either a profession or grad school, until now, something that unnerves even Larry. Meanwhile, Violette lost her best friend from college, and Ryan tells Anita that sometimes her oldest child, the indomitable warrior girl, cries in her sleep, inconsolable. It doesn't help that 9-11 is Violette's birthday, and her friend's loving bouquet arrived more or less as she was falling from the towers, because she called her mother right before she jumped. As she exits on Canal, the cold sunshine is like the muted joy she feels at her daughter's upcoming marriage.

The snow pea leaves at the Hong Kong Grocery are too dry and wilted, and she decides to try the shop on East Broadway, even though it means back tracking a long way. It's Violette's favorite vegetable, and right now, anything she can do for her girl she will. Yet as a light wind brushes her cheeks, reddening them with a healthy glow, her worries are all for Colette. Does she *truly* believe Laura when she says her daughter has talent? This younger child, once afraid of pigeons; this girl, so immune, who now frets as an adult that she might get measles or mumps or some unknown dread disease; *this woman who is afraid of men.* Now, she apparently writes wildly fantastic narratives of male robots-cum-androids, from a galaxy that exists only for war, who are all in love with human girls and are trying to destroy all the boys on earth. She posts these tales on her game website, one she designed herself, using the pseudonym Co-Late, and has a huge fan base of male admirers who thinks she's one of them. It baffles Anita. But Laura has no reason to lie or flatter, and wouldn't, in any event.

Unlike Hui Guo, the sweet-talking "uncle" whom Colette adores and Violette loves but mistrusts.

The fishmonger holds up a large specimen, and its fins flap water at Anita. Hui Guo is like the fish, Anita thinks, fighting his fate. She hasn't said this to Larry because she doesn't want to unduly influence his book. The book she hopes he's finally tackling. She regrets having dragged Laura into it, and is glad that's over. Laura was much too good about things; had Anita known how off base her husband was, she wouldn't have allowed him to keep using Laura as a reader, and she wishes her friend had said something sooner. *You were being too Chinese*, she says when Laura finally confesses that she can't do it anymore because the problem is simply that he's writing the wrong book. *The Chinese endure more than they should.* One conversation between wife and husband ends that relationship, and Anita presses an expensive gift of jewelry upon her friend who refuses to accept any money. Anita has always known how to handle Larry's problems and protests, because he says the problem stems from Gordie and his fears, fears that cut off friends who try hard, who keep trying to know the real him.

The problem isn't Gordie, she knows, it's Larry.

False Gods by Larry Woo, PhD (from the introduction of Larry Woo's manuscript)

"The phenomena following Gordon Ashberry's decision to give away his money can only be understood against the background of Sino-American relations. Zhang Lianhe (*a.k.a.* Minnie Chang) is a resultant product of the modern history of diplomacy, intrigue,

---

[1]"Flying Tigers," the name by which the American Volunteer Group (AVG) of the Chinese Air Force were popularly known was established in 1941 by Claire L. Chennault (1893-1958), who was then a retired captain of the U.S. Army Air Corp. The group's origins are historically anomalous because it was essentially a squadron in the Chinese Air Force created in the American mold at the behest of Madame Chiang Kai-shek who had taken over the leadership of the Aeronautical Commission. In April 1937, Madame Chiang invited Chenault to China so that he could make a confidential study of the Chinese air force. Chennault's status in China prior to 1942 is ambiguous because he was at the time no longer an active member of the U.S. military, and his role was as that of a civilian advisor to the Commission during a period when Japan and China were on the verge of war. Of the AVG, Chennault said: ""My plan proposed to throw a small but well-equipped air force into China. Japan, Like England, floated her life blood on the sea and could be defeated more easily by slashing her salty arteries than by stabbing for her heart. Air bases in Free China could put all of the vital Japanese supply lines and advanced staging areas under attack." Chennault was later to return to active duty with the U.S. Army in the spring of 1942. The Flying Tigers defeated the Japanese Air Force in some 50 air battles without a single defeat; many of the fighter pilots were decorated by the Chinese government, and several were also awarded British and American Flying Crosses. The AVG was officially disbanded in July 1942, but the pilots of

political and economic friendship and rivalry of both nations. In a recent *Newsweek* interview, Zhang says that her interest in Ashberry was first piqued when she learned of his father's role as one of the Flying Tigers [1]. In her now infamous book *Honey Money*, Zhang describes the Tigers as "an organization that marked a turning point in Sino-American relations because it was the beginning of the end of Taiwan's claim to being the Republic of China." (p. 43) While such a claim must of course be read in light of Zhang's prejudices as a patriot of the People's Republic of China, as well as her lack of authority in any area of political or historical analysis [2], she is not wrong in her assessment, further in the same paragraph, that "Gordon Ashberry could not have made the decision he made were he not an *American molded by his own particular Sino-American heritage.*" (italics mine).

"However, Zhang fails to develop that argument, just as she fails to provide an accurate account of what really happened. Her entire

---

the Flying Tigers were absorbed into the 23rd Fighter Group of the U.S. Army Air Forcers, and later the 14th Air Force with General Chennault as commander. There are several accounts and histories written of the Flying Tigers, including a memoir by Chennault, and there are museum displays in the U.S. and Asia honoring the group. As well the group has been the subject of novels and films. The name Flying Tigers was retained for what became Flying Tiger Line, the first scheduled cargo airline in the U.S. that was also a major military charter operator during the cold war era. It was owned by Tiger International which was purchased by Federal Express in 1988 in its bid to become the world's largest air carrier. Mark Ashberry, Gordon's father, flew for the Flying Tigers and likely knew Claire Chennault, although this was not something Gordon could confirm. The esteemed scholar and political scientist Stella Shih, who had been engaged to Gordon although the marriage never took place, believes that the senior Ashberry was a favorite of Chennault, which is something she told me once in passing, but this is not something I have been able to verify. Additional online sources: http://www.flyingtigersavg.com/, http://www.historynet.com/american-volunteer-group-claire-l-chennault-and-the-flying-tigers.htm, https://en.wikipedia.org/wiki/Flying_Tigers.

[2] Zhang Lianhe 張連和 or 張聯合 later went by Minnie Chang (or Zhang). I was never able to ascertain her actual Chinese name as it has appeared in print in both the preceding forms. The first can be translated as "link to harmony or

introduction is a blatant plagiarism, an exact replica of an essay by Peter Haight[3] , Ashberry's godson who was sixteen at the time he wrote it, and there is little else that credibly establishes the account which might have been a young boy's misinterpretation of what he was told. Zhang does not credit her source. She also fails to properly credit her sources about the Tigers. For example, the summary description of the history of Tigers (pp. 45 to 50) is a pastiche borrowed from two texts, a biography about Claire Chennault by Jack Samson[4] and *The Maverick War: Chennault & the Flying Tigers* by Duane Schultz[5] , and at least seventy percent[6] is directly lifted out of these texts. "

***

---

peace" and the second means "united," although both these names follow the same surname or last name Zhang 張. Her origins and age are also uncertain as she is evasive in the extreme. The one time I was able to interview her briefly, she was cagey and unwilling to confirm her credentials; she claims to hold a journalism degree but there is no record of a degree issued to anyone of any of her names at New York University, Columbia or the University of Hong Kong – she has been quoted in various sources as saying she attended all three institutions. She has occasionally published feature stories in the Chinese press, in both Hong Kong and the Mainland, but these are generally what would be classified as "soft" subjects, her impressions as a young Mainland Chinese woman with an entree to cultural circles. An editor of a Hong Kong culture magazine once told me Lianhe slept around with foreign journalists and China experts but could offer no proof other than "everyone knows it's true," and called her a vulgar Cantonese expression that translates roughly as "salty-wet horny slut."

[3] This essay no longer appears to be online as a comprehensive search failed to locate it. Peter Haight does however acknowledge that he did write such a piece although even he no longer has a back up copy as the original word processing file was, according to him, "zapped" from his hard drive when it was struck by lightning. When questioned by his father Harold Haight, who is one of Gordon Ashberry's best friends, how a hard drive could suffer such a fate, Peter confessed it was a deliberate ploy on his part in order to obtain a new computer as the old one was "Jurassic." Apparently Peter, who is mathematically inclined, had calculated the probability of strike by lightning based on an analysis of several weeks of the weather forecast during Hong Kong's rainy season (he was still living in Hong Kong when this occurred) in relation to the position of his

By the time Anita finishes reading her husband's two-hundred page manuscript that the press has returned, Larry is asleep. It's only one, early for him, but she knows he is exhausted from arguing with his editor Auden all afternoon, a bright if overly earnest young man who clearly meant well by traveling all the way from Florida to Brooklyn to meet Larry in person.

She switches off her bedside light and lies awake for another twenty minutes, willing herself to sleep. As usual, his footnotes are as good as, and at times even more compelling than the text itself. *There'll be a way*, she tells herself, to give him the bad news. In the morning.

But the next morning Colette appears at breakfast, red-eyed, and though she says she's fine, Anita suspects she's been crying again.

---

building and the angle of its rooftop. He managed to estimate the probability to a +/- error rate of 3% and placed his computer at exactly the perfect angle for three specific rainy days and sure enough, lightning struck and destroyed the drive.

[4] Jack Samson is the author of *Flying Tiger: The True Story of General Claire Chennault and the U.S. 14th Air Force in China*, Doubleday, New York 1987, one of the definitive biographies of Chennault and the book has been continually reissued. U.S. Senator Barry Goldwater wrote a foreword for the First Lyons Press paperback edition in 2005. In the opening chapter, Samson describes his first encounter with "the highly controversial" Chennault when he was himself a young navigator/bombardier in Kunming, China. The exact date of Chennault's birth is a matter of some dispute, and it appears the date may have been falsified to shave a few years off his age so that he could be accepted into the army. In this respect, Zhang Lianhe shares this characteristic with Chennault as she passed herself off as younger and her actual age is a matter of dispute. Jack Samson suffered from asthma as a boy; coincidentally, Harold Haight also does which was why Gordon never smoked pot in Harold's vicinity. However, more to the point is that Zhang reproduces, in what can only be described as a plagiarized paraphrase, the first four pages of Chapter 2 of Samson's book, from page 21 to the middle of 24. She also copies, almost verbatim, a section on p. 169, beginning "Chennault smiled to himself. It was wonderful what international publicity would do" through to the end of the page "...to Chennault's command in Kunming and wanted him to confirm that he could house and feed the men." At times, it appears that Zhang wishes to identify with Chennault in terms of his brash and commanding manner.

[5] *The Maverick War: Chennault and the Flying Tigers* by Duane P. Schultz, St. Martin's Press, 1987. Why Zhang Lianhe chose this text to plagiarize out of the numerous

Probably over her sister's wedding. Colette is absurdly attached to Violette, complicated by the fact (despite vehement denials) that she has a crush on Ryan. Colette has fallen madly in love with nearly all of Violette's boyfriends from the time she was seven and begged to go along on Violette's first date, and went into a frenzy when told she couldn't. She would live with her sister now if she could, but Anita understands perfectly why her oldest girl needs space from this clinging baby sister, because Colette is still like a child, dependent and, despite an extremely high IQ, constantly in need of reassurance. *Chemical imbalance,* she hears her psychiatrist friend say. It *might* explain why Colette has mood swings and took six years to finish a bachelor's degree in anything. Larry, however, has never been willing

---

other books on the subject is uncertain. One significant feature of Schultz's book is his detailing of Chennault's battles with superiors. A former high school friend in Hong Kong who is a senior accountant at CNN International tells me that Zhang Lianhe frequently argued with her immediate superiors and was known to be a "troublemaker" during her supposed "internship" at the company. In such confrontations, she always brought up her connection with one of the senior VP's at CNN who, it was rumored, was her lover. Perhaps she saw herself as waging her own brand of "maverick war" in the West, as she was known to be a Communist Party loyalist. However, what is curious is why she appeared to desire such a prolonged connection to Western media when she might have fared better as a journalist for the *China Daily* or the *People's Daily*, or why it was she wanted to leave Beijing.

[6] The determination that 70% was plagiarized was arrived at using the following methodology. It was established that X=the number of all phrases of six words or more and Y=the number of all complete sentences in the summary history of the Flying Tigers in Zhang's book. A comparison against the text in both titles referenced was made of all the X phrases and Y sentences using the compare document feature in Microsoft Word (the text of all the books was scanned with OCR software and converted to electronic text files which were then imported into Word, and a visual check made of the electronic documents against the original text by professional proofreaders who were extremely expensive but necessary to ensure accuracy). All identical or similar phrases and sentences were then extracted to determine by word count the quantity of plagiarism committed, and this was determined to be approximately 70% with an error factor of +/- 2% points.

to hear anything of possible psychological problems, and *especially* not about a prescription drug solution, insisting that Colette is fine, just over sensitive. It's so ... Chinese of him! Larry, when he appears that morning, is equally morose and snaps at Colette, and between husband and daughter, Anita thinks she will go mad. In the end, she says nothing to him about the manuscript.

It is not till two nights later, when Colette is out for dinner with a friend, that Larry finally asks. "Did you read it?" He has just finished loading the dishwasher.

Anita pops an orange segment into her mouth and nods.

He switches on the machine. "So?"

Swallowing quickly, she says. "Your editor's right."

"You've got to be kidding?"

"*Tian xin,* 'sweetheart' it's all about timing. If you'd written an article accusing plagiarism, right after her book came out, that'd be one thing. Now, after it's sold as well as it has *and* gone into paperback, a *book* denouncing her book ... well, no one's really interested."

"But I'm right, aren't I? What she did was unethical."

"She is unethical, but four out of your ten chapters analyzing a 'plagiarism' that comprises less than five percent of her book isn't the ethical issue that's important. Unless," she stops, uncertain what to tell him to write since that's his job, then continues. "You're an American pop culture specialist. Are you trying to say that this young Chinese woman created a pop cultural phenomenon *because* she's a plagiarist? The argument's muddled. And why all the political commentary?"

"*You're* the one who said I should write about Sino-American relations. Remember?"

She stares at him, momentarily bewildered, and then recalls her passing remark. "I was joking."

He scowls, looks just like Colette. "I'm *still* right."

"This isn't about right and wrong. The manuscript you delivered wasn't what you were contracted to write."

His face is black, and Anita knows she shouldn't have avoided broaching the subject sooner. Her husband can laugh most things off, but when he's angry, he gets a little out of control. There is a painfully long silence. He is standing by the sink, a towel in his hand, and suddenly whips it against the counter. "You're jealous, that's why you're putting it down. You don't want to see me publish this book."

"*Lao kung!* How long have we been married? Since when . . .?"

"Forget it. I'm going out before I explode."

Anita feels *she's* the one who should explode. Between Colette moping around, the wedding dinner next week and everyone's nerves on edge, and now her husband behaving as if they are back in grad school, running out the door at night to a jazz club just to avoid an argument, she wishes everyone would simply go up in smoke.

All this is partly because of Hui Guo, isn't it, the man who isn't there when he always has been, the man who *still* hasn't RSVP'd to say he'll be there when he knows he should. Violette has noticed this and is hurt. What is she supposed to say or do? Larry's phone messages to him since the beginning of the year have gone unanswered so Anita told Violette to mail the card and hope for the best. Exasperated, Anita looks up his number in Larry's book. It's past ten, but she calls anyway.

"Hui Guo, pick up," she says to his message machine, adding in Chinese, "Confucius says, at fifty, a man . . ." Before she can finish the analect, the phone beeps, intercepted. "Anita?" Gordie's voice is hesitant and, she thinks, fatigued. Or is he drunk?

"*Mo sheng ren,*" she accuses. "What's going on?"

"You're calling about the invitation, right? I apologize, humbly, it was inconsiderate of me. I didn't mean to be a 'stranger'."

"Then you'll be there? Violette will be heartbroken if you're not. And of course, Colette's still *your* sweetest *tian xin*. It's been much too long since we've seen you, Hui Guo *wang*." She adds "king" to his name, the way her daughters did when they were girls, when their name in English for him was His Majesty King HG I.

"Could I ever say no to you, doll?"

"Then you will be there?" She hesitates. "For Larry?"

"Wouldn't miss it for the world. For Larry."

Afterwards, when Larry's cooled down enough to listen to reason, when Colette is coasting on a high because Ryan's good-looking Korean friend has asked to be her date at the banquet (Ryan thus proving himself a loving brother-in-law since Colette *knows for sure*—despite Violette's assurance to the contrary—that the friend wouldn't have done this without being prompted by Ryan) and when Violette is pleased that Uncle Hui Guo will show, Anita no longer regrets her rash decision to call him. Even Stella will be pleased to see him, she's sure, Stella being Stella. Funny how the world turns and transforms in less then twenty-four hours. It suddenly strikes her that Hui Guo is still remarkably fluent, because their entire phone conversation was in Chinese except for—and here she smiles—"doll." He even recalled the Confucian analect in Chinese, about heeding the decree of heaven, although Anita doesn't think Hui Guo is heeding a higher order of any kind. Instinctive, her speaking to him in her native tongue, the way she used to back in the day, back when he and Stella almost were.

Anita had liked Larry's young American friend from the first. He made her laugh, and more important, Larry thrived in his company. Also, they all would talk late into the night about Vietnam and China's involvement, what they knew or didn't know of the Cultural Revolution and all the life that mattered.

The night Larry flirted openly with that Hong Kong princess at a party for all their friends to see, she had watched, flushed with shame. Feeling their two-year age difference (*imagine being an "older woman" in your twenties!*), the difference her boyfriend usually dismissed. Feeling the sting of the history of women in love with men who were, consciously or unconsciously, pursuing their penises. Of course, Larry wasn't exactly her boyfriend, she supposed, because they both agreed to take things slow, especially since she was facing a dissertation committee next semester. But among their community of Chinese student friends, everyone presumed their relationship. The Hong Kong princess, however, was a newcomer to the scene, and irresistibly, only eighteen, most likely a virgin.

It was late in the darkened room, and the party had degenerated into the final pairings for the night. Hui Guo sidled up, holding a bottle of champagne. This was when he showed up to all their parties sporting several bottles. On special occasions, like at the winter solstice dinner last month, he had a case delivered because "even Chinese girls will drink at least a little champagne."

He leaned over and kissed her ear, startling her. "He'll be back, doll," he said. "She's way too porcelain for him," and refilled her glass.

"You're just being nice," she said in English. "Flattering an old lady."

"*Shuo guo yu*, help me practice."

"You know that mature ladies still like sweet language," she said in Chinese, adding gratefully. "You're really our good *peng you*."

"*Gan bei*," he raised his glass. "Let's drink to friendship," and emptied his.

She followed suit. He refilled their glasses and they drank a second toast. Larry, meanwhile, looked up, waved and returned to his conversation with the princess.

He put the bottle down. "Now, I'll be an even better friend." He circled his arm around her waist and led her out to the dance floor where they did a cha cha to everyone's admiring applause because Gordie danced well, and made a much better partner than Larry.

Larry saw his girlfriend with Hui Guo, and was distracted for a moment from being nice to this new hometown girl who was sweet, but so helplessly innocent. The young woman asked in Cantonese, *is the scenery over there fresher,* and he returned his attention to the one he was with, for the moment.

Out on the floor, Gordie said. "For an old lady, you look pretty good. Too bad Larry's in the way."

Anita smiled. "Stop teasing."

"I'm not. You're the sexiest Chinese girl I know." He spun her into a hold and held her with both arms, pulling her tight against him as the music segued to a slow number.

He was making her blush, because everyone *must* be staring. His body was uncomfortably close, and as his hands slid lower down her back, it bothered her how *much* she liked the feel of him. She was floating, light headed, wishing she hadn't drunk so much so quickly. Now, he was definitely embracing her more sexually than as just a *peng you,* and she maneuvered them into an empty side room. Hopefully, no one had noticed.

He backed her against a wall and bit her ear playfully. "Friend, come home with me?"

"Hui Guo!" She ducked her face away as best she could. His palms were firm against the wall and he had her in a cage.

"Don't be so shocked. Larry doesn't know how lucky he is."

"I *can't* go home with you. That's, that's . . ."

"Why not? You like me don't you?" And then he sang, in English, "You're de-lectable, you're dee-licious."

A new slow number started. Out on the floor, Larry and the princess danced clumsily; he stepped on her toes twice. Over her shoulder, his eyes searched the room but Anita and Hui Guo seemed to have vanished.

"You do like me, don't you?" Gordie repeated. "You wouldn't have brought me in here if you didn't." He pulled her towards him. "*Tian xin*, forget him tonight," adding in English, "damn, you feel too good." The flush crept down her neck, spread all over. "Since when?" He leaned down, said in English, "sorry, I can't help myself," and, flinging friendship aside, kissed her. She gave in and kissed back. *Screw Larry*. He hadn't been to see her in two weeks, and *everyone* knew that silly Hong Kong chick was just playing him and face it, she *needed* some relief. When they surfaced for air, she whispered, "Come on Hui Guo *wang*, let's go to my place. It's closer."

Now, as Anita prepares dinner for her husband, she is tickled by the memory, about which she's never felt an iota of guilt even though she knows she should. *Hui Guo didn't need seducing he was a surprisingly good lover*, she recalls. She later told Larry nothing happened, that all he did was walk her home since *my boyfriend abandoned me*, and Gordie corroborated when Larry questioned him. In the sober light of the aftermath, she and Hui Guo agreed, *too much to drink and the heat of a moment, nothing more*, because that was when she knew how truly in love she was with Larry, as she told Hui Guo. She remembers as if it were yesterday, that January morning in '68, admiring Hui Guo's long-waisted, naked body, so unlike Larry's compact form, the one that meshed properly with her own. Later, Hui Guo did truly fall in love with Stella who, unfortunately, was scared of sex—Anita suspected abuse, possibly a rape when she was young but Stella never told and Anita didn't want to ask—which was partly why the whole thing fell apart which Anita understood, even privately sympathized with Hui Guo, and she could have forgiven him pretty much anything, except for making her friend *lose all her face like that* which was too much, even for Anita who otherwise condones pretty much everything else about this friend of her husband's, this uncle to her girls, this man she wishes would return to them because she misses him, this charming playboy who loves women and has never done anyone any real harm. Hui Guo's a good man, and as she hears Larry come home, she reminds herself, *he* must *let Hui Guo know about this book it's the right, the only thing to do. I'll insist. I will*, because she knows her husband needs a little push, from time to time, to overcome whatever is the moment's insecurity.

"My Romance" ends, the last track on the CD. Larry wasn't thinking specifically about Anna when he put on her recording, but played it because he absently keeps music going at all times.

Anita knocks once, then opens the door to his study. "Lunch time. So?"

"When you're right, you're right." It's the day before his daughter's wedding and he has finally accepted the editor's outright rejection. His manuscript titled *False Gods* is officially shelved and he's negotiated an extension with the press. His wife means well, and he is grateful for her honesty. Besides, as she reminds him, he *needs* to get this book out of the way so that he can get back to the real one he wants to complete, his long-standing work on Bugs Bunny and Yogi Bear, a comparative study of his two favorite cartoon characters to determine their symbolic significance for American culture. Long standing because Bart Simpson and the South Park kids got in the way of the research and writing, resulting in his best-selling volume.

But what Anita is asking is something else. "I'll talk to Hui Guo," he says. "It's not about getting permission, I don't think, but I should let him know. I'm glad he's coming tomorrow."

"At least he isn't completely cutting off all relationships."

Larry presses his knuckles against his chin and flicks his thumb back and forth across his lower lip. "How long do you think it's been? Since he's stopped engaging with people."

"You mean, since we've noticed."

He nods, acknowledging her precision.

Anita flips rapidly through the "card index" that Larry says her mind comprises, pulling out facts to support her argument. Her younger daughter Colette complains that Anita is too stuck on facts to understand fiction, a subtext for *my mother hasn't a clue about why I do what I do.* Violette, the older girl who is on the finance management track at GE, is grateful she has inherited her mother's capacity for facts.

She says. " '96, maybe even earlier, but '96 for sure."

Larry frowns. "No way. When I went back home for the handover the next year, he was there, even saw my family."

"That's different. That's like our dinner for Violette. He wouldn't dare not do the right Chinese thing. You know how he is."

"But it doesn't make sense, does it?"

Anita sighs. "No."

"Furthermore, he's not Chinese."

"He might as well be." Anita straightens up the pile of empty jewel cases, stacking them neatly by the stereo. "He's convoluted enough." Larry laughs. "You have a point. Only how come you're so sure about '96? What happened that year?"

"You *really* don't remember?"

The familiar annoyance nags. His voice is curt. "Would I ask if I did?"

"Husband," she says in Chinese, "it was that October they found the remains of those airmen in China. Remember?" She waits for Larry's mind to click out of the haze of devotion to Gordie, and adds, in English "that missing Flying Tigers unit?"

It all comes back to him, the mini rash of coverage that followed about the Tigers' CIA involvement, as well as Harold's earlier suspicions about Gordie's Australian partner, Colin Kenton, even before the debacle in October of '87— nothing to do with Black Monday although that was October also—Gordie's private crash, his company collapsing, his partner's disappearance, the possibility of jail and bankruptcy, but what he is struck by is Anita's ability to locate the precise moment for Gordie when everything turned, which was not the same moment when Gordie's life became a shambles because only in the aftermath, after everyone else has begun to forget and forgive the self-inflicted disaster, did his friend begin to feel the weight of consequences, since this is a man who knows not the meaning of consequences, the way his friends, and everyone else, know.

Anita says. "Delayed reaction. He's always been that way, right? The coverage forced him to confront the truth of his background, and later, some of the reason for his financial crash. Think about it. Harold always said Kenton was a crook, but Hui Guo wouldn't believe him." Her husband's eyes brighten, and she can see him begin to click into data-crunch mode, a sure sign he has an idea worth pursuing. What she's thinking, as Larry switches off the stereo and prepares to join her for lunch, is that her own husband is much the same, operating always on a slight delay or, as Larry once described himself to Gordie, slightly ahead of or behind the beat, never inside the bars, never hearing the score the way it's written. But unlike Larry, Anita can't think in musical terms.

Larry leafs through the pile of news clippings, dated as far back as 1986, which Anita has printed off the internet for him. It's a good thing his wife researches with such meticulous ease, and has conquered the mysteries of search engines. Anita sometimes makes him feel old, even though she is blithe about her retirement and her post-menopausal state, bandying about her fifty-plus years with abandon, because she knows she looks much younger.

His own white streaks—be honest, the white these days is more like a mass with a few, diehard black streaks—make him look older than his years.

Harold's call, earlier in the day, nags. It was a surprise, that Laura would say anything about his book, albeit to Harold who isn't just anyone, and he isn't sure how pissed off to be. It's not that he doesn't like the man, but this new awareness, that he is, has been, perhaps always was jealous of Harold's claim on Hui Guo is unsettling. Life unsettles, constantly. Teaching the annually replaceable crop of college kids, raising two daughters, staying married, all this has taught him to improvise through the changes. Easy to adapt to the outer world we inhabit, *but how do we change the habitat of our inner lives?*

And now, on top of everything, *Harold and Laura?* But he quickly dismisses the more difficult notion and considers them only a dinner table pairing—because the two were seated next to each other at Violette's wedding dinner last weekend—nothing more. Conversation.

The apartment door opens. Violette, probably. His daughter's voice calls through his closed study door. "Where's Mom?"

Larry stretches out a foot and pushes his door open. "Shopping."

"Again?"

Violette is tall, almost five ten, the only really tall one in the family for the longest time until Colette suddenly caught up, a growth spurt at seventeen, like a boy, and now surpasses her sister. The family joke is that she is a changeling, and that their real daughter was swooped up and taken home to China by malevolent spirits. Colette calls this mytho-illogic, since changelings belong to a foreign culture, not theirs.

She steps into his space, leans forward and kisses him. "You look tired, Dad."

"I am. This book isn't going well."

"Mom said it was going great?"

"She's an optimist."

Father and Daughter smile at each other. He has never been as close to Violette as to her sister. His older daughter is independent, self assured, and does not need his approval. Since Ryan, however, Violette seems less prickly. He likes the softer, sweeter girl, just as he likes his new son-in-law, who appreciates jazz almost as much as Larry does.

"Dad, there's something I need to tell you. Uncle Hui Guo, his *laisee* was generous."

"Isn't it usually?"

"No, you don't understand. He gave us a check for ten thousand dollars. Surely that's way too much to accept? Ryan thinks he might have made a mistake. He must have meant to write a thousand."

She shows him the Citibank check with its familiar signature, the long tail on the G trailing, the M melting into the A, the y a squashed signoff. "Please talk to him, Dad. I'm uncomfortable accepting so much."

Larry raises his glasses up onto his forehead and squints at the numbers. "The zero's are quite clear. Hui Guo doesn't make those kinds of mistakes." He replaces his glasses, and flicks his thumb against his lips. "But yes, leave it. I'll talk to him."

She hesitates. "Mom wasn't concerned. She thinks he meant to give us this much."

"What do you think?"

"I think she's right, about him meaning to give this, that is. But I don't want to take it. I mean, he's not like a relative or anything, right?" All her uncles and aunts from both sides have been generous as well.

Alone, staring at the check, Larry wonders if the dinner was a good idea. Did it not impose too great an obligation on relatives and friends? His daughter wanted a quiet wedding, with only immediate family present. The wedding dinner was a concession to her parents, to being Chinese. Ryan's family has not insisted on anything similar. He does not call right away, and waits to speak to Anita first.

***

(From Larry's draft of an attempt at revising his book)

How do we change the habitat of our inner lives? If we are to understand anything about Sino-American relations, in fact, about any relations whatsoever, we must first address this question. The expression *Yee Yan Sai Gai*, which literally means a 'two-person' world, is a useful way to think about this issue.

"When two individuals connect—regardless of background, race, religion, culture, or linguistic, educational and socio-economic differences—the reason the connection works or doesn't is entirely dependent on the confluence of their inner lives. On the face of things, each will seek common interests, mutual friends, similar experiences, to help make judgments about the other. This can lead to their becoming close, or, if they are of the appropriate genders sexually, might lead to physical intimacies that create at least the appearance of a *yee yan sai gai*, meaning a connection that is exclusive, bordered off from others in its lustful engagements. This world, in its Chinese context, is meant to be joyous. In an era where sexual relationships are not necessarily the most intimate connection any longer, a platonic friendship can prove equally as, or an even more joyous *yee yan sai gai* while still allowing room for others.

"Likewise, when two nations speak, they employ the accepted language of international diplomacy, through translators if necessary, and trust that the translations are faithful to the intent, if not the word-for-word communiqué of each party.

"In 1949, when the Chinese Communist Party established its power on the Mainland, forcing the Nationalists under Chiang Kai Shek to flee to Taiwan, America found itself in a *ménage à trois* with the "notion-state" of "China." Although it's tempting to employ the analogy of wife and concubine, the latter being the Mainland, it is actually more accurate to compare that relationship to one of a woman with two lovers, neither of who is her husband. While Taiwan was clearly the more established and constant lover for many years— the sugar daddy perhaps—the romance of the other remained risky yet enticing, a lust which might or might not turn into love.

"America, *Mei Guo*, lit. 'beautiful nation,' is the woman who flirts and teases, understanding her power and capacity to encourage or discourage further advances from lovers. 'Most favored nation' (or MFN), for example, is temptingly dangled, like the promise of sex. The promise is a fantasy. 'Most favored' is what a powerful woman confers on as many suitors as she can, and, if she's a smart seductress, does so by making each lover believe he is the *only* one who can ever truly satisfy her. America is powerful and seductive to both her Chinese lovers, although each one only tells her she's smart in order to get what he wants. In the game of lust, as we know, men ultimately want only one thing.

"A little over fifty years later, America's relationship with China is still colored by this original *ménage à trois*. The dynamics have shifted, and today, it is the Mainland with whom America wishes to cement a *yee yan sai gai*. But Taiwan hovers, persistent. A woman scorned may give way to fury, but a man bypassed has infinitely more to prove."

***

Anita puts down the forty or so pages of Larry's manuscript and removes her glasses. "Husband," she says in Chinese, "The Sino-American relationship isn't only about lust. I counted over thirty references to lust so far. Besides, your analogy's off. Men want more than just sex these days." She grins. "That's what our daughters say."

It is two days later. Husband and Wife have so far failed to agree on what to do about their friend's monetary gift to their daughter. The check sits in the least cluttered corner of Larry's desk, a constant reminder of their impasse. Violette, meanwhile, wishes she never brought the subject up, wishes she simply called Uncle Hui Guo herself, per her first inclination.

Larry's face falls. "So you don't like it?"

"I didn't say that. It's just that you seem to be overdoing the sexual references."

He says. "Laura thought I didn't say *enough* about sex."

"Laura read a different book." She pauses. "I read a different book as well."

He remains silent.

"Also," she continues, "you're confusing the romanizations. First of all, why are you using both Cantonese *and* Mandarin? And for the Mandarin, do you realize you've used both Wade Giles and Pinyin?" The former was favored by Taiwan, and remained for many years the standard romanization until the latter, which originated in China, has more or less taken over as the universally accepted style.

"Maybe I should go back to the first book." Laura's book, he thinks.

Anita rolls her eyes in exasperation. "Don't be ridiculous."

Larry leans forward to pick up Gordie's check and holds it up. "So what do we do about this?"

"Your daughter only gets married once."

"We hope."

"What's the *matter* with you?" Her voice rises and she pulls herself out of the armchair by his desk. "Why are you being like this?"

He can't say what the matter is, isn't even aware that a part of him wishes his wife would tell him to give up writing this book entirely. Laura looms. He stares at his wife, who looks so baffled, upset and annoyed all at the same time, and wants to blurt out *that* lust, the unrequited, unacknowledged, smoldering lust for Laura, one he thought had abated with absence, but seeing her again at the dinner, looking casually elegant, when she touched her cheek to his, *that hair*, long, luxurious, the curls lingering near his neck, he wanted to clutch at her then and there. He squeezed her hand a little too tightly, because she said, *wow, strong grip,* and he apologized, saying, *all these people it's the excitement you know* and looked away before he embarrassed himself further. In all the years of their marriage, lust for another has never been an issue, unlike colleagues who couldn't help themselves around all those college girls, and now, he simply doesn't know what to do. His inner habitat is disturbed, assaulted as it has been by this foreign life form, one he finds environmentally hostile. He can no longer take for granted the confluence of their inner lives, the confluence he depends on that is his love for Anita, and this frightens, terrifies him, more than any of the other changes this time of life brings.

"It's nothing," he says. "I just need more time."

"I'll leave you to it, then. Oh, by the way," Anita adds, just before she closes his door. "You'll never guess what's happened." She waits, the pleasure of suspense in her eyes.

"So tell me."

"Laura has a date with Harold Haight. Isn't that wonderful?"

Another day passes. Larry's turmoil is unbearable.

Husband and Wife finally agree, if only to get beyond the impasse, that he will call Gordie and ask, *why so much.* His wife doesn't mean to be mercenary—in fact, Larry would never accuse her of such, not even in this instance—but Anita is not easily perplexed by what she doesn't understand. She has always been fond of Gordie, and accepts almost anything he does without question. Of course, Larry thinks, she doesn't really know him, but his talent to amuse has always made her fond of him. What more do we ask of friends?

Bill Evans' piano solo on "Laura" plays and the song eventually ends. Larry switches off his stereo, and realizes he's had that one song on repeat for over twenty-four hours. He makes his call, gets his friend's voicemail. "Hui Guo, call me," he says. "We have to talk about this over generous gift to Violette. And I need to talk to you, about a woman," he adds, hoping that this last part will yield a response.

Two days later, Gordie finally calls. "I won't talk about the money. Now, what's this about a woman?"

"Can I see you?" There is a long silence. Larry breaks it. "Why not? *Ni hai shi wo de peng you ma?*"

Gordie replies. "*Hai shi.*"

"Then if you're really still my friend, you won't cut me out of your life," Larry says in English.

"That's not what I'm doing."

"But you are. You've changed."

He starts to sing, "The blossom . . ."

Larry interrupts, deliberately mis-speaks the lyrics. "In *both* your cheeks are fading, fading away. Hui Guo, *ni jai nar li.* What's up, doc?"

"There's no woman really, is there? Not you."

"Do you want to find out or not?"

Larry hears hesitation fight the curiosity he knows, has always known, how to pique. Finally, Gordie says. "Okay."

They agree to meet at the townhouse that afternoon. Larry arrives, rings the bell, puzzled by this choice of venue.

It's been years since he's been to the Gramercy home. He and Anita had come to Gordie's parties before the girls were born, and even then, they usually left early. They didn't fit in a drinking crowd, or so they told themselves, preferring to avoid the true issue, their racial discomfort in his too-white world. After awhile, Gordie stopped extending invitations. To the Woos, it was a sign of his diplomatic sense.

"Hui Guo," Larry says when the door opens. "You've lost too much weight. Be careful you don't disappear completely."

Gordie ushers him in. "Wouldn't that be appropriate for an ash fruit?"

The house is like a womb in which his friend floats, attached but unencumbered. Larry stops in the hallway and stares at the huge, empty living room. Gordie has already gone into the one furnished room, the adjacent space he inhabits with its keyboard, stereo, phone and single bed. There is one chair and a folding card table. The walls are bare, bereft of the art that had hung there for years.

Larry asks. "Have you really sold everything like Harold says?"

"More or less. Some stuff's still in storage. Come, sit. Tell me what's wrong."

Without hesitation, Larry tells of all that lust, that disloyal, painful craving, expelling it, if not forever, then anchoring it into a safe harbor where it cannot continue to destroy him. He articulates this to the only person he knows would understand, the one who will not judge him, or anyone, because that is what this man has always been about.

When he leaves several hours later, after his spirit is relieved, only then does he realize that Hui Guo has evaded him yet again, because he knows very little more than what he knew before, because what his friend said is that they should go to Hong Kong again, *just the two of us*, the way they did for the handover, because that trip, Gordie says, was one of the best—not much jazz to speak of but all that food and hanging out, *didn't we have fun*—and it had been awhile since the two of them have had a good time together. Larry was infected by Gordie's enthusiastic excitement, spoken in such reassuringly familiar tones, that he neglected to confront him about all that other incomprehensible behavior, the weight loss for example. Nor did it trouble him that such a trip could not happen soon or easily, not given his own schedule, although Gordie, typically, repeated what he always says about doing anything with anyone, *pal, whenever you're ready*, lobbing the ball not just into his court but right to where it practically falls against his racket so that the question of readiness is entirely, undoubtedly, unmistakably, *his* responsibility.

When Anita asks later, *so did you tell him,* he lies and says yes. He meant to tell Hui Guo about the book, *he did*, and promises he will since they'll see each other again for sure, on the trip to Hong Kong. It's not a complete lie, he reasons with himself for many months afterwards, or at least until the flight in March, 2003, an argument with himself he cannot avoid because he has never, not once, told Anita *an untruth this real or more significant*. The more he reflects on it, the less he knows why this should be so.

Violette Woo's Interlude

Violette is taller than I remembered. When Colette shot up like a beanstalk, we all ceased thinking of Violette as tall. She is however a tall woman who stands straight, comfortable in her height. An elegant thirty-something who is nothing like the ones in the best-forgotten show of that name who are narcissistic and troublingly immature, or so her mother says.

We shake hands. "Marriage must agree with you," I say because she is showing with her second child. Four months, I reckon.

She rubs her belly lightly. "Ryan thinks it's a girl. He says she's already more rambunctious than Tyler was at seven months."

"You mean you don't know the gender?"

"TMS. Too much science. For us." She grins and for a second I see Larry Woo, the parent she is much less like in character although the physical resemblance is unnerving.

I am only touching down briefly, to vote, even though I already believe Kerry will lose but after the last four years, I will not surrender my vote again as a citizen abroad. Violette's email caught me by surprise, asking to meet if I happened to be in New York. We are lunching at the Harvard Club, her *alma mater*.

As expected, she gets right to the point. "I'm worried about Colette. All she talks about is HG," she means Gordie, their Uncle Hui Guo whom the girls have always called HG among themselves, "about how she wants to follow him to wherever he is. She's making herself sick."

"What does she mean, 'follow' him? To where?"

"Cyberspace, I think," and she tells me about the hours her sister spends on the computer, *researching*, but Violette doesn't believe her, thinks Colette is becoming delusional in some altered reality, and is afraid she might do something drastic.

"Like what?"

"I don't know. Suicide? You know, like those cult groups."

"Gordie's not exactly a cult leader."

"Isn't he? Kinda?"

She is so matter-of-fact about him, this "uncle" she's grown up around, this best friend of her dad's who is almost like family. Does she miss him too, I wonder, or was he just this person in her life, someone she acknowledged but did not think too deeply about one way or another, except when he affects the ones she does love?

"So what do you want me to do?"

"Would you see her, talk to her? She might listen to you. Mom's really worried too."

"What about your father?"

She makes an exasperated noise. "Oh you know him. Always ready to make excuses for HG. And for his precious princess."

Privately I'm thinking I don't really have time, because I'm booked to fly out of the country in less than 36 hours. Violette is looking at me with such insistence though. Not pleading, not demanding exactly, but her whole attitude seems to say, *you owe us this, you know, you have to do this*, and I know she's partly right, that I do have to take care of Colette now that she's in my world. Despite the hint of sibling rivalry, that's not what the sisters are about. Colette totters; under the wrong circumstances, she will slip over the precipice. Those are the ones who need our help, who eat up our time and energies because they can't help themselves, can't survive their genius, or talent, or other-worldliness, or whatever quality it is they possess that makes the rest of us responsible for their lives.

She adds. "Do it for HG? You know he'd want you to now that he isn't around to take care of her."

"Okay, okay," I promise. Why does that man have such a hold on me? Mentally I'm rebooking myself on Continental, out of Newark, because I'll have till the afternoon, and Newark is closer than JFK.

***

The card, the old-fashioned printed variety, announcing both the birth of a third child, their first girl, and a move to Shanghai is a surprise. My mail has caught up to me late, typically, over two months this time because the postmark reads July, 2009. It's Violette's job they've moved for, not Ryan's. She has left GE and relocated for Monkey International. With the card is a handwritten note on the family's personalized stationery. *Come stay with us if you're in town. We have tons of room. Best, Vi.* What made her adopt such WASP-ish sensibilities, I wonder. The announcement card, the stationery, these are not Woo niceties, nor for that matter a product of Ryan's family. Perhaps it is a reaction to their intellectually stimulating but materially understated backgrounds. Larry did tell me Anita was shopping a lot these days, perhaps at her older daughter's instigation.

Coincidentally, I am headed for Shanghai the next morning.

Ryan is out the Sunday I pay my visit. *Racquetball,* she says. The baby is on her hip; the two boys circle their mother, eyes wide with curiosity.

"Your brood!" I hug her and her cheek brushes mine. She is not wearing make up, one of the few times I've seen her so relaxed.

"Our helper's out. Chad move please so Auntie can sit?" Her second son scoots obediently over on the sofa.

"He's already walking?"

She grins. "Dad says he was walking at two and a half, and that Chad is just an early bloomer like him."

"So. Monkey, eh?"

We talk for awhile about her new position, as VP for international finance for this fast-growing conglomerate. Less than ten years ago, we barely knew it existed; now it is looking to go public globally. "Mom said I had to take the offer, that it was too good to turn down and would be great for my career. She said Ryan would be fine." Her husband is a financial editor and freelances from home.

"And is he?"

"Too early to tell, but I think he's okay."

It's that matter-of-fact acceptance of reality that reminds me so much of Anita. "So this didn't raise your mother's Nationalist blood pressure?"

Her lips set in a straight line. "Well, it probably did. She just didn't say anything." She goes quiet a moment. "You know something HG told me once? He said that my mother gave up her political beliefs for love. What did he mean?"

"Who knows? You know how he is," but I'm thinking about CCRAS, the Chinese Cultural Renaissance Action Society, which

Anita supported without Larry's knowledge, lending her name and writings to their cause. How they fought when he found out. Anita's father, who died before she and Larry met, was a KMT loyalist through and through. She probably told Gordie. What their daughters don't understand won't hurt them but I cannot believe Anita is entirely happy about Violette being on the Mainland.

"How's your sister?" I ask.

Her face relaxes into a broad smile. "It's like you said, she just needed time to grow up. I am so proud of that little squirt. Imagine! Listing on the NASDAQ. Too bad HG can't see this."

"It is too bad."

I haven't seen Violette since then but the news is generally good. But the way I'll always remember her was at her Chinese wedding banquet, how radiant she was and certain in her joy. I caught a glimpse of Gordie's face that night looking at Violette. A terrible sadness prevailed, as if he longed for an equivalent happiness. But the moment passed and he was toasting her along with the rest of his table, just being Gordie again.

Five months after March, 2003

Pete's call takes Larry back to that earlier time, some two years before Hui Guo disappeared.

"Of course I'll write you a recommendation," Larry assures his best friend's godson. "Your parents know about this, right?"

"Well . . ." Pete means to say that his mother will be told but somehow, that sounds wrong.

"Right?" Larry repeats. The last thing he wants is Harold confronting him, again, about something that isn't his fault.

"My dad's agreed. Ask him yourself if you don't believe me."

"Okay, that's fine. Email me the details. I'll take care of it right away."

"Oh, man, thanks. That's so great of you."

"Only tell me one thing. Why Hong Kong? If you really want to improve your Putonghua, why not Beijing, or even Taipei?"

"Er . . . I'm learning, I mean, I'm going to learn Cantonese."

The boy was telling half-truths, Larry decides later as he sends off the reference. Pete strikes him as flaky but not dishonest. In high school, he was a bright kid, a bit of a nerd, but outgoing and energetic. After the Haights returned from Hong Kong, Pete changed. The divorce. Never easy on kids, no matter what age they are.

But Pete's call reminds him as well of Harold and Laura Silverstein. Harold, of all people. Anita is delighted for her friend since Laura has been solo for quite long enough since her divorce. What did *Harold* have that . . . *mm ho joi laam*—no longer entertain these foolish thoughts—after all, Larry loves Anita who equally loves him back even though she more or less guesses and even understands her husband's lust, and hence his subsequent jealousy, when it comes to Laura Silverstein.

Two in the morning and Larry cannot sleep. He slides out of

bed as noiselessly as possible and makes his way to the study. Anita sniffs, turns over, but is not disturbed.

At the start of summer, he finally told his editor to withdraw the book. The young man was flattered that Dr. Larry Woo would journey all the way to Florida to meet with him in person. Auden has read everything by Larry on Batman vs. Spiderman, Hanna Barbera and Huck Hound vs. the Warner Brothers' Looney Tuners, the adaptation from comic book to animation of Rocky and Bullwinkle. Larry's books and articles kept him going through grad school to at least an ABD, a step away from his own doctorate, which somewhat eased the wrath of his father, the surgeon, from way back when Auden dropped out of med school. So when Larry said, *but I'll deliver the Bugs-Yogi book by fall,* he was overjoyed because he has been waiting to read it and agreed to all Larry's terms since *Honey Money* was by then less than a non sequitur, and the man's vanished anyway so who cares? Secretly, Auden never thought Larry's book about Ashberry should ever have been commissioned but that hadn't been his call.

Yesterday, Larry delivered the Yogi-Bugs manuscript and he is now sleepless, unable as usual to re-direct energies, concentrated for weeks, on completing the book. In his study, he switches on his computer and re-reads his notes from a few months prior to that last trip with Gordie:

"I think this is only what Laura used to call a "journal pit stop," writing a draft to help flush out my thinking which is not the central writing task. What I need is to remember when and why he first became elusive.

"Anita was right about those dead airmen. Okay, summarize. In October of '96, two Chinese farmers stumbled onto the debris of a plane wreck. It turned out to be a B-24, which disappeared over 50 years earlier with all ten of its crew. The bomber had crashed into the side of Mao'er Mountain, southern China's highest peak. In November, Jiang Zemin presented Clinton documentary evidence. American experts eventually identified the remains of the ten Flying Tigers. These remains were returned to the U.S. for burial.

"At the time, Gordie seemed fascinated by the story. He began to read about the Tigers. It was odd, his taking an interest in them, so many years after his father's death. Previously, he referred to the whole AVG/Tigers/CAT era as 'ancient history, best forgotten,' and would crack jokes about 'fancy flyboys' and 'conspiracy crackpots with nothing better to do.' For several months he read, talked to many people, even flew to Guangzhou where he met someone he claimed was a Chinese Tigers pilot, although I think he must have meant CAT. Gordie's no academic, and I didn't know whether or not to believe in his 'research' if you can even call it that.

"Then at some point in '97, he went through a morose streak, right after we came back from the handover trip. The following year, his half sister (Gail Szeto, investment banker) moved to New York, and for awhile he seemed happy to be fostering a relationship with her (I gathered that they hadn't been too friendly before) although that eventually cooled into a kind of non-confrontational détente, each acknowledging that, at heart, they really had nothing in common except for having the same father, one his sister barely knew at all except for what little her mother told her. It was later that year when he said to me something I found startling, that 'Stella was right all along, my dad was a spy.' When I asked what he meant, he dismissed it, saying something about 'too much money and time' and then he imitated Yogi Bear.

"So what are the possibilities? 1) He actually stumbled onto some information (through research and contact with his sister) about his father that made him despise his heritage enough to want to give away all of his money. 2) He hits mid life and realizes his life has been too frivolous, pointless, and wants to make some amends. 3) He's truly gone nuts.

"Stella Shih, who is the only person I know who ever actually met Gordie's father, says he was charming, delightful, a real gentleman. The mother we all know to be a snob. Stella says they were a most unlikely couple . . ."

Larry looks up at the clock on the bookshelf and realizes he's been reading for over an hour. He is about to stop when it occurs to him that the one set of notes he's never re-read were those following his visit to Gordie's after Violette's wedding. A quick search brings up the notes:

> "Hui Guo was right about my infatuation over Laura—he said he noticed her at the dinner, says he can understand why, which, coming from him, is high praise I suppose—that there's nothing wrong with a desire for a little romance. *I'll take romance, he sang, while my heart is young and eager to fly, I'll give romance a try, I'll take romance.* I was surprised how good he sounded. I mean, I know he has a good voice, but it's untrained. He says he's been teaching himself, mentioned Anna but then he quickly dropped that subject. Well, if he's singing, that's good. A man without a profession should at least have a serious hobby. Imitating Bugs *et al* is all very well, but it's hardly what I'd call serious, since all he uses it for is to amuse his friends.
>
> "But about Laura, he wasn't suggesting an affair. Was he? No, he couldn't have been. Could he?"

Just then, the computer crashes. When it finally reboots, which takes longer than usual, there are all kinds of incomprehensible error messages. Too late to wake Anita, or to ring Ryan, the family's tech support.

It's not my fault.

There it is, defensive again. *It's not*, pause, *my fault*. A pseudo-woman's voice, denying the inalienable right to pursue technological advancement, regardless of pitfalls.

Giving up, Larry shuts down the system. There's nothing more to write of Gordie in any event. The matter is now in the hands of the police and unless they can trace his whereabouts, Larry isn't sure if he'll ever see Hui Guo again. Just prior to delivering the final manuscript of his Bugs-Yogi book, he will tell Anita that the book's dedicated to Gordie. *What name will you use for him,* she'll ask, and he'll reply that he still doesn't know.

III

HONEY MONEY

*By the time I was thirty, I understood that much of
what could said about the children of the rich also could be said
about the nation as a whole and about a society that comforts
itself with the dreams of power, innocence and grace.*

from **Money And Class In America:**
Notes and Observations on the Civil Religion
by **Lewis H. Lapham**

You vanish inside yourself. When "the world" no longer looks, sounds, or feels like you, you find ways to escape, disappear, become invisible. It's like the problem of the "World Series" which less than 5% of the world's population considers a "universal" game, and yet you must now, if you wish to be understood, feel it as universal.

Lianhe has never written this even though such thoughts befit her role as a cultural journalist. Instead, her dispatches in Chinese have been about dangerous American schools, where metal detectors check students for guns. About sexually explicit TV talk and reality shows where people betray intimacies of spouses and lovers, shows, she tells her readers, that they are fortunate to be spared. (Later, she will repeat this when the government bans "Sex in the City" from Chinese airwaves, but this is earlier, rather than later).

She has compared such "vulgarity" to the "disgraceful literary pretensions of those degenerates who turn Chinese women into whores for Western consumption." She means, of course, that best selling underground novel *Beijing Babe Seeks Lustful Foreign Males* (translation, hers), *how* she envied it although she never admitted that to a soul, least of all her mother, the cadre in charge of the government department that oversees publications about the west by Chinese expatriate writers. Her mother, who believes in the power of "uplifting literature."

So when Lianhe stumbled onto Gordon Ashberry's story on the internet, on a sweltering August day in New York City, on a day when the air is cooler if more suffocating with the windows closed in her overpriced tenement Noho apartment, it marked the end of exile. There it was, the story that could render her less invisible in Beijing. The kind of American story that would sell back home and, if translated (she could do *that* herself, oh so easily!) be published in English for readers in Asia and those visitors to China desiring the authentic Chinese point of view. She also seeks the power of being raised aloft, above the fray, to a higher and nobler plane. After all, her mother's best friend ran the office charged with selecting contemporary Chinese books for translation into foreign languages. Both women thrived in their party membership.

And so, as 1998 came to its end, Zhang Lianhe boarded a plane from New York for Hong Kong where she still had connections and clout, although, if asked, she probably would not have so described herself. Later, when asked, she explained thus: "It was accidental, I stumbled on the information on the internet, while researching something else."

Pete Haight, in all innocence, had posted his piece about Gordie on the web, after a rather scattered conversation with his godfather. Despite his unusually high IQ, he *was* only sixteen and viewed the web as a private playground which in fact it was. A personal essay, no less, not even a school assignment, just some musings by a lost soul at a time just before blogs, Facebook and rampant narcissism ruled our entire virtual and more-or-less real existence. His words eventually disappeared, the way gazillions of bytes vanished into that breathlessly thin strato-cybersphere, so that no one could trace its origins. Larry Woo would later say Lian-he cum Minnie probably removed it. Anita was right about Minnie—she *was* an opportunist who got lucky although no one knew how lucky in that first, wildly improbable instance, because she troubled to research Haddon Ashberry, because the name triggered something vaguely familiar, and then of course, Haddon! That famous philanthropist who poured hundreds of thousands into CCRAS and how astonished she was to discover it was a woman.

So she headed for Hong Kong, an innocent stopover on her way to Beijing, although why she needed to stop only she could say since there were more direct routes to Beijing. This was just prior to Christmas, the year no one back home had time for her any longer because she had been abroad just long enough to be out of mind. But it was the season, and the expatriate community buzzed with parties and cocktails and dozens of invites which she sought and accepted, and John Haight (the *uncle*, imagine!), that lawyer who had always had a thing for her although the reverse was not true, hoping to score points, offered an introduction to Gordie once she let on she'd heard through "confidential sources" (John reasoned, *since she already knew, he wasn't breaking confidence*) and naturally, *how* could she say no to such an offer, so irresistibly fortuitous, the only attached thread (not *even* a string) being a dinner date with John (who was generous and only frequented the best, *M* at the Fringe, next to the Correspondents Club, exquisite Frenchy-ish fare) at which she told him with a sad smile that she was flattered, *really*, and if she weren't already in love with . . . *Sylvester, back in New York* (she plucked the first male name that came to mind, having just watched *Looney Tunes* on television prior to meeting him—she *really liked* that bird), she would love to, *honestly*. John was crushed, but since he already had a Hong Kong sweetheart who would have married him in a flash should he deign to ask, he did not despair. In love or its virtual version, he believed, unlike in law, one should persist, even against all odds.

In the new year, after the preliminaries of meeting each other for the first time, Lianhe said. "Gordon, I want to write your biography."

It was the end of February. At the Chelsea Café, on the corner of Seventh and West 22nd, Gordon Marc Ashberry frowned over his latté at this woman who barely reached his armpit. She bordered and might have exceeded thirty but dressed low twenties, with too many body parts exposed for the season. Plump and sassy, fluent with an accent. He corrected her. "Gordie."

She hesitated, in awe as she was of this tall, disgustingly handsome and reserved *gweilo*. "So Gordie, can I?"

"Why?"

"Because your action is exemplary."

"My life isn't. Besides, it wasn't supposed to be public knowledge."

She chugged her espresso and squashed the emptied cup into a pulp. These "devil-folk" *gweiloes* were weird, she thought, no matter which foreign land they came from. "This isn't meant to be, like, a full-blown *biography*, more like a long essay. After all, you haven't done anything particularly remarkable until now, right?"

"Flatter me, why don't you?"

They sat side by side at the counter near the front door. A cold blast caught them every time someone entered. Gordie had agreed to meet because she came with an introduction from John Haight whom he'd known forever. John's older brother Harold was his best friend and also a lawyer and the two men once saved his ass big time. Harold currently represented Gordie's charitable interests.

She continued, the true meaning of his last remark lost on her. "It's not your life I'm interested in, but your family's. Your mother was on the board of several charities, including CCRAS, and your father flew with the Flying Tigers. They're both, like, American heroes, right?"

He looked at her dubiously. "Really?"

"Well, they both played somewhat significant roles in history and society. Also, your ancestors went to China. What I want to know is why you would give away their money. Readers in China would find that interesting."

He couldn't help noticing that she did not refer to it as "his" money. "Oh, then you're writing this in Chinese?"

She was insulted. "Of course."

"In that case, no problem."

She looked surprised. "Really?"

"You heard me. Listen, got to run. Give me a call to schedule interviews whenever you're ready."

He left, his cup still full, and, though he would never tell Harold, pissed at John's indiscretion and lack of taste in women.

Lianhe tried to follow him out, but he raced ahead and disappeared around the corner of twenty-third street, heading west.

She hadn't expected him to agree so easily as she told Leilei that evening.

"Lianhe," Leilei began.

"Call me Minnie. I want my friends to get used to my American name."

"Even in Chinese?"

"Why not?"

Leilei shrugged. The two women had known each other since kindergarten in Beijing, although their paths split when they were fourteen. Leilei had entered Hong Kong illegally, found her way to the U.S. and lost sight of Lianhe for many years. Then, out of the blue, her friend had shown up in New York last year, as a grad student in journalism at Columbia, although from what Leilei could tell, she didn't seem to spend much time going to classes, and could afford to fly back to Beijing and Hong Kong frequently. Lianhe was staying with Leilei and her husband temporarily because she had apparently lost her lease, although by now, it had been over three weeks.

"Okay, Minnie."

"He's very good looking, by the way. Tall and slender, no beer belly like most American men. And he has this beautiful baritone voice, like he's singing when he speaks. He makes me go wet down there."

Leilei blushed. Her friend's rampant lusts embarrassed her. "Shut up. You don't even know him. How good is his Chinese?"

"So-so."

And then Lianhe was off, to work on her latest idea, which meant tying up their computer again for hours, the one from Taiwan loaded with Chinese Windows. Why her friend's expensive new laptop only had American English Windows was something Leilei didn't understand and, even though she knew she should have, didn't raise with Minnie-Lianhe. She resigned herself to cleaning up the apartment—her friend was nothing if not messy—and promised herself, *tomorrow, she would tell her it was time to move out.* If she was procrastinating, she preferred not to acknowledge this because what use, after all, was admitting the truth if you weren't going to do anything to change things, at least, not as long as you didn't have to?

Not even one of those any-Chinese-girlfriend-will-do boys, Leilei told her husband in bed that night. *At least those ingratiate themselves by speaking well. I don't know why she wants an American boyfriend so badly. She'll only be disappointed again.*

Chou-wen was half asleep. His wife's friend was a pain, and the sooner she moved out the better. What disturbed him most was the way Lianhe came on to him, right in front of Leilei, although his wife never seemed to notice, absorbed as she was these days by the pregnancy, almost two months along.

"Go to sleep," he murmured, stroking the small swell of her body. Her hand rode his, following his rhythm, the rigid fingertips barely touching his knuckles, a legacy of inadequate heat in Hong Kong and New York. But those days were long over. He had found this amazing woman and married her, and now, she was no longer an illegal, unable to make a decent living. Soon they were both asleep.

"*How* long did you say you've been a writer?" Gordie asked, as they began the first interview. Lianhe cum Minnie had arrived at his home without tape recorder, notebook or writing implement, and requested paper and pen.

She sighed. "Look, I know you think I'm a flake, because I seem so unprepared, but someone knocked my bag off my shoulder onto the subway tracks and the train rolled over it. Honest. I'm not as dumb as I look."

He glanced at her and stared off in the distance, an aversion not lost on Lianhe.

Her tiny eyes and nose were like the wrong size buttons and she had too-round cheeks. Had Gordie bothered to reflect, he might have said she resembled a blowfish. Glasses would have balanced things out. Not *ugly* exactly, but . . .

"Okay," he conceded. "Shoot."

"So, like, was this some kind of post-modern gesture? Redefining the essence of the inheritance tax, as it were?"

Gordie grinned. Perhaps this would turn out better than he anticipated.

Half a year later, when preparing for the lawsuit, Gordie could not recall a great deal of those first two hours they spent together, except that he laughed a lot. Harold pressed him to remember—*had he signed anything, demonstrated how to forge signatures perhaps, since his mimetic abilities extended to handwriting?* Gordie did not think so. The document that appeared, with his signature, pledging a million dollars to an organ transplant center in Beijing, looked entirely genuine. It was witnessed by Zhang Lianhe and dated the day of their first interview, but by then, all her interviews were done and she had become elusive, unreachable, her cell phone number having been long disconnected. Leilei and Chou-wen, whom Gordie had met a couple of times with Lianhe before she moved out of their apartment, could shed no further light on Minnie's whereabouts.

"She can't just disappear," Harold Haight declared.

It was Sunday night in the middle of September. They were in Gordie's almost empty townhouse in Gramercy Park, the exception being the study off the downstairs vestibule which Gordie had turned into his temporary living space. This was only, as he had told Harold, until he could make arrangements with a realtor to sell it.

"And," he added, raising his glass of scotch, "you're insane."

"Yes she can, anyone can, and no I'm not. She hasn't disappeared. This is some kind of game she's playing."

Harold, fatigued by a long week of too much alcohol, his own difficult marital situation, and despair at his former college roommate's unaccountable behavior, hiccupped. He readjusted his position on the floor, but could not get comfortable. "C'mon, quit with *your* games. You don't give a shit about whatever silly scam she's trying to run. Even the organ center has gone quiet, now that they know we're not going to back down. Trust me, the problem's over. But you, why all this? How do you think you're going to live once all this is gone?" He waved at the barren room and shifted his bulky physique again.

Gordie, lithe and as slender as when he was twenty, appeared not to notice his friend's discomfort. "I'll figure something out. I always have."

"Gord, we're not eighteen. The protest is over. Don't sell the townhouse.

"I want to."

Since Gordie had begun what he called his "re-distribution of wealth" over a year ago, there were moments Harold wanted to *weep.* His best friend was transforming before his eyes, like a magician creating an illusion on stage. But his friend was real, breathing, living, the same as he had always been from the afternoon they met, when Harold had tossed his bag onto the bed on the left side of the dorm room, stared at Gordie rolling a joint and declared, "I'm allergic to smoke–Asthma," to which Gordie had replied, "then I'll take the weed outside," and always had, guarding the clean air of their room with a vigilance as if his own lungs depended on it.

The phone rang, its metallic echo loud through the vacant space. Harold heard Gordie say, "Leilei! Hey, is the baby out yet?" and then a conversation in Mandarin ensued when suddenly, in English, the exclamation, "holy shit!"

"What is it?" Harold roused himself off the floor, leg half asleep.

Gordie returned holding the phone, its cord stretched around the corner from the hallway. "She's going into labor. Chou-wen's out of town."

"Address?" Harold was already onto 911 on his cell.

A red streak ran from the temple to the chin on the baby's face. Under the lighting of the maternity ward, it looked like a scar.

"It's terrible," Leilei said. Chou-wen sat beside the hospital bed, holding her hand. He had left an urban planning conference in Chicago to meet their first newborn child, a premature daughter.

Gordie and Harold, who had stayed through the delivery, stood on the opposite side and gazed at the new parents. Harold was wallowing, nostalgic for his own children's births.

"It's not so bad," Gordie said. "The doctor said it'll probably fade."

"But what if it doesn't?" Leilei said. "It wouldn't be so bad if it had been a boy."

Chou-wen's fingers brushed the discoloration on his forehead. An unconscious gesture. "Shh," he told his wife. "Don't worry. Be happy it was a safe birth, thanks to our friends." He smiled gratefully at the two men. Strange that his wife's troublesome girlfriend had led to this connection. Gordon, Chou-wen decided, was more than okay, and by extension, so was Harold.

Harold said. "So why were you calling, Leilei?" He ignored Gordie's glare. It wasn't the thing to ask, he knew, not now, but loose ends made him physically ill.

Leilei sat up and exclaimed. "Oh, I almost forgot. It was about Lianhe."

"Lullabelle," Gordie said. "What, did she surface?"

"Surface?" Leilei looked puzzled.

Harold, who spoke no Chinese but by now had learned how to communicate in a half-foreign tongue, rolled his eyes. "He means, did she contact you?"

"No, but I heard from a friend that she published a book last month in Beijing. About you." She pointed at Gordie. "It's very popular. The title is *Tian Tian Mei Guo Feng Fu*, which means something like *Sweet, Sweet American Fortune.*" Her energy flagged, and she leaned back, still puzzling over the verb "to surface."

"Well, damn," said Gordie. "The little ... so she did it after all."

What no one expected was the almost back-to-back publication of an English version, translated by none other than Minnie herself, which appeared in Beijing that winter. Within months, Minnie Chang had acquired a US publisher, and *Honey Money* appeared in time for spring (easy, since the Beijing press simply printed more copies with a different cover in a co-publishing deal brokered by none other than Minnie herself), and Gordie found himself a hero, especially on the internet, among the young, privileged, slumming crowd of all the major urban centers worldwide who deemed it fashionable to decry the capital markets and dynasties that spawned and nurtured them. The same crowd, and its loyal hangers-on, who thrived on the all-encompassing "whatever" buzz—a lack of meaning being the essence as long as the media hounded and chased and created infamy—and who made the internet seem bigger than it was.

Spring of 2000 was memorable on many counts. The war on terror was still in the future. The media blitz following the publication of *Honey Money* had begun but was not yet overwhelming. And Zhang Lianhe or Minnie Chang, a.k.a. Lullabelle at least to Gordie, was more than merely solvent for the first time in her adult life.

Minnie (since hardly anyone she associated with now could pronounce or even knew her Chinese name) invited three female acquaintances to lunch at Windows on the World to celebrate. She had invited a male acquaintance first on his own but he declined.

"You look fabulous," pronounced the first woman, because Minnie had lost weight and acquired a new hairdo and clothes.

"Stunning," agreed the second, as she ordered a bottle of expensive Chardonnay.

"It's a perfect new look," declared the third.

The three New York women, all young, connected and upwardly global, were not above flattering the latest potential media darling. The first was a "journalist" (she inspired others to write, given her family's inside connection to political power), the second was "in television" (or rather, slept convincingly with the TV woman who counted), and the third did media relations for the publishing industry (sadly, she needed to make a living ever since Father drained the trust fund, illegally). Not one had read *Honey Money* but each could speak authoritatively about the book as if they had.

Minnie beamed gratitude, but was not entirely fooled. The meal, she calculated, would run up her credit card over two hundred dollars. But she smiled and chattered with these women, all of who would be responsible, in some fashion, for launching her forth into even greater fortune and fame. Female solidarity, as long as a rival love-interest wasn't in the picture.

"So why's this guy so reticent about public appearances?" asked the second as she tasted the expensive wine.

"He's shy," Minnie replied.

"*Everyone* wants to be on television at least once," she said, nodding at the waiter.

"What about a magazine profile," said the first, "somewhere soft core, not like," she wrinkled her nose, "oh, I don't know, not like *Harper's*."

"He won't do interviews at all."

"Obviously," said the third, "Minnie will just have to be the front person. After all, she is the author."

They all nodded in agreement, at both the wine and this sage insight.

Their seeming casualness masked ruthless ambition and street smarts. In the months that followed, the trio turned Minnie into a recognizable celebrity that even *The Wall Street Journal* would profile. For Minnie, it was a long and lucrative fifteen minutes. She was feted in Beijing and New York. Her mother, now deceased, would have been proud.

By the end of summer, Gordie was forced to delay selling the townhouse, to avoid anything else that might draw public attention, much to Harold's delight.

"You're the establishment's nightmare and philanthropy's dream," Harold said when Gordie called to say he would postpone the sale. "Do you know how many trust fund babies are suddenly taking an interest in their wealth?"

"That wasn't the point."

"What is the point, Gord? You still can't explain why you're doing this."

"I guess maybe I still don't know."

"You know your trouble?"

"Like you won't tell me?"

"You don't think things through before you act. You never have." Harold resisted mention of the whole arms trading fiasco, well over a decade ago. He had gone out on a limb to rescue Gordie that time, co-opting his brother John for reinforcement, but then, wasn't that what friends were for?

"Zip it, Harold."

"Hold on there, bud, I'm still your lawyer and . . ." but the phone went dead. These abruptly terminated calls were becoming a pattern. He was about to hit redial but thought better of it. Give the man a day or two, he decided, he'd come around. Harold was nothing if not patient and eventually, he would wrest some sense out of Gordie and terminate this, this, ridiculous . . . *charade*. That's all it was. Surely.

Two days later, Gordie left a voicemail on his cell.

"Lullabelle showed up. She said 'You're so American. That's how you could give away your money and not even know why.' Can you beat that? Some nerve, huh?"

Harold listened to the message twice. Typical Gord, not a word about what mattered, like how to get in touch with that damned woman. But what he did hear, clear as a bell, was Gordie making almost the *exact same declaration* about himself, two years earlier, when he first announced that lovely lucre was his nemesis but that now, at last, he had an exit strategy. *I'm American. That's why I can give away my money without having to have a reason.* Didn't Gord remember? What was this, early Alzheimers?

Two years later, and Zhang Lianhe is now Minnie Chang, author, who flits between New York and Beijing as long as someone invites her. Now here she is, as the very short story of *Honey Money* draws to its close, in New York, wondering what to do next in the era of dwindling royalties. For one thing, she is still on a student visa, just barely, and half hopes to get legal help from Harold Haight or one of his acquaintances. It is a long shot, she knows, popping into his office like this. *Chutzpah*. What New Yorkers often say they admire.

Harold recognizes Minnie Chang from her photograph. Because they haven't met till this moment, he sees only the attractive and poised figure she now cuts and not the overweight and clumsy woman Gordie described. He signals his assistant to leave the door open which Tim does, pointedly, offended by the woman's demeanor towards him, which changes as soon as he presents her to Harold.

She enters his office tentatively and hesitates before taking a seat. "So you're the best friend."

He suppresses his desire to be rude. "What do you want?"

She cocks her head, a half smile on her lips. "Can *you* forgive me?"

"You hardly seem contrite."

"That's because you don't know me. Being Chinese, I find it hard to show my emotions openly."

He wants to remind her that he used to live in Hong Kong and knows plenty of emotional Chinese, so she can cut all the "it's a cultural thing" crap, but decides against this. "Look, I know you and my brother are acquainted, but if you don't mind, I am busy. What is it you want?"

"So why did you agree to see me?"

"Miss Chang . . ."

"Minnie, please. May I call you Harold?"

"No."

She stands up. "All right, you're upset. Perhaps another time you'll agree to see me again and let me explain." Her eyes narrows. "I'm not some kind of monster." And with that, she walks out of his office.

When she's turned the corner down the passage towards the elevator bank, Harold tells Tim. "Don't put anymore of her calls through."

After Minnie leaves Harold's office, she stands for a moment on Water Street, wondering where to go next. Harold's office is located at the eastern end of the Financial District, furthest away from the wreckage of the World Trade Center. He was understandably cool. What she hasn't told him is that John Haight has kept his distance since the publication. What she had counted on was that John and Harold, despite their being brothers, probably didn't talk about these kinds of things or much of anything for that matter. It was typically American.

She is getting nervous. Although the paperback's selling—certainly enough to earn back her meager advance since Impermanent Press had not expected success of this order—*Honey Money* is still below that all important radar. Just before Christmas, someone said *movie deal*, and for a week or so, she imagined herself in Hollywood, talking to the likes of Richard Gere or Hugh Grant, both potential male leads in her eyes although the latter would have to do an American accent (she assumed he could since, after all, even *she* could). But that fizzled out, just as translation rights haven't sold. "Cult following," a label she dreads, is already bandied around about her book. It is not *Wild Swans* or *Shanghai Baby*, despite her very Chinese perspective (the original book continues to sell fabulously well in China), although sometimes she thinks perhaps *that's the* problem, being a Chinese who only journeys to the West for convenience (that is the truth about her, is it not, and as her mother always said, writers must be truthful). She is a patriot and proud of it. She owes it to her late mother to brook no disdain by the Party.

But that doesn't mean she can't use a green card.

Harold appears at the door of his building, and turns in the opposite direction. For a moment, she almost follows him, but reconsiders. Leilei. She should go see Leilei. Her friend will be pleased to see her again. Heading west to what remains of the N/R line, she boards the subway and goes uptown.

The door to their building is ajar so she let herself in without buzzing. Chou-wen is home. "What do you want?" His abrupt hostility startles her; she hadn't expected it.

"I was in the neighborhood and thought it would be nice to pay Leilei a visit?"

He doesn't open the door or invite her in. "She had to take the baby to the doctor."

"Will she be back soon? Maybe I can wait."

"She might be late."

Minnie whips out her cell phone. "Does she have her hand phone with her? I can ring and see how long she'll be."

Just then, the elevator opens and Leilei appears with the baby, completely negating her husband's tale.

"Hey," Leilei said. "How are you? Come on in. Chou-wen, why are you standing in the doorway like that?" She glares at her husband who glares back. The baby burps, gurgles and grunts. As her friend follows her into the apartment, both women spend the next few minutes cooing over the miniature human.

Chou-wen puts on his coat. "I'm going out for awhile."

Leilei frowns. He leaves anyway, even more annoyed than at the initial sight of Lianhe, wishing he'd been ruder so that she would have left before his wife's return.

"So why," Lianhe begins. The door slams and she glances up. "So why didn't you come to any of my book parties? You did get the invitations, right? I haven't seen you for ages."

Leilei busies herself with placing the baby in the playpen, and keeps her back to Lianhe. "Oh, you know how things are with a new baby."

"None of our friends came to any of them," Lianhe continues. "Everyone's upset at me, aren't they?"

"Come on, Lianhe, what do you expect?

"Minnie."

Leilei sighs. "Lianhe, you have plenty of new friends, right?" She pours tea into a tumbler and hands it to her. "I've seen your picture in all kinds of news magazines. You're famous. And rich. People get jealous, that's all." Despite everything, the admiration in her voice is unmistakable. It is Lianhe at twelve all over again, winning the national writing prize for her essay, making her whole school proud and she, Leilei, the best friend could bask in adulation as well. "You look very good too," she continues, fingering the cashmere cloak Lianhe has draped carelessly over a chair. "Such nice clothes."

"I had to lose over ten kilos. For all the photographs." She looks at the baby across the room. "Your son's so big already."

"Daughter."

"Oh."

"Her name's Mei-lan, and her English name's Alexandra."

"Mei-lan. Your mother's name."

"Yes."

Both women are silent, remembering. Years since Leilei has seen her mother or her family. Illegal immigrants, as she used to tell Chou-wen when they first met, can have no family except the new ones they create.

Lianhe speaks abruptly. "My mother died the year before last, waiting for a new kidney. She never knew about my books."

"Oh no." Leilei places a hand on her friend's shoulder.

"All those people, people she was good to, none of them did anything to help her," Lianhe's voice turns shrill. "I was desperate. They could have pushed her up the waiting list. She *deserved* it. She shouldn't have died."

"Shh, it's over. Don't upset yourself."

Lianhe begins to cry. "There's been no one I could tell. I don't have anyone anymore."

Leilei rises, goes over to her friend, and takes her in her arms, saying "Shh, you still have me." Lianhe weeps. So complicated, Leilei thinks, this way of the world. She hadn't known about the mother's illness. Her friend's odd behavior—that silly forgery, trying to steal Gordon's money for the organ transplant center in Beijing—it all begins to make sense now. Lianhe was just trying to bribe her way to a kidney, that was all. It had just been an unbelievably stupid and convoluted idea.

In fact, as Leilei tells Chou-wen that night over dinner, *she's always been somewhat bullheaded. She was very surprised that Gordon stayed in touch with us and I told her she just didn't understand how to relate to people properly. That's always been her problem.*

Chou-wen selects a mouthful of snow pea leaves with his chopsticks. "She's a selfish whore," he says as he chews.

"Don't say things like that."

"But it's true, isn't it?"

"Even so, you still shouldn't say that. It isn't nice."

He shrugs and continues eating, grateful that his wife no longer extends herself over much to this "friend," this woman who brings nothing but trouble. Leilei tells him that Lianhe's visa will run out soon, and what he thinks is *good riddance, she'll have to go home,* while Leilei talks on and on about how they should try to find a way to help and doesn't he know an immigration lawyer?

Zhou Chou-wen's Interlude

"Why does everyone want to write a book about Gordon?" Chou-wen says. He pronounces it Gorr-don, to rhyme with Don, and curls the r Beijing-style.

"I'm not writing about him," I say.

I've just heard Professor Zhou's lecture on Cincinnati's urban planning which he gave at City University of Hong Kong. His particular interest is the use of eminent domain by city governments; he characterizes this power as akin to that from "the barrel of a gun" and analyzes US models that can be compared to urban planning in Chinese cities, Shanghai and Hong Kong being two current case studies.

He looks at me dubiously.

"Honest Professor Zhou, I'm not," I half tease in English.

There it is, that proud glint because I call him "professor." He likes this tiny sign of respect from a former student, especially a Chinese one, and even though he wasn't a professor then, I used to call him Zhou *lao shi*, which sounds like honest Zhao but means teacher. Even though his years in America have democratized him—*please not Professor, he says, not from you.* Even though he knows I'm only half serious, the lapse is deliberate and I do this because to reinstate a little lost pride is, after all, a worthy endeavor. He, like others who ended up in the West, had to work their way back up to where they used to be in China.

"Okay, I believe you."

It's only a month and a half since Gordie disappeared in March, and we're smack in the middle of SARS. I've just returned from Hainan Island to where I escaped for a few, SARS-free days. Chou-wen's lecture was badly attended. He had considered cancelling it because so many public events have been rescheduled.

The Pacific Coffee in Festival Walk, an adjacent mall to where we've headed, is virtually empty and we have all the comfortable sofa sections to ourselves.

"This is nice," I say. "It's actually a pleasure being in Hong Kong when public is private."

He frowns. "Surely this is not a good thing?"

"Gordie would think it is."

He ponders this, and I imagine a mind like a cityscape, one that keeps re-arranging itself until things fall together into all the right spaces. "But he's such a gregarious man why would you say that?"

I tell him then all about Gordie's disappearance and his shock is palpable. "You're wrong, he can't possibly have disappeared. He's probably just playing a joke on all of us, you know how he is." Then. "I'm sure that's it. After all, he promised to come to our baby's full month dinner and Gordon doesn't break promises, right?"

"Congratulations. Didn't know Leilei was pregnant."

He beams. "Yep. Due in June and the doctor says this one won't be premature."

"Good going for an old man," because we're roughly the same age, pushing fifty.

"Young wife, young heart."

As long as I've known Chou-wen, I don't know him well. When we were both grad students, he was my Mandarin tutor, but I lost track of him for many years. He was part of the early crop of Chinese sent to U.S. universities after President Carter officially reopened relations with the People's Republic in '79. Only he didn't want to go back, and to stay on, did a paper marriage with a willing American friend. Later, he helped Leilei legalize her status when he married her; she's twelve years his junior. It was Gordie who reconnected us in New York.

Now, it is again Gordie who brings us together, the way he does so many people.

"Minnie's book," I begin.

"Yes, I know, she's silly, irresponsible, the whole shebang."

I like the way he inserts *shebang* into his Putonghua.

"But only in English," he continues.

"You read it, then?"

He hesitates, and I'm guessing he hasn't. Chou-wen is a real scholar and does not presume to pronounce on work he hasn't actually read, as some do, relying on the skim or abstract or summary by a research assistant.

"No, but Leilei read both versions, and made me read at least the first chapter of the Chinese one. When my wife's right, she's right. The book in Chinese is a serious book, and does not have the same opportunistic tone of the English. Nor the flimsy research, apparently."

He goes on to say that the original Chinese text is actually Lian-he cum Minnie's story, as opposed to Gordie's story of giving away his money, which is only summarized in one section. *According to Leilei,* he notes, her friend wrote about her own life in the U.S., about how alienated she felt, and used Gordie's act as a way of showing a difference in cultural values that contributed to her alienation. The English text was less a translation than a completely different book, a sensational, rather than a thoughtful one, and was significantly shorter. An easy read. "After all," he concludes, "Lian-he really is a Party child. Her parents marched with Mao."

"I didn't know that," I say. "Makes her seem less of a . . ." I want to say "bitch" but that seems inappropriate somehow. Chou-wen may be more American now than he used to be, but he doesn't swear in English. So I say, "bad person."

"Oh I don't know about that. That woman's a moveable disaster, untrustworthy, and always will be."

INTERMISSION

Bino and I are in a limo, headed for JFK. He's off to Manila and I'm headed back to Hong Kong. Things are tense. We don't see each other nearly enough given my transnational life where I inhabit the flight path connecting New York to Hong Kong (and lately, even the South Island of New Zealand, though that's *really* another story). We're in a stretch limo, white, because DeLillo wrote it for us back in 2003 and time has passed and now I'm X-woman, wrestling with Gordie, making it up as I roll along. Sometimes not so merrily.

X-woman, says Bino, *it's all so white in here.*
Bino is dark chocolate Asian while I track somewhere along the spectrum between Meyer lemon and chocolate. The thing is, we both surface from time to time when the fiction becomes too real.
I say, Chinese is white in American.
Yellow, he replies.
Lousy color.
Okay, okay but you know what I mean.
We're all white, like the ghosts of *gweilo, gaijin, farang, et al.* We pretend like our race and complexions really mean something but we've been whitening, lightening, de-tanning, demeaning anything darker than white.
Fashion?
Fashion is mindless. Our brains are whitewashed.
North and south. Like Italy. Spain. You name it. Not dead white poets white.
You don't think so?
China wasn't wholly colonized, not by the white man I mean. Not the Mainland.
China colonized itself inside and outside the Wall, and before the Wall it kept moving its borders, shape shifting, until their language became our language thanks to some accidental oversight by the British garrisons. At least in Hong Kong and now, even on the

Mainland. English is just another thing to conquer, to make ours.

And what happened to "Chinese English"?

That's Linguistics. Not the way we write.

X-woman, it's time for a daydream. You're raining too hard on all the parades that march to different drummers.

Umbrella Country. You said it in your first book, didn't you?

Shelter me, my dear.

From the rain or the language?

Write. Just write.

Okay, okay, back to the sewers we go.

IV

GORDIE, HAROLD & ALL THOSE HAIGHTS

If dreams are made of imagination,
I'm not afraid of my own creation.
With all my heart, my heart is here for you to take.
Why should I quake?
I'm not awake.

from the introduction to **"Isn't It Romantic"**(1932)
music by **Richard Rodgers** • words by **Lorenz Hart**

1

Pete was not wrong about his father's pain. The first time Gordie tried to tell Harold that Isobel was cheating on him, Harold was a tad distracted. He was in the midst of closing a huge deal for his firm and had not slept more than a couple of hours each night before heading back to the office. Gordie was staying with Harold in Hong Kong.

What Gordie said, because he knew Pete was out that night, was "Go home, Harold. You'll lose Isobel otherwise."

"I am home. She just needed a break is all. She'll be back."

"Not if Trevor has his way."

Harold glared at the man he called his best friend, the one he would risk almost anything for, and often had. "Naaah, no way. We're okay, you know just minor problems. Besides, even if she were to—not that she would, mind you—she's over him, has been for years. It's called 'trust,' something that happens in marriage, Gord. You should try it sometime."

It was mid summer of '95. Around Easter, his wife told him that she would be going home for the summer. Harold Jr. was starting college in the fall—at UC Berkley, because he couldn't get into Yale or any of the other big three, much to his father's consternation—so it made sense that she go back, to help him with his cross-country move. *Sure,* he'd said, and not thought further about it.

What Isobel had said, a few weeks prior to that was, *Harold, I hate it here.*

It had been a quiet Saturday evening. No society event or enforced business dinner with too much booze. Isobel gave their Filipino helper an extra evening off and cooked. The boys were out, Harold Jr. at the clubs and Pete was, as always, at Marcel's or so his parents thought (Marcel's parents thought their son was at Pete's). Harold had actually made love to his wife, something that hadn't happened in awhile. The effort exhausted him and he barely heard what she said.

"Uh huh."

"I'll go crazy if I stay much longer. I just don't fit."

He was on the fringes of sleep, his lids getting heavy. "What doesn't fit?"

"Me. The wives, all they talk about are their maids, about how stupid they are, how they never do anything right. Don't they know how lucky they are to have domestic help? Who has that back home? Who?" She meant the expat wives of the other investment bankers at the firm or other of Harold's business associates.

"And," she continued, "all they do is start on the wine at noon and this goes on all afternoon. Half of them are smashed by five."

"Smashed," he responded, but Isobel heard the deadening sleep in his voice and shook him roughly.

"Harold, please wake up."

He rolled over and his girth shook. Isobel grimaced. Her husband had gotten fat in the two years since moving here. How had that happened? Harold grunted and she knew it was over, he was down for the count, dead to the night. She switched off the bedside light and resigned herself to post-coital wakefulness.

At least he lasted long enough to make me come. How had this happened, the husband who was and always had been her wonderfully compatible lover, how had he become this *bang, squirt, thanks, snore* in the rare moments they ever did it at all? This man who never listened to anything she said anymore? In fact, how had all this happened, his leaving tax law and the practice he'd been with since they first met, his wanting to prove himself, or something, in this lousy rat race of deals and gold-out-of-straw world? Harold did not belong in investment banking, certainly not in Asia; that was what was making him crazy and why he was letting himself go with too much food, booze, all that stress. Why they no longer lived like a family. Why Harold was no longer her best friend. Why this was just another one of many frustrating conversations, at least for her.

That night, Isobel left their bedroom and sat on the verandah of their luxury flat for hours. The city's verdant splendor along the hillside below, and their enviable, untrammeled view of the harbor and Kowloon, once so enchanting, was invisible to her now. She was not given to self pity or depression, and even in those tougher moments of life—*when Mom died so unexpectedly that it killed Dad less than a month later* or *Harold blowing a gasket because Junior didn't get into Yale*—she could summon up that Yankee fortitude, the inner strength required to move on, with a reliable dependency borne of character and upbringing. She was a Whitman who did not sing a song of herself but of the *there but for the grace of God* anthem. Ever grateful for her well being—an only child of older parents, well loved, well educated, well married with boys of whom she could be proud— what more did a woman want? She even had religion and Harold was, despite himself, still a good Catholic boy, and this was how they had raised their sons. That night she sat for hours, this woman who did not whine or despair or relinquish discipline because she was the tough who got going when she should. That night, this woman wept.

At one of Gordie's numerous townhouse parties, in the long-gone evenings of wine and gardenias, Isobel was sipping a champagne cocktail, trying to decide if her host was a potential mate. She had met Gordie casually, several months earlier through a classmate from her art history days at Smith who claimed she wasn't interested. The man was a little too rich for her blood, Isobel knew, being a dentist's daughter from Northampton, Massachusetts, but able to hold her own in this Ivy and Seven Sisters crowd thanks to frugal but doting parents and a scholarship. Isobel had just turned twenty-six in this summer of '77. She worked at a gallery in midtown and was hearing the maternal clock chime. These days, she was very interested in any man with potential, although there were nights her interest bordered on desperation.

A masculine hand landed lightly on her back, caressed bare skin. "Miss Isobel Whittington, I believe?" Gordie said. "May I introduce Harold Haight?"

She turned to face a stocky, dark haired man, built like the wrestler he was. Tall enough to be presentable. But such a serious and anxious face! "Whitman," she corrected, adding, "and no, not related."

Harold saw a not-too-tall, pale redhead, whose eyes flashed like an Atlantic tempest. Her plunging neckline was wholly justified. Attractive. Probably willful. His interest rose more than a notch. As they shook hands, he asked. "Not related to whom?"

Gordie gazed upwards at the heavens. "For a lawyer, you're sadly illiterate. But excuse me," and he was off to make other introductions. Realizing, Harold squeezed his lips in a grimace. "Slow, I'm afraid. Sorry."

The self effacing blush stirred Isobel's maternal instincts. She smiled, showing off a sexy overbite and full lips, her other good features. "Don't be. I don't read him either. Now where is it you practice and how do you know Gordie?"

A week earlier, Gord had offered to invite Kathleen O'Mara for Harold.

"Why?" He demanded. "Don't you get enough of your own action?"

"Come off it Harold you *know* I wouldn't. She's a nice girl, *and* your sister's best friend. How can I invite Patti and not her?"

"They're not so close anymore. Besides, Patti's all wrapped up in Richard and the wedding these days. They probably won't come. *Don't* invite Kath."

Was it his imagination or did Gord seem pissed off at the mention of Richard? Harold had always suspected his buddy was sweet on Patti—*that would have been grand for sis, and Gord*—but she didn't give him the time of day, always being such a wise ass. *No interfering*, he had decided, tempted though he was in past times to encourage his friend because Gord was basically shy, despite the way he carried on. Richard was a good enough guy but . . . here, he shut down. It was exhausting, listening to the parents. So what if Richard was Jewish? As long as Patti and he worked things out, why did that matter? In fact, it bugged him that his parents were being such a pain, given all their liberal crap. Their last family dinner a month or so ago ended badly because he wound up slamming his fist on the table—*I don't care, there's no way I'm voting for Jimmy Carter!* Pop had turned purple and Mom looked ready to cry. Even John—Judas—ducked out, unwilling to argue that one, while Patti and Richard went silent as he nursed his hand.

Now, Isobel Whittington, *Whitman*, was leaning too close, disturbing him with cleavage. He blinked, breathed deeply and trained his eyes away, but then she had that mouth with those dark crimson lips which were moving, saying, "Catholic school, nuns in bat wings, the whole nine yards."

He smiled at her, more than a little dreamily. "Me too."

"But a good education," they began together and laughed.

"Say," he said. "It's hot in here, isn't it? How 'bout going for a walk?"

"Love to," she replied and bent down to slip her sandals back on, and he caught a glimpse of lace that almost revealed what he knew must be God-given, perfect breasts.

Isobel let him touch her a little that night, here and there *nothing too rude*, and gave him her number. It was late when he got back to his apartment and recalled, *shit, Kath*, because he was supposed to go over to her place that night, something he would never in a million years confess to Gord, because his buddy didn't understand, *a man needed relief*, because unlike Gord, there weren't a dozen willing girls to bed because they wanted his money, or at least, his good looks, a dozen or more girls Gord regularly strung along, promising nothing. Harold knew himself and his own family too well. The girl he finally bedded for real would be one he could bring home and marry. No way Kathleen O'Mara would ever be a Haight. *That* would be worse than even Patti and Richard Kahn. Gord didn't understand. It was a Catholic thing.

He picked up the phone and replaced it without calling. Too late now, and besides, things might be changing, his luck might actually be turning now that his possibilities at the firm seemed more secure. Kath was smart. Anyway, she slept around, *sure she did, always had.* Kath knew the score and wouldn't complain.

So midsummer, mid nineties, Asian economies booming and the deals flying a kilometer a second, Harold was in no mood to hear bad news about anything, least of all from Gord. His buddy was in town for their once-upon-a-time annual midsummer boys' night out, a longstanding tradition, and even after life changed radically so that "annual" lost its standing, they managed occasionally to pull one off. What puzzled Harold was why Gord seemed so serious, not wanting to drink, only wanting to "talk." Like a woman.

The two men were standing in his living room.

"I mean it, Harold. The Isobel I know wouldn't leave you alone for longer than a week, maybe two."

"Forget about it. Let's go get a bite. What about a steak? My treat."

"And that's the other thing. You, are, fat." He spoke slowly, spacing his words the way Harold did, in deliberate imitation.

That was when Harold took a swing. Gordie ducked, and his punch landed on the oblong, columnar, standing lamp, a heavy affair, which wobbled on its base. His hand bled where it caught the edge. "Fuck you Gord."

"Shit Harold, what the hell's wrong with you? Here, let me see that." They could have been in college again, Gordie nursing a Harold wound, physical or otherwise. The two men did not talk about Isobel's adulterous urges again that night and did get drunk—cocktails and two bottles of the best Amarone, which Harold was only too pleased to pay for, glad that he could now be the one to treat Gord instead of the other way around—which was all she wrote.

In September, Isobel returned to Hong Kong as promised, but there were problems with their house, she said, and before Harold knew it, his wife was "commuting," more or less, taking care of their home in Montclair, New Jersey—she even brought home Terror, their half-breed Rottweiler, from the kennels—and suggested Pete come back home to his old school. Pete refused, because he loved his school in Hong Kong where he was popular for the first time in his teenage life; neither parent, but most especially Harold, could deny their son his bliss. By spring the following year, it was clear Isobel would remain State side indefinitely. Harold gave up their large, expensive, luxury rental, paid for by the firm, and he and Pete moved into a smaller flat in the city complex connected to the Pacific Place tower where his firm was housed so that he virtually lived where he worked. At least it was a short commute.

The night Pete overheard his father's howl, he witnessed something he'd never imagined. G hugged his father as the latter bawled, saying, *it's okay, it's okay, you'll be okay, I'm here,* and though he wouldn't swear to it afterwards, he thought he saw his godfather's face nuzzled in his father's hair, and that he was kissing his head, the way you would a dog or lover, which one he wasn't sure.

When Pete rolled out of bed the next morning, a Saturday, he was surprised to see G flipping pancakes. Harold was at the office.

"There's fresh squeezed juice in the fridge. Breakfast?" he offered.

Pete nodded.

"Blueberries or plain?"

"Plain. Where's Esmeralda?" He meant their helper. "Why are

you making breakfast?"

"I sent her to the market with a shopping list. We're having prawns for dinner. You like prawns, right?"

He nodded.

"So," Gordie continued, "school's good?"

"G, what's going on?"

"What d'you mean, kid?"

"I heard you and Dad last night."

"That's unfortunate."

"Also, what are you doing here?" Because it was spring, right after Easter, and not a time his godfather normally visited.

"I need to consult your father on some legal matters, but maybe that should wait."

"Like what?" But what Pete was dying to know—*was it true, his mother sleeping with someone else, someone named Trevor, who was that?*— but somehow, he couldn't say this to G because it just seemed too absurd to be real. So even as Gordie told him—*I'm planning to give away all my money to charity*—Pete could not later say for sure that he fully understood what G meant. He wasn't paying complete attention, he didn't think, as he later told Marcel and what his friend said was, *all his money, is he crazy?* And Pete said, he didn't think so, and that was what made him ponder this for a long time afterwards, and to write about it, and to post it on his private cyberspace at a time before the world used the web as ubiquitously as it does today. His essay was a private meditation which began "My godfather G is a good man, but strange."

Gordie said to me once that even if Pete, who was only sixteen at the time, did understand what he was doing, it was *entirely without malice,* and consequently, he never blamed Pete for a thing.

2

True to his better instincts, Gordie delayed discussing the legal matter with Harold and time slipped away as it will. On February 10, '98, his fiftieth birthday, Gordon Marc Ashberry had a net worth of a little over US $43 million. His liquid assets comprised sixty-six percent. Only ten years earlier, his worth was more than quintuple that, but large sums had gone to pay the U.S. government, thanks to his swindling ex business partner Colin Kenton, who had conveniently vanished. For Gordie, it had been unreal, watching all his money disappear. His mother Rosemarie had no idea about all that of course, despite the gossip in their world. Rosemarie didn't listen to gossip except when it suited her.

By now, Harold had resigned from Merryweather Lind and was headed back to New York and his law practice. He frequently told Gordie he was too liquid. If not for Gordie's brush with the Feds, which had cost him such considerable fines, plus the losses sustained as a result of *not* declaring bankruptcy, his worth could easily have been six times that. Probably more, if Harold were permitted to manage the portfolio, as Harold knew he ought to be doing since his *best friend had zero sense when it came to money.*

Gordie was born Gordon Haddon Ashberry in a year of the rat. Had he been born just fifteen days earlier, the way Harold had, he too would have been a pig. It was something Harold frequently reminded Gordie of during his Hong Kong stint, when he immersed himself in the study of just enough Chinese culture to do business in that city. *Pigs are lucky, rats are not,* although Isobel's betrayal silenced that jab. When his father Mark died, Gordie was a couple of months shy of turning twenty-one, and changed his middle name legally to Marc. Rosemarie wondered at this, but was too overwrought at the time by the revelation of Gail Szeto's existence (the girl was sixteen), and her husband's posthumous instructions to confer legitimacy on this half-Chinese bastard in Hong Kong (by a whore, no less!), that she did not question her son's strange action.

In late May, Gordie sought out Harold at his office in lower Manhattan. There were still unpacked boxes in the corner, and the empty newness of his space, as well as the rest of the premises, was evident.

"It's only forty-three million," he said. "Hardly gargantuan as fortunes go."

Incredulous, Harold stared at his friend from across his desk. Since his return to New York two weeks earlier, Gord had been evasive, and not because he was traveling. He wasn't even going to be around for midsummer—which Harold had come to regard as their tradition—the fortnight Isobel and the boys used to vanish to the Jersey shore prior to his joining them and he could be a bachelor again for forty-eight hours or so. Finally he said. "You want to give away, just give *all* of it away?"

"I started making a list of charities and then realized it was more complicated than that. Figured you'd know how to handle this."

"And what will you live on?"

"Relax. What's up doc with all this high anxiety?" He grinned, continued. "You're being way too Elmer Fudd-ish. Look, I'll keep enough to get myself started up somewhere. I guess."

Harold's eyebrows valleyed into a frown. "You guess. And how much do you suppose enough is?"

Gordie glanced out the window. A late afternoon sun ray bounced off the roof of the Staten Island ferry, illuminating its path of relative velocity across the water. He turned back to his friend. "I don't know. Twenty, maybe?"

For a moment, Harold breathed a sigh of relief. "Oh so twenty mill, well . . ."

"Thousand."

"Jeez Mary Jos, Gord, do you have any idea how *little* twenty thousand buys?"

"Even in Bumfuck, Iowa?"

"You're moving to Iowa, now, are you?"

"Just a figure of speech."

Harold, who was seated behind his desk, stood. He was portly, weighing almost two hundred fifty pounds, which did not sit well. Although only three inches shorter than Gordie, who was six-one, he looked wider and more squat than he actually was, because the fat had concentrated around his middle, dragging his body down towards a lowered center of gravity. His shoulders tended to slump, which did not improve his overall appearance.

"As your lawyer," he began, and coughed.

Gordie said. "You should look after that cough."

Harold waved away the concern. "It's nothing. Listen, I can't let you do this. It's ill advised."

"You're my lawyer. You have to do it."

"I register my dissent."

"But you *will* do it?"

Harold moved out from behind the desk and began pacing. "This, is, some, kind, of, joke, right? Hahahahaha. Now, let's, go, get, a, drink."

"You're doing that word spacing thing again."

"No, I'm, not, and, don't, change, the, subject."

Gordie rose from his seat. "Got to run. Think it over, okay, and let me know how to do this. I'm counting on you." He headed towards the door.

"No, you, think, it, over . . ."

But Gordie had already leapt down his Wabbit Hole.

It was the mother's death last year, Harold believed, that unhinged Gord. He had never wanted to say it, but always thought there was something too cloying and sick in his friend's relationship with his mother. The only child thing probably. Rosemarie Haddon Ashberry had been pretty even when she finally passed on at eighty-two. His practice did not handle the Haddon estate—that went to one of the larger white shoe firms with an established trusts & estates practice— so Harold was not privy to details, although he was aware from the comments Gord made over the years that Rosemarie's financial and legal affairs were muddled and full of charitable excess.

Isobel rang in the midst of his reverie from their home in

Montclair. His now ex-home.

"Oh, you," he said. "Gord just left. He wants to give away all his money to charity."

Isobel took in the news, uncertain of its meaning. She did not like Gordie, although, if asked, she would not say she disliked him. He was just one of those irritants that came with her husband, although what she really wanted was to make Harold understand her situation. "Well why not, he's got enough," she said.

"No, you don't understand. *All* his money."

"That's ridiculous. What will he live on?"

"My point, precisely."

She moved the cordless to her other ear, stooped down to leash Terror, who was prancing, impatient to urinate. "Harold, tell me about it some other time? Listen, Trevor and I have been talking..."

Harold stiffened. Despite the separation, over a year by now, he still could not talk about Trevor. "What about him?"

"We'd like to get married eventually. I mean, it only makes sense."

"Over my dead body," he said, and slammed the phone down.

Isobel stared at the buzzing handset. So that's the way it was going to be, was it? Well at least he knew now. She opened the door and followed Terror out as he strained in his desire to exit.

Of course Harold would say that, she thought, as she yanked Terror's leash. He pulled her along the sidewalk, past the Jensen and Schwartz residences. Puzzling, this thing about Gordie, and if she guessed correctly, the two would be knocking back more booze than they should later that night. Harold didn't need booze, or food. What he needed was a diet.

Isobel waved to Gina Schwartz, smoking at her picture window. Gordie had had a brief fling with Gina, oh, several years ago now, long over, when Ed, Gina's husband, did that three-month stint in Athens alone for his accounting firm. The Schwartzes had no children, which was part of Gina's problem; Isobel knew this hadn't been by choice. The *stories* Gina told of Gordie chaperoning her around Manhattan's clubs—she always had been a wild one—sat badly with Isobel, although Harold thought it was *all just in fun, generous of Gordie.* Harold, who remained completely in the dark, despite the spotlight of guilt, so evident.

The trouble with Gordie was the trouble with Harold. Gordie could do no wrong in her husband's books, even when he *was* wrong, disastrously, illegally, morally wrong. Gordie who didn't work, who didn't know the meaning of a mortgage or responsibility, who had more money than sense, who still looked as terrific at fifty as at twenty-two when she first met him, who gave her the gift that was Harold, the man who still loved her despite Trevor and other disappointments and boulevards littered with shards of dreams.

Harold did not drink with Gordie that night. Instead, he went to the gym, an odd destination for him, and parked his corpse onto the rowing machine. That was what his body felt like, a large, ungainly corpse, one that would require at least two men to lift onto a stretcher when he croaked.

And you will croak Harold, his doctor had warned only last week. *Sooner than you think. Your heart won't take all that weight.*

He pulled hard on the oars. His leg muscles twitched as all his limbs moved in rhythm. Sitting wasn't the answer, he knew, but the treadmill looked too forbidding. Earlier, he'd been pissed off that Gordie left so abruptly, not even stopping to have a drink. But as his pores erupted sweat, he was grateful for this brief attempt at exercise. Fifteen or twenty minutes was all he could manage and then he sat in the steam room, wishing that fat would just melt away on its own. Time oozed. He nodded off momentarily in the silent mist. When he emerged, his earlier hunger pangs had eased and he sat at the juice bar where a concoction eased its way down his throat.

Later, when he stepped out into the evening, he almost headed for the Path, his connection to New Jersey Transit, a rail commute that was still second nature despite the years in Hong Kong and the reality of his life now.

What he didn't expect when he got home that evening was a call from Pete who said, *in your neighborhood can I stop in I'll bring Chinese?*

So within minutes. "Pater-man. Hey," said Pete. He placed the brown paper bag on the counter in Harold's studio apartment kitchen.

His father smiled. "Hey." He felt the customary—was it protectiveness?—that welled up whenever he came in contact with this son. Why it was that way he couldn't say, just that he had known, from the time Pete was a baby, that this one was his, the way Harold

Jr. had never been and who now increasingly would never be.

"I called G," Pete continued. "He says I can do it if I want to badly enough."

"Do what?"

"Study Chinese at Yale."

"And you're sure about this?"

"Dad, I want to live in China like Uncle John. Like we did. That was the best time of my entire life."

"Hong Kong's not the same as being in China," *and,* he was thinking, *you're nothing like John.* "Give life and college a chance, okay? There's no hurry to declare a major before you've checked things out."

"You're not going to take *her* side, are you?" His voice took on the same peevish inflection that sounded exactly like Isobel's.

"Hold it right there. This isn't about taking sides. I just want you to be sure."

"I *am* sure Dad. I've thought about it *all* year."

"Your mother's only thinking about your academic strengths," but even as he said this he knew the argument was moot, as his son's facial disgust conveyed. Pete had a perfect score in math on his SAT's without even trying and had been too advanced for his advanced math class. His verbal score was almost as high. College acceptances had come much easier for him than for his brother. "Well," he corrected, "she's thinking about your future."

Pete was gazing at him with Isobel's eyes, the plea insistent. "Dad?"

"I'll talk to her."

And then he began to tell Pete what Gord wanted to do, and his son listened, rapt, although he never mentioned G telling him as much two years earlier back in Hong Kong. For Pete, it was startling to watch this play out in reality, something which till now had merely been imagined, unreal, a G thing as all G things were, just this side of insane, something that was good for a fiction, which was what he considered the piece he wrote about all that. Harold had thought of nothing else during the time at the gym and the twenty-five minute commute home. The telling was cathartic, as if this information relay could somehow solve the puzzle. As if by sharing his confusion, his son could cushion its rough edges, the way Pete filled the distance between himself and Isobel, the distance Harold could feel but not give voice to. It wasn't till later that he wondered at Gord not mentioning his son's call, an extraordinary event, by any reckoning.

Pete had called his godfather that afternoon out of desperation. If his mother had *her* way, he'd still be in diapers. He had been furious that his father had let her corral him back to the U.S. right before graduation, so that he missed the parties and fun with his friends, all for some dumb party Trevor hosted to celebrate his something or other, at the Plaza no less. Dad was invited but hadn't gone. Who could blame him? It was unreasonable, the way Mom could be at times, and worse now that she was playing society girlfriend to Trevor. What did she, and his brother who actually came back East for it, see in that man anyway? It was tough too, living back at the old homestead with his mother, especially now that the Pater-man was in the city on his own.

"Chance," Gordie said. "I did the Chinese thing by chance."

"But you're almost Chinese," Pete protested. "Larry Woo says so."

"He's pulling your leg."

There was a silence of wires crossed.

Pete caught his breath and then spoke quickly. "You have a Chinese sister, don't you?" It was risky, mentioning that. His mother, when she told him, had added, *and don't you dare tell your dad I told you.*

"Half."

"Sister or Chinese?" he shot back.

Gordie, much to Pete's relief, laughed. "Both."

It was no secret about Gail Szeto, not anymore. Even in Rosemarie's world, people knew, since Gail lived and worked in New York these days, a senior VP at Northeast Trust, and acknowledged Gordie quite openly as her brother.

Calmed now by his audacity, Pete did not regret making the call. He couldn't however resist adding, "Your dad was quite a dog, huh?" parroting G's own words.

"Watch it, kid," was the man's reply.

And then Pete let out all the pent up frustration, about his parents' separation, and Trevor whom he despised, about how he hated being back in the U.S., how he missed his friends back home. *Isn't Marcel coming over,* G interrupted once to ask, and Pete said maybe, that if he could swing a visit to Yale this fall he would. He missed his life, he told G, this wasn't life, meaning the suburbs with Mom. *I wish I were like you, G, you don't have to answer to anyone,* he said to which Gordie replied, *be careful what you wish for, kid.*

In November of '68, after Nixon beat Humphrey, Gordie's father had engineered a safe landing in the Cessna on their private airstrip in Greenline, stopped the plane, and died. The engine had still been running. He was fifty-nine and did not get to attend the presidential inaugural ball, to which he was invited but to which Rosemarie, in any event, would have refused to accompany him, enamored of the Kennedys as she was then and still mourning Bobby K. in an unusual display of partisan disloyalty.

After the reading of the will, when the Gail Szeto bomb exploded in Rosemarie's face, Gordie held onto his mother's arm as they left the lawyer's office.

"He knew," Rosemarie said. "That damned lawyer knew and didn't stop Mark, didn't have the . . . *decency* to come to me."

"Now Mother, you know he couldn't do that. It's not his fault Dad . . ."

"Don't defend him."

"I'm not, but . . ."

"Oh, be quiet."

He shut up then, the guilt of his own complicity a bar to further defense.

Rosemarie, her bereavement now replaced by hostility, glared at her son. Surely, *her* Gordie didn't know. Or did he? She had always disliked his accompanying Mark on flights to Hong Kong, as he had done through his boyhood, not that her late husband ever gave her much choice in the matter.

They arrived at Mark's Thunderbird, the car Rosemarie despised but it was the chauffeur's day off and Gordie was not about to drive the Town Car. Rosemarie did not drive. Gordie opened the passenger door. Rosemarie leaned her hand against the top of the door frame and collapsed forward.

Her son's arm encircled her waist, bracing her. "Mother, are you all right?"

She sobbed, crying harder than she had during the funeral three days earlier, a funeral with few mourners because at the time of Mark's death, he was a recluse of sorts, at least from what little of their Greenline society remained, spending most of his time flying covert missions abroad for the government under the guise of his part-time pilot's job with Pacific American, and had cut himself off this way for over ten years.

Resisting Gordie's attempts to usher her into the passenger seat, she remained in her collapsed state. Her mascara was streaming but who cared? Certainly not Mark. Perhaps he never cared. Anger and sorrow roiled as a strange relief coursed through her. What did anything matter now?

"Mother, please," her son said, softly. "Let's go home."

They remained this way for some time, five minutes perhaps, possibly longer. Rosemarie finally pulled herself together, got into the car and allowed her son to close the door. She cleaned the streaks off her face and powdered her nose. As Gordie started up the engine, she said. "He might as well never have come home."

Her conviction was fortified over the next few weeks, and she suspected, correctly, that Gordie must have known more than he let on, that Mark had lied and hidden way more than she guessed. Oh she knew! Only a *moron* wouldn't have, that her husband wasn't faithful, that he was not what he pretended to be. They had made their pact years ago—he did his thing and didn't interfere with her money or life, and she would ask no questions. But death meant an end to that farce. Only *why* did he have to be so petty and mean, humiliating her this last time? It was beneath even Mark.

That Christmas, Rosemarie threw the biggest house party she had done for years. It lasted through January 1. Even some of old Greenline turned out for it, the ones who hadn't attended Mark's funeral. James Townsend, her former neighbor did, on December 29 all the way from Italy, *sans* the Mrs., but he just happened to be passing through. However circumstantial, Rosemarie was pleased to see her girlhood beau.

What Gordie did was defy her by asking Jimmy Kho to advise her husband's mistress of Mark's death; Jimmy, however, wasn't able to locate her for several months. He also went to Hong Kong in summer the following year. There, she presumed he met Gail and her mother, and arranged U.S. citizenship for his half sister the way his father wanted. He was twenty-one and could do what he chose. Or so Mark would have said.

Rosemarie was home when Gordie returned from the trip. She

stared at this son who had overnight become a stranger and said. "Don't tell me. I don't want to know anything about them. Nothing." She did not even offer her cheek for the habitual kiss.

"But..." he began.

She held up her left hand; the martini glass tipped precariously in her right. "No buts. It's my turn now and I'm going to call the shots for a change. I'm changing my will. You've got your father's money, his townhouse and the Block Island place anyway, and there's the trust my lawyers set up of course, but everything else of mine goes to charity, including our home." She paused, knowing he did not fully appreciate the extent of what she proposed to do. "Unless you promise me that not a cent of my money will go, in any way, towards the upkeep of that, that..."

"Mother, I don't want to talk about this."

"Won't you promise me, Gordie?"

"No, it's just..."

"No?" She brought the full glass to her lips and drank half the liquid in two, long swallows. Her voice rose. "No?"

"That's not what I meant, Mother."

"Then *what* did you mean? You boys are all the same, no better than my father who ruined Mother's life." She raised the glass, downed the rest and declared. "My best revenge was being born female!" Placing the glass lightly on the coffee table, she mustered all remaining dignity and tottered towards her bedroom, even though it was only six o'clock, their cocktail hour.

Gordie picked up the glass and brought it to the kitchen. "Such melodrama," he said to Reginald, their butler.

"Master Gordon, there's something you need to see."

Opening a cupboard, Reginald pointed to the row of empty gin bottles he had held onto as proof to show the young master. Only then did Gordie begin to get an inkling of the impact of what his father, and now he, had done, and the price he might have to pay for the rest of Rosemarie's life.

What even Reginald didn't know about—Reginald who heard what rattled in all the closets in the village of Greenline—and what Rosemarie *absolutely* had no inkling of, was that a Marc A. Aden (really, Marc Ashberry Aden) had once breathed and lived. He was Gordie's half brother, many years his senior, a posthumously decorated war hero. He was born before Rosemarie entered Mark's life, from Mark's younger days in Europe, so the illegitimacy wasn't quite the same as Gail's; his parents had put the brakes on marriage to their son's Italian-French waitress girlfriend, although Mark managed to arrange U.S. citizenship for his son and regular cash payments without his family's knowledge.

Mark had told Gordie in a drunken fit, furious as he had been at his son at that moment, shortly after Gordie's eighteenth birthday.

What Gordie never forgave his father for was not that he told him about Marc, but that he made it so obvious Marc was the son who *should* have carried the Ashberry name as more than a middle initial. The ace fighter pilot lived in the shadows of a marred paternity, but had flown with his father in Korea, a time when Mark Sr., at 42, could still command a squadron (too old, yes, but no one crossed Mark Ashberry or the power of his connections), and ensured his son was under his wing. Marc Jr. was shot down out of the skies over Vietnam in the summer of '67. He more than earned his silver star. His death made their father prouder than Gordie, alive, ever could.

Gordie, the draft card burner, a burning done in private which he then rubbed in his father's face after Rosemarie had gone to bed. *No son of mine is a coward goddammit Gordie-boyyyyy! Why the fuck aren't you like Marc?* And then, Mark told him.

3

Patti listened to her brother rabbit on about the man for whom she still had a soft spot.

"Harold, Gordie's an adult. He can do whatever he wants."

The Haights had originally planned to do Thanksgiving at her home this year because, Isobel claimed, she couldn't face the prospect of another burnt turkey, the cinder star of last Thanksgiving. Harold and Patti's mother, by way of dinner table conversation, wondered aloud at her daughter-in-law's inattention last year—*early menopause, perhaps?*—which would have been fine had she not said this in front of all the boys. It was a problem, these early signs of dementia. Patti's two sons and Pete would not shut up about blood that day, egging each other on more and more until Harold lost his temper and yelled, extremely loud, after which they simply nudged each other, silently, under the table.

But here it was, Thanksgiving, and no Isobel who was already separated from Harold and dating Trevor for our whole world to watch, or Harold Jr. who no longer came back East for Thanksgiving, not since college at Berkley. For Harold this family affair, one perennially significant for the Haights—if not for the Kahns—one for which he made a point of heading back State side with the family every year even after relocation to Hong Kong, was fading to less than a shadow. He added an extra helping of mashed potatoes and a second roll to his plate.

Patti raised her eyebrows. "You'll get fat."

"He *is* fat," Pete said.

Harold dug in, oblivious to familial pressures. "Patti, talk to him.

He'll listen to you. He's always . . . respected you."

Richard Kahn, Patti's husband, spoke up. "Yeah, give him our bank account number. We take donations. We're not proud."

Patti frowned. "Shut up, Richard. There's nothing I can say. It's all too bewildering."

Richard, who did not know about his wife's former thing with Gordie, one that predated him in any case, said. "Maybe the force of good goes with him. You know, spiritual journey, all that jazz? What's the diff? He's not going to starve."

"But he hasn't a clue how to make a dime," Harold said.

Richard shrugged. "He seems to have done okay so far, racing around in that Jag. Didn't he take you for a ride Trish, when was it, last Thanksgiving, right, no, year before last, '96, wasn't it, or was it the year before?"

Patti felt her skin go hot. Only her husband called her Trish, which Gordie wickedly used the day he had taken her for that ride, and they stopped and made out, swiftly and savagely, not shy in the least (unlike their very first time, when she was seventeen) and she hadn't resisted even though she wanted to, even though she knew he was simply horny, *no other reason*, and she sucked him off as she used to, something she never did for Richard who wished it but wouldn't ever dream of asking. She had walked back into Harold's house that afternoon, the damp patch on her skirt, she was sure, visible to all, but everyone had behaved as if nothing was amiss until she wondered, had it all been a fantasy, this lust, unfulfilled, so easily re-ignited by a youthful crush?

"So will you talk to him Patti?" Harold was insisting, cutting across her memory.

"Harry, must I?"

"You've got to. He barely talks to me anymore."

"Well maybe . . ." but her brother's expression brooked no refusal. "I'll try, but I'm not holding out much hope."

"Do it soon, okay? He wants to sign papers for Christmas, god help him. An atheist, and suddenly he goes all religious on me. Promise, sis?"

"Okay, okay. Can we talk about something else please?"

Patti's call, in the middle of Hannakuh, caught Gordie by surprise. "To what do I owe this pleasure?"

"I promised Harry." She waited. When he did not respond, she said. "So can I come see you?"

"Doll, you can come anytime."

The innuendo was typical, and predictable, yet his voice still gave her goose bumps, *even now imagine!* Almost fifty and boring to her once-so-adoring sons who regularly lamented, *Mom quit that,* no matter what she said or did. Over the next few days, their laments did not trouble her. She was re-invigorated, *growing younger by the hour,* at the thought of being alone with Gordie. The last time they'd been alone had been in his car, Thanksgiving before last, Patti realized, as she rang the doorbell to his townhouse.

"Hey." He leaned forward to kiss her cheek and ushered her in.

It was only the fourth time she'd been in his place alone with him, and the last was when they were young. The three-story dwelling on Gramercy South (the basement was a wine cellar cum storage, uninhabited), was lighter than she remembered. She had held onto a memory of dark wood paneling and furniture that she, in her early twenties, could only describe as "antique, probably expensive." The front room looked sparse, uncomfortable. The divan on which he once undressed her seemed extraordinarily narrow, and she could not imagine how the two of them had ever fit upon it.

She was surprised to see bread on the table and a plate of olive oil. Plus a small oil lamp. His little joke, she assumed, to remind her she was a Kahn, albeit secular, his way of saying, *see my tribute to your Hannukah.*

"Gordo." She used her private name for him and searched his face. That Bugs grin was missing.

He smiled, a little sadly it seemed to her. "Only to you, doll."

"You've . . . changed."

He sang. "The blossom in my cheek has gone?"

She did not recognize the tune. "Harold sent me, you know. I didn't think this was any of my business."

"So how's the world of investor relations?" Because Patti wrote reports for an agency.

She shrugged. "Doesn't change. Profits up, great performance, profits down, we speak of future potential."

He cocked his head. "I've always had a thing for brunettes." His green eyes gazed through her, like a cat's. "Pretty Patti. That's how I always thought of you."

"Did you? I wouldn't have guessed." She blushed, an unfamiliar sensation, and turned to face the window, keeping her back to him. The park was gray as winter raised its mantle.

He spoke to her back. "What do you want me to say?"

"Don't say anything, Gordo. This is about me and Harold. It's some Catholic thing or sibling thing. Nothing I can properly explain. But I had to come so that it wouldn't be a complete lie." She continued staring out the window.

"Only half lies, huh? *Little white lies?*"

"You should know." Yet what she suddenly felt was an overwhelming urge to cry, which she quickly squelched. Days, imagining, even *dreaming*, waking up as wet as a teenager, yet now, she couldn't look at him.

He said. "I'm sorry."

She spun around, startled. "Whatever for?"

"For you, us, everything. I wasn't . . . nice to you."

He seemed physically in pain, and she wondered, was it some illness about which he refused to speak? He seemed thinner than she recalled, and slightly frail. She moved towards him but he backed away.

She stopped. "I should go, shouldn't I?"

"Yes." He no longer looked at her, and stared into space instead.

"It's all right, Gordo, about everything, really."

He led her to the front door. "Goodbye, Patti Haight."

When Harold asked how she made out, Patti told her brother that it had been a waste of time, that the man made up his mind and nothing she, or anyone said, would change things, *no, not one whit.*

Afterwards, when she thought about that encounter, she felt it was the closest he ever came to expressing some kind of love for her. She couldn't say why she felt this—the years had made them strangers, meeting occasionally via Harold on those familial occasions that offered little privacy—yet she was certain this was right, that Gordo did love her or was trying at least to offer some mode of love.

Harold would never know, or understand—what could she say about her big brother, two years her senior, the one she and John used to call *Dunderdick I* out of earshot when they were kids—and Richard who must *never* know . . . *Richard's the husband, isn't he? The decent one, the one Harold likes,* as Gordo said the last time they were truly intimate, there, at his townhouse. A week before her wedding when he was riding solo. She had come *this close* to calling it off with Richard because Gordo had been tender, the sweetest lover ever, pushing every emotional button she possessed—*he knew it too, surely he knew*—that it almost broke her heart until he said what he did. *Husband. Gotta have one, right?* And laughed as if she and he were, and always had been, nothing more than a colossal joke.

Gordo. The first time, Harold had brought him home during spring break of their freshmen year. The Haights lived in Spring Lake along the Jersey shore where Mr. Haight was the Catholic high school's math teacher, later their principal, and Mrs. Haight (formerly, Donoghue) executive secretary and the real power behind the throne of the largest law practice in town. As a child, Harold was fond of noting they really lived in Sea Girt, close to the border of Spring Lake, but the latter was what his mother preferred to say, because it had been her childhood hometown and for her at least, if not anyone else, still held the glamour of the "Irish Riviera" as it once was less ironically known in her grandparents' time. Their home was large and quite new, on Brooklyn Boulevard, built in 1950. Harold pulled her aside and whispered, *be nice, the guy's a fish out of water among the middle class.*

The Haights did not serve alcohol before or at dinner.

"That was a surprise," she heard their guest comment to Harold afterwards, "given how much you drink."

"It's a Catholic thing." Harold undid his jeans to re-arrange his shirt.

Patti saw her cue to push open her brother's room door, which was ajar.

"Goddammit, sis," Harold exclaimed. He turned his back on her to button up his fly. "How many times have I told you . . ."

She batted eyelashes in mock haste. "God hears children who swear. Besides, we shared a bath in our youth so there's nothing I haven't seen."

Gordie guffawed. That was when she decided he was okay.

Harold said. "Don't encourage her. What do you want anyway?"

"Take me along to the drive in?"

"Get lost."

John, ten years younger than Harold, scrambled past at that moment. "Yeah, take me too!"

Patti and Harold glared at him in unison. "Vamoose!" He slunk off, wiser but unrepentant.

"Come on Harry," she begged. "Be a sport. You know the car's the only place to drink. I won't be a bother, promise."

"You, shouldn't, be, drinking, and, don't, call, me, Harry."

"I'll tell the parents what you keep in the attic, in that box behind the stack of old *Reader's Digest's?*"

He glowered. "Little snoop."

Gordie gazed at her expectantly, and she continued as Harold turned furiously red. "He likes to read, you know, don't you Harry? 'The Easy Come Seduction Craze That Ruins 50 Girls a Week,' or 'I Was Held Prisoner on Nympho Island,' or," and here she winked at her brother's friend, "you'll like this one, 'The Secret of Madam Gordon's Bawdy House' and my all-time favorite 'American Men Can't Handle Women'?" These were story titles from her brother's *True Men Stories* collection, one he had discovered in their late uncle's attic and read voraciously since puberty, and to which he bought later issues. His parents would have had a fit had they known.

Gordie was by this time doubled over with laughter and Harold was making strangling gestures at her.

It was time to play her ace. She slid into the room and closed the door. "Kathleen O'Mara asked about you." She pretended to inspect her cuticles, but her eyes remained trained on her brother's face. "I happen to know she's free tonight, and you know Mom won't object if *I* invite her."

The edge of Harold's lips creased into a grimace. He was hooked. Later, as the three of them left together, Gordie touched her arm lightly when they arrived at the car. "Who's Kathleen?"

She looked at him properly for the first time that night. There was a sweetness about him plus a disarmingly cute grin she liked. "You'll see."

His face, when Kathleen appeared, was one of those priceless moments of her girlhood that Patti prized. O'Mara's red leather mini defied the concept of skirt, and when she unbuttoned her jacket, also leather, it was difficult for both boys not to stare. Kathleen long had the hots for Harold, and Patti knew her brother wouldn't resist, despite his disparaging remarks in private. For a brief second, she felt the familiar twinge of jealousy—what girl wouldn't for that mass of gorgeous auburn hair—although, as her brother did that rapid blink thing, followed by the intake of air, Patti thanked whatever heavens ruled for her own lean, long-jumper's physique, and legs, and height, and yes, even her less-than-flatteringly flat chest because she never envied, no matter what all the boys might crave, those O'Mara tits, which Kath used to bandage and deflate when they were both thirteen and her poor friend would cry herself into a fit over all the catcalls and nasty boy talk that had once meant only pain and shame.

In the car, she and Kath sat in the back seat, and Gordie turned round to talk to them. To her. His eyes wandered towards the edge of her skirt as she crossed her legs. Should she smile back? Kathleen nudged her hard when Harold said something and his head turned away for a second. By the time he turned back, she had discreetly undone one more button on her skirt, and re-crossed her legs, hiking the skirt up further. It was a good thing, she thought, that she'd worn the pale yellow sweater, the one that fit snug but not tight, as she smiled at him, her nipples hard, pressed against the lace of her bra.

They parked at the drive-in. Harold opened her door. "Out, sis."

She slid out obediently to effect the seating exchange.

There were still odd occasions, long after she and Gordo had called it quits, that the memory of that first time in her brother's old Dodge could make her wet, catching her unawares. It had been a strange and tense encounter. They sat next to each other, the popcorn on the seat between, his eyes never leaving the screen. She would have had to have been *blind* not to notice his erection, and the way he discreetly shifted that sexy butt of his, trying to rearrange his jeans. When she thought of it now, she wondered if that hadn't been the real turn on, watching him desperately trying to concentrate on the movie while Kath and her brother made out, noisily, on the back seat. Something about secret, uncontrollable lust tantalized her, gave her courage. Imagine having the *gall* to reach over and unzip him— and she had moved quietly, swiftly, without her brother realizing a thing—releasing his stiffness, folding her right hand over it and jacking him off into a Kleenex! *How quickly he came.* Patti didn't know whether she ought to laugh or cry now, years later, at this old home movie of her younger self, licking her fingers afterwards, pretending aloud how much *I just love popcorn salt, don't you?*

What she hadn't expected, what completely floored her, was when he slipped into her room later that night, punctuated by Harold's snores beyond the wall, and went down on her while she was half-asleep until she came, so hard, *four times for sure,* that she had to bite her knuckles till they bled. Before he left he whispered, *don't tell Harold. He said he'd kill me if I touched you,* and then kissed her.

The boys departed the next day, but just before they left, Gordo did that silly Bugs grin of his and blew her an air kiss when Harold wasn't looking, and she waved with her band-aided fingers and was *hooked,* more firmly than her brother ever was by Kath whom he managed to resist on the marital front until Isobel appeared to claim him, a choice for which Patti only half forgave him, despite her love and acceptance of her sister-in-law over time.

Patti never told anyone, not even Kath, about Gordo. Why she didn't know since she used to tell Kath *everything,* and still couldn't say as the years passed. Once, Kath asked outright, after she and Patti visited the boys at Yale the first time and she and Harold disappeared all weekend, but Patti shrugged indifferently and said, *Gordon's nice, generous with the beer and dope, we hang out and have fun, but he's definitely not interested.* So she lied, something she'd never done to Kath, as if Gordo needed to be protected, Gordo, the man for whom she saved herself, offering up her virginity which he turned down—*who would believe that?*—and yet, he had, holding back while they made out for hours during which he would elicit uncontrollable multiples until she physically hurt, and him saying, *damn, girl, don't you ever quit,* as if trying to stop her from falling in love with him, as if he could. What had *that* been all about?

Now, as Christmas neared in the present moment of family and what should be nothing more than a silly secret of youth, Patti found herself drenched in recollections of this man she once was convinced was the only mate she could ever possibly love.

Patti Haight's Interlude

Had it been rape? Patti and I would consider this whenever we met. Gordo surprised her, she admitted. Brandon was three, and she and Richard were already contemplating a second child. Parties at Gordo's, especially New Year's Eve ones, were boozy and wild, too many people wandering the spacious three-story townhouse into its nooks, hands landing in the wrong places, like his. But she kissed back and then things got heavier, hotter, and then, *even though she said no*, he fucked her. In the back room on the top floor. The maid's room, except that Gordie didn't have a maid.

"It's rape," I said the first time she told me. "He penetrated you against your will." It was early in '82, the soonest I could manage a visit after Gordon's birth. Gordon had almost been a Labor Day baby, she said, just missing September 7 by minutes.

"No," she insisted. She burped the baby and repeated "no," more emphatically this time, and, "don't say 'penetrate' that sounds so clinical."

"So it was . . .?"

"I let things get out of hand."

"You do that with him, don't you?"

She sighed. "But then, we wouldn't have our Gordon, would we?" and she nuzzled his child, cooing in her Mommy voice that seemed so at odds with the investor relations writer from Manhattan.

Only I knew, and possibly her brother John, that her second son was Gordie's progeny. Patti was sure from the start. An odd certainty, but it carried her for years before any real proof. After all, as she confessed to me much later, she and Richard had a long afternoon of sex the very next day.

I had gazed at her in admiration and horror. "But how could you do that?" We were at the Plaza, doing Winter Solstice drinks. She had been recounting her indiscretion with Gordo in his Jag just a few weeks earlier at Thanksgiving before dropping this second bomb.

Patti sipped her second Cosmopolitan—this made me cringe but

Patti was like that, would order these *faux* sophisticated drinks in her charming ignorance. "Plus," she slipped the lemon slice off the side of her glass and brandished it, "we had just woken up and I hadn't showered from the night before. My heart was going a marathon a minute, I tell you, so afraid Richard would catch on."

"Jesus, Patti!"

"I know, I know. I'm a slut."

"Only because of him."

"I guess."

The moroseness had crept into her voice and posture; Patti is nothing if not lapsed, but Catholic guilt casts long shadows over her although she'd never admit it. She loved Richard Kahn, I knew that, and would never do anything to really jeopardize their marriage. Which is why I still wonder, even now, why Gordie had such an effect on her? Perhaps it really was a little of the glamour of his wealth, he being the boy she wished were next door. I decided to try a different tack, to stop this confessional slide into cliché.

"You promised you'd tell about the paternity test."

She brightened. "I was right of course, always knew I was," and now her grin was wicked, the Patti I knew as a girl. "Seize the moment, right? Wasn't hard with him all over me in the Jag to get a DNA sample."

I laughed. "But why were you so sure before?"

"Rif lip."

"Huh?"

"R-F-L-P, that's the way it's pronounced. Restriction fragment length polymorphisms, the way DNA tests used to be done."

By now I was thoroughly hooked. "And you know this because...?"

She hesitated. I sensed a big revelation. "Let's just say," she began slowly, "I have friends from college who have influence in blood banks to get enough of a sample for the test. And of course," she looked straight at me, "you won't ever tell him I stole his blood to check, right?"

I was too flabbergasted to speak.

She continued. "I'm AB, you know, a pretty rare blood type. Both Gordo and Richard are O. My Gordon's got A type blood which fits with either guy as the father which was convenient. But I just knew, even without the RFLP, which may not have been as accurate as the tests now but was pretty damned close enough."

She sat up straight and the moroseness was replaced by a flippant determination. "So that's that," she declared and I knew the subject was closed for good.

What more could I say? I clinked her glass. "So now you know beyond the shadow of a doubt, right? C'mon, drink up, Vassar Virgin."

***

The proximity of the two encounters would surely create some uncertainty in a person's mind, you'd think. And even though I didn't call her on it, she had to have been lying about the RFLP test. Hell would freeze over, no, *disappear* before Gordie ever gave blood. I was with him once for a blood test and was shocked at his pallor; the man cannot stand the sight of blood.

Still, it was her fiction, and who was I to rewrite her story?

She never told Richard that I knew of (or "Dickie" as Gordie called him, his green eyed monster sneaking through). Besides, Gordon was Richard's favorite cousin on his mother's side so their child was his namesake as far as anyone knew, it complemented his brother's name Brandon, and young Gordon (who was always Gordon, never any other name) looked enough like Patti to pass. Nor did she tell Gordo, at least I don't think she did. But Patti doesn't tell you things, not really, even though she appears to. It's the way she is and when you've known someone as long as I've known Patti, you forgive her this little flaw because Patti is such fun, such rare and tenacious friendship and you know she'll always be a barrel of laughs, good for a drink or ten (all the Haights are fish).

What I never told Patti was why Gordie wanted her both those times. He tells me these things. Sometimes. Well, most of the time, though Gordie being Gordie will always pervert the truth. It was Rose, of course, Jimmy Kho's daughter who worked for Gordie for awhile, whom none of the Haights knew. Gordie is Gatsby times ten, the daisy chain being longer than it should be for any man. He was lusting, Rose was teasing under the guise of innocence (staying married to a gay man you'd have to say, she's no innocent, right?), and Patti was where he could park a little of that lust. There you are, not very nice, is it? But Gordie isn't very nice, despite his being that man in our lives. We put up with him, is all.

***

The last time I saw Patti it was at Porters on Seventh, near 23rd. *Right round the corner from the Chelsea Hotel*, she said. *Big drinks, sexy bartenders.* I'm not sure whether she meant the women or the men, but she wasn't wrong about either. I could see the beginnings of silver which, true to form, she did not dye or streak or damage that beautiful brunette head of hers. Her hair is still shoulder length and shiny-brushed, and there are times when I look at her that I see the little Catholic schoolgirl in her silly pale blue uniform and ponytail. She'd put on a little weight, nothing tragic, but enough to say, the beginnings of fleshy flops and folds. The talk, as always, turned to Gordo.

"Have you seen him?"

I nodded. "Of course. You know I do."

She didn't say "lucky you" which I suspected was going through her mind.

"He can't help it," I reassured her. "He needs me."

She ordered a Californian Chardonnay and I wondered at this suburban choice. Patti's been, or tried to be Manhattan all her life, always working in the city, preferring to switch jobs when her firm moved out to Jersey, even though that would have shortened her commute to ten minutes, refusing to acknowledge her suburban roots and routes, even during those maternity sabbaticals she took after each of her boys was born. Richard's the opposite. He did the home office consultant thing as soon as he could do so successfully and shoots hoops in the driveway with the boys after school; he feels the empty nest much more keenly than her. I sometimes think that's what kept her in heat over Gordo. It's that Gramercy townhouse, that city boy aura of his, that careless cosmopolitanism that's in his blood.

We were contemplating the first anniversary of 9-11. Patti lost several friends in her finance world that day and she, like certain New Yorkers I know, invoke those numerals the way certain Hong Kongers utter *luhksei*, 6-4, meaning Tiananmen. The conversation with Gordie about Patti that I hadn't yet had then, because it happened later in Lausanne, would change the way I would eventually come to feel about her. But in our moment of too-sweet Chardonnay (I gave into her choice because a bottle was cheaper than wines by the glass), I heard a new bitterness in her voice.

"Richard's having an affair."

This was unexpected. "Are you sure?"

"He's careless. There are bits of her all over him."

I refrained from the wise ass remarks on the tip of my tongue. "Is it serious?"

"I don't know." Her face contorted—you know, that strange, painful, middle-aged look of defeat but not resignation—and then she smiled, not wickedly but tight, poured a third glass and signaled the bartender to bring a second bottle, much to my dismay.

"Fuck him," she declared. "If he needs some twenty-something sex-in-the-suburbs bimbo with boobs falling out that even his own sons wouldn't screw, then he can go babysit his mother instead of me." Her mother-in-law had moved into a home and the Alzheimer's was becoming unmanageable.

So she did know who, and she probably also knew how far gone he was. Funny how it always came back to boobs with Patti, Pancake Patti as her brother John used to tease, making her cry way back when tears were not, were never withheld.

4

"G.I.B.," Gordo had said, as he pulled out of her mouth. "That's what Harold is."

They were in the back seat of his car, "killing time" on a drive to nowhere while Kath and her brother monopolized the room. It was just spring, almost a year to the day from their first, playful time as almost-lovers. Both Patti and Kath were eighteen and could no longer be considered jail bait.

Patti's jaw did a double take at the suddenness of his exit. She maneuvered herself off the floor of the car and climbed astride him before he could zip up, riding her crotch against the tip of his still hard penis, reveling in his agony. Whenever he pulled a non-sequitur, she knew he was just trying to avoid her. "What are you talking about?"

He pushed her off and zipped up. "Guy in the back. Military terminology for the gunner or, later, the radar intercept officer. In the early days of air combat, before planes were equipped with firing systems that the pilot could maneuver solo, gunners were the ones credited for successful attacks. The guy in front, the pilot, was more or less just the chauffeur. That's me and Harold, he's my guy in the back." He paused. "My dad told me that. He used to be a fighter pilot."

"You don't say." She pushed up her skirt and straddled him again, bracing herself against his shoulder and the window. He was still hard. "Gordo, make love to me."

He stuck his hand into her panties, cupped her buttocks and closed his eyes. "To the Virgin from Vassar? I can't. Harold would kill me."

She tried to move but he held her still. "And that's the reason we keep doing this?"

"You want to save it for the man you fall in love with, don't you?" His eyes remained closed.

She gritted her teeth, debating. Finally. "Is Stella saving it for you?"

He opened his eyes and pulled his hands out. "Who told...?"

"We have ways of making our Harry talk."

"Kath, wasn't it?"

"Ask me no questions, I'll tell you no lies."

"That's *my* line."

"Not anymore."

He removed her completely and they didn't speak for awhile. She regretted mentioning Stella because it diverted his attention.

It was unique, the pose she had kept up for him. With other boys she dated, she was more demure, less of a wise ass, and far and away more virginal. Kath had reputation enough for them both—unfair really, since Kath was diehard loyal to Harold (who really *didn't* deserve her) and Patti necked with a lot more boys than either her parents or Harry guessed. Gordo knew, though, because she told him what a tease she liked to be, because telling him always seemed to turn him on.

All the next year, her first at Vassar—the Haights were nothing if not brilliant at acquiring scholarships as Gordie noted, because Harold had one at Yale and later John followed in both his siblings' footsteps at Harvard—there was a distance between them. *Not,* as Patti admitted to herself, that Gordo *had ever given her cause or otherwise promised anything* since all she and he were, were "playmates." And that should have been that. All that year, though, she knew she was kissing *him,* and not the one she was with, nor any of the ones who *begged* the maidenhead she refused, waiting, believing in . . . *what?*

In the summer of '69, after months of listening to Harold repeat, *Gord and Stella,* engaged, *can you beat that,* Gordie called her, out of the blue.

"Hey doll. Come see me in New York?"

"Gordo? That you?"

"None other."

"Some stranger. I barely recognized your voice."

"And who else calls you 'doll'?"

On the bus to New York, Patti couldn't help thinking she was making a huge mistake. Oh, he was always cavalier, that wasn't the problem, but such a long silence, months, and then, this. For the first time, she suspected he knew that she would do pretty much anything for him, not that she minded him knowing. What she did mind was his sudden willingness to use that knowledge to his advantage. It was a side of him she hadn't seen.

It was early summer. Patti had remained at school where she had a summer job on campus, and Harold was interning somewhere in the city. Patti feared she might run into her brother, but as Gordo said, it was a big city. She had agreed to stay the weekend, but as soon as she saw him, at his townhouse, she wished she *had* made some arrangement to crash with a girlfriend as she had initially planned to do. There was something different about him, a coldness she didn't recognize, an arrogance of which she was slightly afraid.

He took her bag. "Aren't you going to kiss me?"

"Eventually." She kept her voice light, trying not to betray her nervousness.

His eyes swept over her. "I've missed you."

"You should call more often."

"I was . . . otherwise engaged."

"So I hear."

It was then that he led her to the divan where they kissed. Patti's mind scrambled all over the place and the kiss was awkward and clumsy. *What else did she know to do with this man except make out?* This thought intruded, her brain refusing to shut up, and despite everything that followed—his hard edge softened with the hours and he reverted to the silly boy she first fell in love with—she was troubled by the *lack* of anything they really had, and how she had enshrined hope in him through her ridiculous parody of "being in love."

Patti lost her virginity that weekend. There was blood. *Damn, girl. I don't believe it,* Gordo whispered. *You were telling the truth.* Patti wasn't sure, would never be certain because she was half asleep, but later that night, she felt the empty space next to her in bed, and could have sworn she heard music, and possibly, although it might have been a tomcat on the prowl, the sound of someone weeping.

And there it was, Christmas, a season Gordie despaired at facing alone in New York, and a visit from Patti of all people, evoking a forgotten time. For years, Christmas meant travel to places where the climate made snowy images ludicrous. There was always a party somewhere, parties like the ones his mother used to throw at the Greenline estate, especially after Mark's death, where hordes of strangers laughed over the music and kissed each other, hordes in the later years that were rainbow colored, culturally diverse, evidence of a global soul, or at least, globe trotters who agreed upon how to party. But in his mother's last years, as she became frail and unable to socialize, he had spent Christmases alone with her.

So, early afternoon Christmas Eve, he got into his Lamborghini and headed home to Greenline, to the Haddon estate.

Mark had purchased the Gramercy townhouse, which Gordie inherited along with a sizeable trust because Mark spent little for a man of his wealth. His father flew. That was his only real passion in life as Jimmy Kho, also a former China Air Transport (or C.A.T. as it was known) *cum* Flying Tiger pilot, once told Gordie. *Flying, and fucking the wrong women, that was Mark.* Now everyone was gone, even Jimmy who finally expired, never having awakened from the prolonged coma. Everything was history. Why remember? Lately, Gordie remembered too much too often, which horrified him.

Lately, Gordie seldom flew.

His Cessna was on the lawn outside the house, right by the driveway. Sacrilege, yes, but there was neither a full-time gardener now for the massive grounds nor the contingent of chauffeurs and maids his mother maintained to upkeep their oversized home. Just Reginald the butler, and his wife Annabel, the housekeeper and part time cook. Even Chef was gone.

The house was dark as he pulled up the driveway.

Reginald, who heard, had the lights on and front door open before the engine stopped.

"Master Gordon," he said, the barest hint of surprise in his voice. "You're home for Christmas."

Gordie removed his driving gloves. Reginald removed his bag from the trunk, saying, "Annabel can defrost a bird, but the wine cellar's a little sparse I'm afraid."

"Scotch?"

"Always."

It had been several months since Reginald had seen him and he thought the young master looked thinner, if that were possible, and unusually somber. Death was of course a serious affair, but surely, over a year was a sufficient bereavement, and it was his mother's time, after all? Gordon would always be "the young master," as long as he remained unmarried, although Reginald conceded to addressing him as "Sir" when he remembered, and "Mr. Ashberry, sir," in the presence of Rosemarie's guests. It was lonesome these days, just him and Annabel rattling round the silent mansion. And it was hard work, now that they were no longer young, keeping the place presentable for when the realtors descended with their clients.

1998 was neither the best nor worst of times for real estate. As his mother's estate executor, Gordie had, to date, turned down three purchase offers, citing either price or his own schedule as excuses. His mother had left him even less cash than he expected—*less* than half a mill—but assigned him the responsibility of liquidating the estate for the benefit of her numerous charities. Gordie was both annoyed and grateful. If nothing else, it meant access to the homestead for a little longer. Reginald never let on that he could practically hear Rosemarie's laughter, reveling in the fact that *this* responsibility her son couldn't shirk, *so there.* Harold, when he heard, was aghast, and almost blurted out to his buddy *what a bitch*, but checked himself, although he had said to Isobel in private, *it'll break his heart. He loves that place.* Isobel was sanguine. *His own fault*, she said. *Cutting off the hand that . . .* But Harold knew it wasn't just about money. The Greenline home was Gordie and he couldn't imagine Gordie without it.

Rosemarie's lawyers were impatient with him, but Gordie had never liked them anyway, and most of all was irked that Jack Hwang's nonprofit would benefit from the estate. Reginald agreed, and since his and Annabel's pensions depended on Gordie, they were inclined to support whatever delaying tactics he employed.

"He's crashed," Annabel whispered to Reginald. Unlike the latter, she wasn't English, but years of marriage to Reg had altered her accent although she maintained a fondness for American slang.

It was only nine thirty. The previously full Black was down to less than a quarter. "Poor boy," Reg said. "This isn't like him. He drinks to enjoy, not to despair." He stopped then added, "like his father."

"He's terribly sad. Didn't even make a joke when I brought in the bird. I've never seen him like this."

They stared at Gordie, asleep on the drawing room sofa where Rosemarie had slept many an evening after cocktails, only to awaken at three or four in the morning, demanding her dinner, which was served without question. It had been her pattern for several years after Mark's death, until the arrival of Jack Hwang.

Jack Hwang was everything Ashberry men were not—circumspect, gentle, ruthlessly kind as opposed to merely ruthless—and back in '78, Rosemarie had been smitten. Gordie, after meeting him the first time at one of his mother's parties, cautioned. "Rosemarie, Jack's making eyes at you." His mother spun around the drawing room, the detritus of the party surrounding them at midnight. *"Ma, he's nearly breaking my heart,"* she sang.

"And when did *you* start singing such drivel?" because his mother had always been strictly opera and classical.

"Don't be jealous," she said, because Rosemarie knew, perfectly well, that her son was not only jealous but afraid of any barriers to her affection.

A week later, Rosemarie was in Manhattan and Gordie brought her to an opening reception for an exhibit at the Asia Society, one of her sudden new interests. Jack was a friend of the curator's and squired Rosemarie around as if it were his own show. Jack was seven years older than Gordie and a year younger than Anna, the woman Gordie was secretly seeing at the time. Rosemarie was sixty.

"Your mother," Jack addressed him, "ages like a Chinese woman. She could pass for my older sister." He smiled at her as she tittered like a schoolgirl. "Only *slightly* older."

Gordie glared at those exquisite Mandarin features. "Is *your* mother here?"

Rosemarie said, "It's so tragic about Jack's mother, the Koo-man-ting and all that."

"Mother, it's the *Guomindang.*"

Jack's eyes glazed over, which might also have been due to an involuntary misting. "I still get a lump when I think of her . . . sacrifice." There was a reverential, five-second silence and then he addressed Gordie again. "You're a Chinese scholar, I understand."

"In my case, 'scholar' is beyond hyperbole. I studied a little."

"Muqin de ai shi tian de ai."

Rosemarie touched Jack's arm. "What did that mean? It sounded so beautiful."

The two men spoke simultaneously.

Gordie said, "Mother's love is heaven's love." Jack said, "Mother is heaven."

Height gave Gordie some advantage and he tried to stare Jack down. He was ignored. Jack brushed his hand lightly against Rosemarie's, and then he held onto her elbow and arm, like an escort, as the three of them continued to walk round the exhibit. It wasn't till much later that Gordie learned Jack's mother had been killed in Taipei by a hit-and-run driver. Jack had been four. The Kuomintang had nothing to do with anything. By then, Rosemarie had become the largest single donor to the Chinese Cultural Renaissance Action Society, or CCRAS, a new non-profit which Jack founded.

Gordie found support for his position: neither Larry Woo nor Harold Haight had liked Jack. Larry dismissed him as a sham Kuomingtang nationalist, trading on Taiwan's historical relationship with the U.S. He said this in front of Anita who disagreed but did not say anything. Anita told Gordie she did not trust Jack Hwang, as she could find no one in her circle from Taiwan who knew anything about him or his family, although she would later change her mind about him.

Harold didn't simply dislike Jack. He loathed, despised, and completely mistrusted Jack. He also wanted the Haddon estate account, mostly to protect Gordie's interest, rather than for his firm's benefit. If he were in charge, Harold knew, he would make sure Gord wouldn't just fritter away his inheritance since the man hadn't the slightest idea what to do with all that money.

Which was why now, in 1998 of the post-Thanksgiving, pre-Christmas haze of work and parties and too much loneliness, Harold tried once again to reach out to Gord. Patti had been useless, less than useless, something he didn't quite understand about his usually resourceful sister.

Meanwhile, up north at Greenline, Gordie slept.

"Should we put him to bed?" Annabel asked.

"That would be difficult."

She studied his long limbs. "Yes, I suppose it would." Then. "Remember Stella Shih and Samantha Nelson? Such attractive girls.

He always had good taste."

Reg grimaced, but his wife did not notice.

Annabel continued. "And Mimi Townsend, wasn't she a delight? But sad about the tragedy, her dying so young. What was she, nineteen?"

"Something like that."

"She and Gordon got married, remember, when they were six? Over at the Townsends'? We were the witnesses." Annabel smiled at her memory. Gordie—she called him that despite her husband—had been a *wonderful* little boy, filled with the promise of life's joy, and Mimi, an exuberant and happy child, had been his best friend in Greenline till they were sixteen, but even after their falling out—it hadn't really been so bad—a friendship remained. They were the same age, but it was a problem, this village with so few families, Annabel felt. A child needed lots of other children. There had only been two other boys close in age, from acceptable families that is, and Mrs. Haddon Ashberry despised the Townsends, not that she was *rude* or anything, even having them over for parties and drinks. But working as long as she had for the Ashberrys, Annabel knew. Overheard remarks, disparaging. Oh, the Townsends were different—and here she paused in her memory—truthfully, they were downright odd, what with that nutty twin brother of James Townsend, Mimi's father, who lived with them, dressing up in ladies' clothes and god knows what else. Everyone knew. And their being *Democrats*. Quite shameless. What really upset Mrs. Haddon Ashberry though—and of this Annabel was certain even though Reg never agreed—was *Mrs. Townsend*. She was Italian, sensual, glamorous, and Mr. Ashberry was frank in his admiration of her, *not*, of course, that there was anything there, Annabel wasn't implying, but well, you can always tell when a man's prick is tickled—and here she giggled to herself at the thought, imagining Reg's distaste at *such language my dear!*

Reginald studied the sleeping man. Not a boy anymore, pity, not that his boyhood was all that glorious. Difficult life, not that he showed it most of the time, what with all the laughter and parties, and women when his mother wasn't around—Annabel had *no idea* of all those *other* women he brought in through the back door, late at night. Blue-blooded society girls and god knows what else, in their evening silks and European shoes—how many Cinderella leftovers had he retrieved the mornings after when Gordon had driven the girls home to elsewhere in Connecticut or New York or Massachusetts? Sad, really, that he should end up like this, alone. This place, this house, this village. That was the problem. Mark Ashberry was the devil incarnate, all wrong for a Haddon girl, not like James Townsend who *belonged* here. Reg knew that was the real cause, one he'd never mentioned to Annabel because why gossip? Besides it was ancient history that Rosemarie and James had possibly once almost been lovers . . . passed along by his uncle who had buttled for the Haddons and had remained in the home with Rosemarie when she married Mark Ashberry, after her parents died. Parents who hadn't approved of James because of his brother, apparently, which seemed awfully unfair, Reginald felt, since it wasn't James' fault if his twin was a fairy. The Haddon house where Reginald first came to as a boy, orphaned by his parents' sudden demise, to the only living relative he had, and the teenaged Rosemarie had been sweet, kind, lovingly gentle. Didn't matter now, did it? He wondered where the Townsends had gone, back to Northern Italy perhaps, to her family the Truccos? Mimi's death was a hard blow. Reg didn't think they ever recovered.

But Mimi! *What girl, Mr. Reginald,* she had declared at six, her expression certain, brooking no argument, *wouldn't want to marry Bugs Bunny?* And Reginald had only been able to nod his head in agreement when faced with such stellar logic.

5

It was the evening before Christmas, 1958, and all throughout Greenline, sounds of grown-up parties emanated from lit houses. The Haddon estate was no exception. Rosemarie threw the most lavish and elegant affairs, while Annabel decked out the back room behind the kitchen with a festive warmth to appease chauffeurs and other members of the servant class who trailed behind the guests. Occasionally, the odd *au pair* isolated herself from these festivities, as one did this evening despite their gardener's persistent flirting, which Annabel thought a shame. When push came to shove, despite education, *you may as well be one of us because you'll never be one of them.*

Reginald appeared, a broken champagne glass on his tray.

"Oh dear," Annabel remarked. "Isn't it a little early for that?" Because it was only six thirty.

"This was a genuine accident," he responded, and swept the shards into the garbage. Outside, on the airstrip, a rattle of engine. "They're back."

Annabel peered out and sighted the dark outline of the Cessna. "Thank goodness for that." She watched as Mark Ashberry brought the plane to a complete stop.

Reg joined his new wife at the window. "It's wrong of him, coming back so late, especially with the boy. Madam's furious enough as it is."

"He probably didn't mean to. His incoming flight from the Orient might have been delayed, and anyway, Gordie so loves these trips. The child needs some time with his father he gets precious little as it is."

"It's going to be a long Christmas."

When Reginald murmured of her family's return, Rosemarie held out her emptied cocktail glass for a martini refill. Then, she returned to her guests—and they were only her guests—paying special attention to the well-mannered, if mannered, young man who had just arrived, assistant to the curator at some foundation Rosemarie patronized, a young man who clearly had eyes for no woman other than the stunningly graceful Mrs. Haddon Ashberry.

That night, Mark did not make an appearance. Gordie raced through his bath and dashed into the party, hair still slightly damp. Sighting his mother, he edged his path through the crowd. "Darling," she said, two cocktails further along in the forty-five minutes since Reginald first informed her, "it's about time you came home." She unlinked her arm from the elbow crook beside her.

"Hello Mother," said the boy who, even at ten could reach her cheek to kiss it. "Where's Mimi?"

"The Townsends were busy."

The young man next to Rosemarie frowned. Gordie's appearance was an unhappy reminder of a husband's existence. Fortunately, the kid didn't hang around and he soon re-positioned himself as the evening's escort.

Gordie did not feel an iota of jet lag. A grand adventure coursed through his veins, of landing on the slenderest strip of runway in Hong Kong, of crossing the harbor aboard the Star Ferry's lower deck where the sailor let him hold the gangplank rope, of scrambling to the top of Lion Rock with his father on a sunny day which felt nothing like the winters he knew.

On his first and only trip there, two years earlier, they had both flown as passengers. This time, Mark was piloting the Clipper and had allowed his son into the cockpit at the landing into Kai Tak. Gordie had maintained a brave face, since he wouldn't act otherwise around his dad, but he had actually been scared silly by their approach into the tiny British colony, where it felt as if the plane would crash right into the gray, murky sea. Minutes prior, he shut his eyes briefly as they circled the tops of ramshackle buildings along the Kowloon hillside, certain they could not clear that tight, air traffic path. Now, safely back at last, he was bursting to brag of surviving all these dangerous moments. But Mother was preoccupied, playing host to all these strangers, and Mimi—how could her family be busy at

Christmas?—was nowhere to be found.

He knelt on the window seat in the dining room and cupped his hands to the glass. Peering diagonally across their grounds, he could just make out the lights at the Townsends'. So they were home! For a second, he struggled with a guilty twinge at the idea of leaving his mother's party, but a greater impulse of self-preservation prevailed. Grabbing his parka and boots, he braved the depths of unplowed snow, and trekked the shortest path across the blanketed lawn towards the home of light and warmth.

"Gordie, boyyyy," his father said the next day. "Where you been?" Mark was in the atrium dining room, eating lunch. Not a sign of the previous evening's detritus remained.

"At the Townsends. Mother said I could sleep over," he lied, although he had told Annabel and that was truth enough.

"Really, your mother did?" He returned to scanning his mail.

Reginald appeared. "Would you like a ham sandwich, Master Gordon?"

"No thanks. I'm as stuffed as Mrs. T's goose."

"I heard they'd ordered one," Reginald remarked and departed.

Gordie was about to leave when his father asked. "So who was there?"

"Just the family."

"And what was the crazy man wearing?"

"Uncle Arthur's not crazy. He's just different," because James Townsend's twin brother lived with the family, sang Broadway musicals to his sister-in-law's piano accompaniment and cross-dressed.

Mark's ulcer did a somersault. His voice rose. "That fairy prince is not your uncle! Don't you ever call him that."

"Yes, sir."

Calmed, his father unfolded the letter from his broker. Year-end dividends looked promising, he noted, pleased. "And was Mrs. T. wearing anything?" He asked without glancing up at his son.

"*Dad!*" Gordie protested, and left.

How he wished he had never told Mark about that accidental glimpse of Mimi's mother, disrobed. Bragging, Annabel would have said, destined to end badly. Of course most *everyone* knew their last gardener posed for Mrs. Townsend, during her painterly phase; he had been fired and replaced when Rosemarie finally caught on.

Gordie happened by one afternoon—school hours during which he'd played hooky and no one would expect prying eyes—and there they'd been, both of them in a state of undress that did not resemble a painting session. He stared, dumbstruck, as pre-puberty roiled. Luckily, they didn't see him. The thing was, he'd meant the disclosure to be his and his dad's secret, which it was, except that ever after then, he couldn't help noticing that whenever Mrs. T was over, Mark looked at her in a way that embarrassed Gordie.

But nothing, nothing was worse than when his mother finally crawled out of her room, and began again with martinis at three. Gordie tried, but did not succeed in evading his parents, given that it *was* Christmas, after all. The session ended with his father drinking more than customary, a glass being smashed in the fireplace, and Mark leaving the house early evening before dinner and screeching down the driveway towards the city. Just prior, Mark had said, "fuck you, Rosemarie," to which his mother, eyes glazed and no longer unhappy, replied, smiling, "don't swear in front of the child," even though Gordie had already gone to Annabel. *There, there,* she said to the boy who was forcing back tears, *they're not really angry at each other.* Gordie had dinner alone that evening, because Reginald said it would be bad form to barge in on the Townsends' again, while his mother dozed on the sofa in the drawing room. Mark did not return till mid January, when it was time again for him to go abroad, to where, only he knew.

As Reginald predicted, correctly, it was a long and arduous Christmas season.

***

Gordie awoke to his ringing mobile. The voice on the other end was certifiably drunk.

"How, could, she, do, it?"

"Harold? That you?"

In the background Harold said, "Ahhh, fuck off," followed by an equal and opposite retort.

It was 02:00 and Gordie's head hurt. He needed to pee. "Slow up Harold, what're you talking about?"

"My wife. Fucking Trevor. Fucking, a, third, rate, trial, lawyer. How could she?"

"You've had too much, buddy."

"Pretty, boy, Trevor. You, and, he, get, along. *Don't* you? Don't you?"

"Where are you Harold?" Gordie stood up, unsteadily, and headed for the bathroom.

"Some hole in the city."

Unzipping, the relief! His bladder, if not his head, a little less weighted, Gordie focused. "If you're not home then come up here. Greenline I mean. I'm not in town."

***

Harold looked around the bar. Where *was* he? The sound of Gord, speaking in full sentences, sobered him. In fact, Harold already knew that Gord was not in the city because, despite his inebriation, he had called the Gramercy line first and left a rambling message that boiled down to "so where the fuck are you?" a message left often during the past couple of years since returning home from Hong Kong.

He went silent momentarily. "I'm broke. Walked out of the office without my wallet. I've spent all the cash in my pocket."

"Get in a cab. I'll cover."

Once in motion, what struck Harold was the fact that this was Christmas Eve, so this was beyond bad, this was *disaster*. Hadn't he promised Pete they'd meet? The other thing—*had* he really forgotten his wallet and if so just *how* much cash had he been carrying, and throwing away? But inside the rolling movement of the yellow car his mind collapsed and he was soon asleep.

When he showed up in Greenline three and a half hours later, he was less drunk, having slept most of the way.

"Not even on the map," the driver repeated. "I circled twice, looking for the turnoffs. And *he* wasn't any help," thumbing at Harold, "saying, 'coast, coast, just go coast,' like *everyone* should know, like Route 66 or something, and snores off so loud to rattle the windows, louder than a caravan of camels." He was Egyptian or Pakistani or maybe even Iraqi—Harold couldn't tell in the half light where Gordie stood by the driver's side window, payment in hand—but his indignation was plural. "Mister you got something smaller?" He held up the bill. Gordie replied. "Keep the change. Celebrate whatever."

Harold, half out of the cab, awoke abruptly. "Gord! It's a *thousand bucks,*" and then, in rhetorical disbelief, "who the hell has thousand dollar bills?"

"Hey, thanks!" The driver's indignation eased, but then, he looked puzzled. "You sure this is real?"

Gordie grinned. "As real as a two dollar bill, pal. Look at me, would I lie?"

The driver stared beyond the man who paid him at this peculiarly shaped structure, with its long and unnecessarily curved driveway, and then looked at Gordie's face. Deciding not to press his luck, he drove off, muttering in Arabic.

***

Pre-dawn light veiled the house, the "elf boot" Harold had first been introduced to back during their college days. His friend led him through the foyer straight into the vast drawing room under the stairs. The row of French windows opened out onto a sloping lawn that led to the sea. It was chilly, but Gordie had lit a fire. The mess of the evening before was gone. A coffee pot and rolls sat on the low table. Reginald and Annabel, deafer than they used to be, were still asleep.

"Here, this will help," he said, handing Harold a cup.

Harold sipped. "Fine Christmas, huh?"

"No worse than last year," because that had been shortly after Rosemarie's death and Harold had invited, no, *insisted* that Gordie not be alone and had had him over to their Christmas. Gordie was morose, even slightly snappish, and Isobel, finally, unable to stand the gloom he cast over her family's festivities, had told him to leave, which started a fight between her and Harold—the last, since by then Trevor was more than ready, parked and waiting to take her away for good—and then the two men left, right in the middle of Christmas Eve dinner and went on a binge in the city for which Harold paid, painfully, having gotten punched in the mouth for saying the wrong drunken thing to the wrong drunken guy at around eight thirty in the evening, Christmas day.

"Gord, we can't keep doing this. We're getting too old."

Gordie did not reply.

After a long while, Harold spoke. "She's left me, Gord. It's really over," and then, as the faint glimmer of early sun appeared, began to weep.

His jag eventually calmed. Gordie unfolded a handkerchief and handed it to him.

Harold took it. "Thanks."

"You could have had Kathleen O'Mara instead, you know. You two would still be together I bet."

"Dickhead." He rolled the handkerchief into a ball and mopped his cheeks. "You're probably right."

"You know I am."

Dawn was clearing the horizon. "But look at it this way, Gord. We wouldn't have Pete then, would we?"

"No," Gordie agreed, "we wouldn't. As usual, you're right on that last word."

Harold was not a man who cried, let alone weep. Hours later, after a long, very hot shower and the restful ease of a clean, well-lighted bedroom, he stared at the Atlantic, his mind sharpened and clear. This was *war*. No ands or buts. Let Trevor provide if he wanted to marry her; his responsibility was now only to his boys. And Terror, the dog.

Gord had let him blather on for over an hour, saying very little. *You warned me, didn't you,* Harold repeated. *Isobel hated Hong Kong, as did Harold Jr.*, and when the two of them returned to the U.S., (unlike Pete who *thrived*, minding Esmerelda, eating on schedule, and doing so well at the international, geek-friendly school), *you said* go home, *and I procrastinated, because things were complicated at work, but also, I never believed she'd go back to that man.*

Despite opportunity—what married man *didn't* confront that most breakable of commandments?—but Harold himself, *never*, not in a million years. In this new light, Gord's unassailable despair following his mother's death, crystallized for Harold. It was what you didn't know, *what you didn't want to know* that got you in trouble, tripped up your heart, devastated your world irreparably. Much more than sin, cushioned as that was by remorse and absolution.

6

By Harold's reckoning, it had been a fast courtship, and before long he and Isobel were spending most weekends together. A year after their meeting, he'd made up his mind to marry her. The problem was a ring, which he began saving up for monthly once he'd decided. Five months later, he only had seven more to go.

"Harry," his brother John advised, "you're pushing it. What's the diff? A small diamond will do. I can get you a deal in Hong Kong." As an American, John Haight was early, back then before Carter finally embraced China, in heading out to Asia. To everyone's surprise, the baby in their family had become fluent in Japanese and post-college, was interning in Tokyo on his way to Hong Kong, *and* learning Chinese. Mrs. Haight would have preferred him closer to home, but John did what John wanted and ultimately, no one ever really objected.

"I'm not giving her some fake Chinese rock. It's Tiffany's or nothing."

"Does *she* know?"

"What're you, nuts? You don't *tell* a woman these things."

Dunderdick's going to lose her, John told Patti. *Talk to him, sis,* because even John, years away from any kind of long-term commitment, could see that Isobel was not just impatient, she was outright hostile. John had arrived home a week before Christmas and was crashing at his brother's in the city. It was plain that Harry wasn't getting as much as he should have been for a man who was virtually married, and was a mean pain in the butt as a result. John knew from where he spoke, he being the easy going one, the one girls hung onto even as he slid out of their grasp.

Patti, anxious herself at the tedious arguments involved for a Catholic-Jewish wedding next spring, only half cared. Besides, she wanted Kath to go get Harry once and for all, before it was too late, *goddamn it, girl, why you let him push you around I'll never know, he's only my brother and you know I'll shut my parents up if they get out of hand.* It was in this mood, as her wedding day drew closer, that she went to see Gordo *one last time, promise,* she whispered to whatever god she still trusted, and crazy Gordo, happy to keep their secret treated her so well she couldn't help herself—*why are you being so sweet you're going to make me cry*—but then he laughed and when she got dressed that rainy afternoon, it was the one and only time she raised her voice at him, *I'm just your Kathleen O'Mara, aren't I,* and left in something of a huff, only to be assuaged at the wedding when Gordo was perfect to everyone, even Richard, and sent the most expensive present on their list.

In the spring of '77, The Kahn-Haight wedding was memorable on many counts. For one thing, it was a double wedding, one for the groom's family and the other for the bride's, covering both religious contingents and wardrobes, saddling each family with a separate tab. But it ended the impasse of prolonged negotiations that erupted from the initial proposal for a civil ceremony by the couple concerned. For Patti and Richard, it was their last concession to family. Patti conceded to the rise and fall veil thing and ceremony under the huppah, while Richard got through the "love-honor-and-obey" speech and wedding mass in church, complete with the mangled chords on the organ (the Kahn boys grew up notably secular, a fact not lost on their envious Haight cousins). Also, Isobel was in a flattering green dress at Patti's Catholic wedding, *a little short, isn't it,* Harold remarked on first seeing it, only meaning that her legs weren't her greatest assets, but Isobel took it all wrong and kept him out of her B&B room by offering to share it with one of the bridesmaids, something she took pains to mention to Mrs. Haight who later said to her husband, "such a *nice* girl, our Harry's Isobel. Considerate and well brought up, not like you-know-who," glancing at *that* O'Mara girl, maid of honor (*Patti was such a stubborn girl, always was*) who, even in a nice bridal party, looked every inch the illegitimate *slut* that she was.

At the Haight reception, Kath was cool towards Harold, *not that he could blame her but hell, they were over, she was a big girl and he never promised anything, right?* And it had been awhile since they'd run into each other since he became serious with Isobel and ended things with Kath over nine months ago. But then he watched her slow dance with Gord and as the next number came up, his brother took Isobel to the floor. So Harold went straight for Kath, *she let Gord put his hands pretty damn low there*, and pulled her a long way down a secluded path. His temper was rising and no matter how much he breathed, he couldn't hold it back.

"Harry, what the hell do you think you're doing? You're hurting my hand."

He didn't answer and continued to drag her along.

She stopped walking and yanked at his arm, hard. "Cut it out."

The woman was *strong*. He stood still and stretched out his arm. "What, were, you, doing, and, don't, call, me, Harry."

"Slow down. You're doing that spacing thing again. It'll trigger your asthma, you know it will. You don't want that to happen here, do you?"

"I'm, not, doing, anything, what, were, you, doing?"

"Okay that's it. Calm down or our friendship's terminated."

He took a deep breath, knowing she was right, hating her for it and wishing he didn't, *what didn't he... what?* Hating himself for being pathetic. She reminded him, too easily, of who he really was. "Kath, what were you doing with Gord?"

"With *Gordon?* Are you out of your mind? He's your best friend."

"I don't want you with him."

"I'm not 'with him' and besides, it's none of your business. Is it?"

"I'm making it mine."

"You can't. You have no right and you damn well know it."

Things would have taken a worse turn, but Gordie had followed them and stood in front of Harold. "Hey," he said. "It's Patti's day. Don't wreck it."

Kath, meanwhile, walked back to the party, found John Haight and said, "what's with your brother?" And Isobel, having no idea about any of this, annoyed at being abandoned and a tiny bit tipsy, was pleasantly piqued when there, surprise, was Trevor Silverstein, who happened to be someone's date, someone currently off in the ladies room, which gave her time to flirt, shamelessly, and they made a date, *it's Harold's own fault*, she whispered to her god who, about this tiny sample of his flock, was probably too busy rolling around some cloud in laughter to listen to the protest of prayer. Trevor, as only

Trevor knew, engineered this phony date, knowing Isobel would be here, but could not be accused of cutting in improperly on Harold, since *she* suggested their assignation, not he.

What Gordie did, what Gordie offered when he and Kath were dancing, was for her to crash at the townhouse for a week or so between leases.

"I'm just doing her a favor," he explained over Harold's protests.

"Touch her and I'll kill you."

"Why Harry," he mock-batted his lashes, "I didn't know you cared."

"Cut that out you jackass."

They were in Chinatown at Wo Hop's, which Harold agreed to only because it was dirt cheap and he was counting pennies which, even by Harold's standards, was decidedly lean, beyond his normal frugality. It was Sunday evening, a month or so after Patti's wedding.

Gordie took the bill. "Let me. I can't stand the agony."

"Dickhead."

"C'mon, I'll buy us a round."

They headed to the upper West side, near Harold's home in the seventies. Harold insisted, because it meant they could take the subway before it got too late. Generally, they drank at Gord's, but a taxi from Gramercy was a luxury. Besides there was work in the morning, something Gord didn't have to think about so *he can do the cab*, Harold reasoned and Gordie, true to form, went along with whatever his buddy suggested.

A week later, Harold dropped in at Gramercy. Gord was out but Kath was home. Harold already knew that because he called ahead and got the answering machine which his friend only turned on when he was abroad. In fact, Gordie was at that moment on his way to Hong Kong, which Harold knew but had temporarily forgotten. So his surprise, when Kath opened the door, was at least subconsciously a pretense, although what he told himself, what he tried to tell himself, *in the neighborhood, give it a shot.*

"Can I come in?"

Kathleen was in jammies, her version being a long T-shirt that reached to the middle of her thighs, because it was a warm night and with Monday a work day an early night was in order. She stared at him, surprised.

"Gordon's abroad. Surely he told you."

"Gordie."

"Patti calls him Gordon."

"She does?"

"Harold, what do you want?"

He could feel the shortness of breath, the uncontrollable impulse to speak staccato, that "spacing thing" which all his intimates knew only too well. *How could he forget about Gord's trip! What must Kath think?* He was also ashamed. Breathing in hard, he said. "I owe you an apology."

She opened the door and admitted him. Three hours later, energies expended by their inevitable sexual wrestling match—*never, he never could keep away from her not since the first time they met when Patti brought her home to dinner and he couldn't keep his eyes off her sitting beside her that time had been one of the worst agonies of his teenage years*—Harold leaned his face into her neck and said. "Marry me?"

"Are you nuts?" She rolled him off her, sat up in bed and slipped her T-shirt back on. And then. "You don't mean it, right?"

"I've never meant anything more in my life." He reached for her face with both hands, his palms smoothed the rounded cheeks, *like baby fat*, this face he had known for so long and so well. Her auburn mass had come undone, sliding out of the band that held her ponytail of curls. Her naturally curled lashes, her father's perhaps, and the hauntingly large green eyes, just like her single mother, the town's diner waitress who had gotten pregnant at fifteen with Kath. O'Mara was her mother's name; her birth certificate read "unknown" for the father. Kissing her lips lightly, he added, "we love each other, don't we?"

"Quit going soft on me. It's not you," because what they shared, what they did for each other was drink hard together and more than simply *talk* dirty, they were dirty, very, very dirty, unleashing their ambitious, street fighting natures—strained by the civility of their respective work worlds—when they connected in the throes of bodily heat. She sat up, her back against the headboard. "What's happened with Isobel?"

"Nothing."

"Harry, you know you're the worst liar in the world."

"Trevor Silverstein's proposed." When Kath didn't respond, her face in something like shock, he continued. "He brought her a ring that might as well be the Hope diamond. A two-carat rock, and a necklace to match. The necklace is worth almost as much as the ring."

Kathleen shook her head. "She *told* you all that?"

He nodded. "Kath, I can't compete."

That was when Kath got out of bed and tossed him his clothes. "Of course you can," she almost said *Dunderdick* but didn't. "Isobel didn't accept, did she?"

He looked at her pleadingly. "I've *almost* got the ring. Just a couple more months."

"Did you tell her that?"

"I *can't*. She'd tell everyone, *and* that mother of hers. I've got my pride."

"Can't you borrow from Gordon? He's generous and won't mind."

There was a hesitation, and Kathleen swore later to Patti that Harold was mad, really mad, and trying hard not to let on. Finally, he said. "He hasn't offered and I won't ask."

Patti's heart leapt when she heard. *Yeah. Good old Gordo*, because she suspected he rooted for Kath. But all she said to her friend was, "and you let Harry get away with treating you like that? Kath, that's unconscionable."

"Don't worry about me, it's fine. I'm over him." And then, with a wink at the best girlfriend she ever had, added, "besides, around Harry, I'd never get out of bed. You've got to change the sheets sometime."

Stella Shih's Interlude

When Stella (surprise!) contacted me at my summer place in Bergen, it was to say she would be in Oslo in a couple of weeks and was there a chance I might come over to meet her? I had to ask—*business or pleasure*—because Norway was a little far afield for her, and I've never known Stella to travel for pleasure.

"You took the train?" Stella asked. She hadn't even shaken my hand yet.

I laughed and gave her a hug. "Well, you haven't changed, oh Grand Inquisitor."

As it turned out, I *had* taken the train over the mountains, because the view is irresistibly spectacular in summer and a stunning white palette in winter. We met at the Grand Hotel because Stella is nothing if not purposeful about her choice of location, the more public and obvious the better. Out in the open, for all to see, because that way nothing seems covert.

Once we sat down, she asked. "He's gone undercover, hasn't he?"

"You should know. If you don't who does?"

"I don't."

"Aren't you still . . . ?"

"Yes."

Stella doesn't ever say "C.I.A.," doesn't ever acknowledge her connection out loud. Mark recruited her of course, which Gordie never knew till much too late, long after he'd left her at the altar, because he thought she'd been his father's lover. At least I *think* Gordie eventually found out. Stella's never said and I've given up asking either her or him.

The waiter came by and she ordered us coffees. "No one knows where he is."

"And you want to see me because . . .?"

"Don't you know?"

I wondered why she had drawn her conclusion so quickly since this was only a month or so after his alleged disappearance. Stella's like that though, makes up her mind quick about pretty much everything. "So why did you want to see me? Just to ask this?"

"Yes. Oh no, of course not, you knew that though, didn't you? I think I'm in love."

"Anyone I know?"

She didn't answer at first, but then she nodded and said, "He's married."

And this was when she became silly, almost a girl again, as she made me lean over to whisper in my ear the name of Gail Szeto's husband, Jim Fieldman. I frowned, and forced myself not to say anything too sharp because I know she's sensitive, despite her seeming self confidence. But to be infatuated with Gordie's . . . and here I had to pause because what do you call a man's half-sister's husband? His half-brother-in-law? Isn't that beyond the limit?

"You're not really his type," I declared. "He likes tall women."

"Love," she said, "is not about type. Or height."

"What then?"

"Pheromones."

That's when I knew, *she's a goner.*

***

The first time I met Stella, it was about half a year after her disastrous non-wedding to Gordie, right after she had returned from Taiwan to where she had retreated with her parents to recover. She was softer then, more feminine, and wore those slightly too girlish dresses for an adult woman. Pastels, especially pale pink, sleeves gathered, disastrously puffed with lacy edges and frills. Except for her awful taste in clothing, which has improved over the years, Stella Shih is Gordie's type: petite, long hair, thin, shy, a little bookish, attractive enough but not exactly what anyone would call pretty. Stella walked, often for hours, and she told me that she and Gordie would easily spend half a day walking the shoreline of his Connecticut home, just talking.

Anita introduced us, because she had told Stella I could help her get over Gordie, and we had a *dimsum* lunch in Chinatown where our conversation was mostly in Chinese, interspersed with explanatory

English. Anita occasionally interpreted my Cantonese for Stella because she only spoke Mandarin and mine was non-existent back then.

I had asked. "Have you seen him? Talked to him?"

She shook her head.

"He's a wreck." But what I said in Chinese was *he has difficulty getting over it*.

"He should be," Anita said, because she wasn't talking to him then and it took her quite awhile after all that before she would be civil again.

"Did you give back the ring?"

She held out her left hand; the diamond sparkled.

Anita interjected. "I said she shouldn't. She can sell that for a lot of money."

It was square cut, at least two carats, but I knew it was nothing Gordie would have chosen. Mark. It had to be Mark who bought that. Also, it wasn't the Haddon diamond, the one Gordie would later give Sammi. That was when I first had an inkling that perhaps Stella and Mark were more than friendly, as Gordie suspected, although it wasn't as if they could have known each other for very long since he died before their wedding day. But as I gazed at this older woman, she seemed so young to me, even though she had to be at least six years or so my senior (I would later learn she was even older than that). It wasn't just her youthful appearance and demeanor. There was something frighteningly invisible about her, almost as if she was lost, a woman without a face or identity or self.

Over the years I would bug Gordie. *What was it about Stella?* And all he would ever say was *oh how do I know? Who understands why we do anything?* He did admit once, but only once, what I've come to believe is the real reason. *I had to keep her from floating away,* he said. *She was so ephemeral. Like a bubble.*

7

Harold is both pleased and *nonplussed* to get the Woos' invitation to their daughter's wedding banquet. The red envelope, hand written with his name and office address, *looked too utterly exotic not to show you, unopened,* his secretary says as he hands it over with the afternoon's in-box. The calligraphy on the card, translated for the benefit of those illiterate in Chinese, reads Zhou-Woo, a *pinyin*-Hong Kong-CantoEnglish combo. Violette's fiancé's family all are fluent in Chinese, his Norwegian mother having been stationed as director at the Shanghai branch of a shipping company, which was how his parents met. How he and Violette met was another story entirely, one not fully understood yet by either Larry or Anita.

He notes the Saturday date in his pocket diary, the one Pete calls Jurassic.

It is shortly before Valentine's Day. Harold's personal assistant Tim White discovered the rift in his boss' marriage three years ago on February 12, when he was told to cancel Isobel's annual floral bouquet, one Harold has had on autopaid renewal forever, or at least since the first time he forgot the day and caught hell from her. Harold had actually agreed to return to the firm early in '97, just before the Asian economic crisis hit. Harold predicted the crisis correctly, a prediction that fell on deaf ears at Merryweather Lind, which was what decided his return to law. Tim has been with Harold since his return.

"But he's a *guy*," Harold had protested to the firm's human resources manager upon being assigned Tim. "I need a secretary."

"Personal assistant," she corrected. "All partners get p.a.'s, and we don't discriminate here in case you hadn't noticed? Besides, he's been with the firm seven years and did a superb job for Case."

But Linda Case was litigation and *female,* he protested privately, as Tim sat across from his desk during their first "conference." Tim had been warned Harold might be "difficult."

"I'm detailed oriented," Tim said, "and working nights doesn't bother me. I can use the overtime."

Harold gazed at the young man, who had toned down his attire for their first meeting, as the song "Y.M.C.A." flashed. Bad enough that the firm's expansion meant strange new practices—during his absence, the firm had become less of a tax law business and more of a real partnership with multiple practices which Harold accepted, reluctantly—but *this* was beyond the pale.

Undaunted by his new boss' silence, Tim continued. "I know I haven't worked in tax, but we used to do a lot of cross over with the practice when I was in litigation. I don't make mistakes, ask Linda. I would have followed her over to," and he named the firm to which she had absconded, "but I like my colleagues at old Mort. It's like home here."

"Rebecca used to bring me coffee," Harold said, referring to his former secretary, an older woman who had since retired. "And she'd go out to get me lunch," he added, hoping to daunt him.

Tim didn't miss a beat. "That's the 'personal' part in my title." He paused. "C'mon, Mr. Haight, give me a shot. I really don't bite? And I promise, no cross-dressing, at least not during office hours."

Despite himself, Harold's lips wrinkled into a smile. His tolerance had improved as a result of working in Hong Kong, where he discovered that a raised voice did not improve comprehension, but that a little allowance for second language speakers of English went a long, long way.

Tim, as he has since discovered, also arranges dry cleaning and laundry pick-ups and deliveries, healthy but non-geriatric meals-on-wheels, private trainers at the gym, as well as other necessities for a man without a wife, not to mention absolute discretion at all of Harold's venting. Things are better these days; the firm moved down to the Wall Street area last year in the wake of 9-11 when the price of real estate crashed, and his new office is larger, more comfortable, with an enviable vista. Also, Harold no longer carries as much weight, and his doctor pronounces the progress acceptable.

He glances again at the red envelope, which is neatly sliced open. His firm's name, Morton, Talbot & Hayden (formerly, Morton, Talbot, Hayden & McDuff until the removal five years prior of the fictional founder—a long standing joke—as a concession to expansion sensibilities) is inscribed perfectly straight, as are all the address lines. Did—here he glances at the invite again—Violette do that? He tries to recall her, but all he can conjure up is the face of a sullen eight year old sulking in a corner at some Chinatown restaurant, on the occasion of the "full month" celebration following her sister Colette's birth, at Harold's first-ever Chinese banquet, shortly after the death of Chairman Mao in 1976.

"Do you think he's really dead?" Gordie had asked.

The news that September day was full of Xinhua's official announcement regarding Mao's death. Harold frowned over his beer. Gord was sprawled in the front room at Gramercy, where he now lived most of the time. Harold was not paying full attention to what his friend said because the problem that nagged was his promise to Isobel concerning Sammi.

"Listen to this," Gordie continued, "The People's Republic says, 'we will never seek hegemony and will never be a superpower.' What d'you think of that?" He was reading the complete text from Reuters which Larry had acquired and copied for him. "Oh, and get this, here's one of the man's thoughts, 'a man's head is not like a scallion' . . ."

"Gord," Harold cut him off, unable to withstand the pressure much longer, "you know that dinner Larry & Anita invited us to, the, what d'ya call it, 'full moon' thing? On Saturday night, a week from tomorrow?"

"Month. Full month. Portends well for a baby's prolonged survival. What about it?" His eyes were still on the announcement.

"Pay attention, Gord. This is important. You want to bring a date, right? I mean, I'm bringing Isobel."

Now, his friend looked up. "What's it to you?"

"It's like this. I need a favor, a really big one," and then posed the problem of Sammi, adding, "don't think of it as a date. Think of it as helping me out with Isobel."

Gordie frowned. He knew Sammi vaguely. Pixie face and thin lips. Perky and petite. A fox.

Back, back then in the time of Anna, it had taken Harold forever to wheedle the truth out of Gordie. The catalyst was Samantha Melinda Nelson. She was New England blue blood, with an inheritance less than Gordie's but certainly enough to demand she marry one of her own. More important, she was one of Isobel's closest friends. By now, Gordie and Anna were already a three-year-long, on-again, off-again, more-or-less thing, although Larry was the only one who knew.

By the end of the evening, Harold asked for the third time. "So will you take Sammi?" because Gord was still "thinking" about it. "I really need this, buddy."

The appeal, and persistence, finally worked, as Harold expected. He was in the second quarter of seeing Isobel, and to present the *fait accompli* was the feather he craved.

So on the night of the dinner, the foursome filled a third of the table reserved for non-Chinese guests.

Anita was radiant. Childbirth agreed with her. "Hui Guo! So glad you could come," she greeted. Baby Colette was burbling quietly in a corner, calmed by Por Por's ministrations. The paternal grandmother smiled at Gordie who waved and mouthed *gong hei!* Behind her, Violette scowled, jealous at her loss of supremacy.

Gordie kissed Anita and handed her two red envelopes.

"Too much, Hui Guo," she said. "Why two?"

"Two couples."

Anita hesitated, but then, bearing in mind the cost of child rearing, accepted both gratefully, knowing that these would be exceedingly generous since Gordie was like that. Besides, as she later said to Larry, he could afford it anyway so no big deal.

At their table, Harold said. "What were those envelopes for?"

"It's a tradition. A small token of money as a gift."

"I didn't give them anything. I mean, I sent a present when the kid was born. That's enough, isn't it?"

Gordie nodded. "Oh, sure. This is just Chinese tradition."

Isobel said. "It's only a token, right? Like a dollar or something."

"Right," Gordie lied, unwilling to reveal his thousand dollar gift. "So, want to hear the menu?" He picked up the card on their table. "We begin with bladder of snake."

Everyone laughed. Sammi's eyes twinkled and widened. "You can read all that?"

Gordie turned the card right side up. "Even upside down," he said. "You *are* funny," Sammi said.

As Harold recalled the evening, they laughed a lot as the brandy went to their heads. Afterwards, Isobel maneuvered things so that Gordie would take Sammi home. Gordie obliged, because he couldn't not, even though he was in a hurry to see Anna, and also because Sammi was cute and laughed at his jokes, coaxing a full-scale Bugs Bunny imitation out of him, something he had begun to think he was getting too old for, being two years shy of thirty. He was late to Anna that night, and she noticed for a change, a slight pique showing at this breakdown in unadulterated worship, so all was well in Gordie's world.

The next evening, Sunday, Harold insisted they meet for a drink, his round.

"Isobel says," Harold began.

"Simon sez, put your ass in gear," Gordie retorted.

"Hey, what's your problem?"

"Nothing. But you're about to give me a lecture, right?"

Harold drank half his pint, trying to find the right phrase. The trouble with women was that they got on the phone to each other the morning after and Isobel was the type who wouldn't let anything go.

"Okay, what did Sammi say?" Gordie asked.

"How did you know ...?"

"It's a woman thing."

"Sammi thought you were in a rush to get rid of her last night. Even if you were, and I don't know why that'd be the case, you could at least have been polite."

"When a man's got to go, he's got to go. Besides, you can't kiss a girl after a Chinese banquet. The spices revolt."

"What's with you anyway? Sammi's a nice girl, and she is your type. You and I both know that. Gord, you can't just keep fucking party girls."

"What makes you think I am?"

Harold downed the other half. "Because you're no monk."

Gordie pulled out Anna's head shot from his wallet. He'd stolen it from her portfolio two years ago because she wouldn't give him a photograph. Handing it to Harold, "that's why."

Harold stared at the bitter chocolate complexion, uncomprehending. "Why what?"

And Gordie told his friend everything, or rather, everything of his passion, love and desire for Anna Kavanda (not her real name) of the past three years. Harold listened, half comprehending, interrupting to ask what her real name was, and was astounded by Gordie's reply that he didn't know, on top of which the woman was something like *eight years older, possibly as much as ten,* as if the four-year age difference with Stella wasn't bad enough *at least she looked young this one's obvious you can tell even from the photograph.* None of what Gord said registered, because it was too insane, too infatuated, too wrong-headed and muddled, the way Gord always was, always, *irritatingly,* too much.

The upshot was that they drank much too much, arguing. Provocative, Harold thought him, and the bartender in the dive he had chosen for its cheap drinks was beginning to worry about these two frat boy types slumming in his neighborhood, thinking, they're going to end up in a fist fight.

At twelve thirty, the bartender said. "That's it. You're both cut off."

Harold at twenty eight was a testosterone brick house. He glared at the man. "My money not good enough?"

"Listen, pal," the bartender began.

"Harold," Gordie said. "Time to go home."

"Fuck you, Gord. And you," he leaned towards the offending party, finger extended, and almost jabbed him in the eye.

The bartender struck aside Harold's hand. "Get him outta here."

Gordie complied and dragged his friend outside. The cool air masked the stink of the lower East side, since this was long before *faux*-heme had transformed an urban war zone into fashionably overpriced real estate. Gordie looked around for a taxi, but few yellow cabs plied the area on a Sunday night. He was too drunk to drive, but that seemed the only alternative. His car sat before them, surprisingly unscathed. Harold was gesticulating, talking loudly into the quiet of the streets.

"Harold, shut up a sec."

Harold, the fresh air sobering him for a brief moment, pulled away from Gordie's grip. He shook his head, looked back at the door to the bar, and registered the fact that he had just been debarred from a hole. Then, remembering back to the morning, to Isobel's chilly remark, *he's* your *friend, do something,* since Sammi's phone call *interrupted everything—sleep, hangover recovery, sex*—Gordie at that moment resembled the enemy, the one impeding his path to happiness, or at least, to Isobel. All the old anger resurfaced in Harold at Gord, the man who wanted to be Chinese back in the days of Stella, that his friend could be so cavalier, so goddamned idiotic, so . . . *wrong*, about everything. Harold, the rapidly reforming liberal who knew better, who believed in civil rights and still registered Democrat although voting was another matter, who even had Black acquaintances, this Harold started to say:

"Gord, you're, a, nig . . ."

"Don't you dare say it."

"Just calling it like I see it."

And Gordie hit him. They fought there, in the streets, till both men were bloodied and blue, only this time, it was Gordie beating up Harold and not the reverse, as it had been back in the time of Stella, when Gordie had been the dishonorable one, since dishonor takes turns among friends.

Gordie had returned to that Harlem club, night after night, until Anna could no longer ignore him. The night she finally agreed to join him for a drink, he found himself short of cash.

Anna burst out laughing when he couldn't pay. "White boy," she said, "just for that I'll buy the drinks."

Gordie, never at a loss for a wisecrack, and who rarely blushed, turned pink. "I feel like a fool," he said.

Her eyes devoured him with a gaze worthy of Mae West. "For a fool, you are kinda sweet looking."

"And you're magnificent. Your voice . . . " Her gaze discomfited and he simply stopped, unable to speak.

"So what is it you think you want with me?"

"I want," he began, "I want you to teach me to sing. With you, I mean."

At five eleven, she was taller, and more shapely than any woman to whom Gordie was ever attracted. *Goddess*, he called her, after the first time they had sex. Her rich, velvet mezzo tones promised honeysuckle, and the physical reality did not disappoint. Within months, he asked her to move in with him.

She said. "Into *Gramercy?* You're joking, right?"

They were in his car after her gig, outside the club. They only met in the early morning hours when her gig was over. Even on nights when she did not perform but agreed to see him, she would only do so late, after midnight, vampire-ish. And they seldom met. He felt lucky if it were more than once a fortnight. Once, she refused to see him for two and a half months.

"Why not?" he countered. "You'd have more privacy and space than in that tiny room of yours, not that I've seen it since you won't take me there, but you complain enough. Plus I have a piano. You could rehearse with your accompanist."

She snorted, the high-spirited whinny of a prize thoroughbred. "Boy, I can't afford your space."

"We're not talking money," he almost shouted. "What d'you take me for? And why do you keep calling me that?"

She was unmoved, her voice scornful. "That what?"

"Boy."

She slid her hands between his thighs, extracted the gasp she wanted, and said. "Because that's what you are."

He tried to switch on the ignition. She stayed his hand and unzipped him.

"Anna," he said. "Not like this again. Please?" But she ignored him, released his erection, pushed back the driver's seat and climbed on top. He lay back, locked the door, surrendered, not daring to object lest she denied him even this.

She left him to drive home alone after he came. They had spent just under forty minutes together. Except for the very rare times she went home with him—three, four times perhaps in the four years of their relationship, if you could call it such—this was the pattern of how they met and loved. She never wanted to meet his friends or society, although Larry Woo was the exception because he came to the clubs. When he did see her in daylight, which happened only once on an afternoon around other musicians, it was to listen to them rehearse, to hear her perfect every phrase, every line, every modulation in pitch and intonation. Anna was the reason Gordie learned how to hear, really hear, all that jazz.

The second time Gordie saw Sammi, it was as she arrived at one of his mother's townhouse cocktail receptions later that fall. This was shortly before Anna left him in the new year for her long-time Congolese lover in Paris.

"What are you doing here?" she asked, pleased.

"I live here. Why are you here?"

"Oh you're *that* Ashberry."

"Yes."

Since meeting Jack Hwang, Rosemarie regularly co-opted the townhouse for Manhattan events. Her practice annoyed Gordie, who disliked this invasion of privacy, although he never complained. This evening's reception was to celebrate the founding of some new arts organization, one to which Jack only had a tenuous connection, making things a little more palatable to Gordie since this was really his mother's affair.

Unlike their first "date," Gordie more than glanced at Sammi this time. She was wearing a skimpy cocktail affair, and despite her compact figure, he could tell that what the décolletage revealed was all her own. Also, there were those legs.

Rosemarie sailed towards them. "Melinda Nelson, isn't it? How lovely you look."

Sammi leaned into an air kiss. "Hi Mrs. Ashberry. It's Samantha. Sammi."

"*Are you?*" Her eyebrows grinned. "Well, your mother calls you Melinda."

"That she does." She laughed, and Gordie saw the even teeth, the pretty mouth, the delicate lines of her eyebrows and those naturally long, dark lashes.

"Gordie, be a good host and get Samantha a drink. She's one of my hardest working volunteers."

He obliged, returning with a glass of wine just as Jack Hwang appeared and looked right past him. "Sammi, darling," he kissed her cheek and his hand gave her waist a squeeze. "How good of you to come."

She smiled, but it was merely polite as Gordie couldn't help noticing. "Wouldn't have missed it for anything."

"By the way, about the fundraiser…" and for the next few minutes, Jack monopolized her with talk of aggressively polite money. Gordie waited. At one point, she glanced at him and their eyes locked for a moment, and he was surprised by the disappointment he felt when her gaze returned to Jack.

"And so," Jack was saying, "you will come to Rosemarie's place, in Greenline? It'll be a grand occasion and we'll need all the help we can get. I'll be happy to give you a ride up." He suddenly seemed to notice

Gordie. "Oh, and you'll be there too, Gordon?"

Gordie stared down at Jack who looked less smug than usual. He handed Sammi the wine, his arm cutting right across Jack's face, and said. "Only if Miss Nelson's there," and smiled somewhat less than politely at her and she reciprocated with the giggle of a smile.

Jack glanced from Sammi to Gordie and back. "Yes, well, excuse me. I have to mingle." He touched Sammi's arm lightly. "Lovely seeing you. We must do lunch," and turned around to the next group.

Sammi sipped, leaving no lipstick imprint, looked up at Gordie and said, softly. "Who needs to 'do' lunch?" Her nose did a dainty wiggle, and Gordie leaned close to her ear and whispered, "let's do later." She gave him a pretend shocked look and replied, "catch you after we've *mingled*," just loud enough for Jack Hwang, whose back was to them, to hear, which he did.

In fact, all they did later that night was talk. Gordie took her to dinner, and they sat for hours talking all about being who he was, the kind of world he came from and could inhabit, and she instinctively understood, because her own inheritance afforded her an ability to use education for something other than merely earning a living. Gordie vented a little about Jack, at which Sammi sighed, said, *your mother's very attached to him and he's not a bad guy, means well and everything, but he is just a little, oh, pushy don't you think? He's been asking me out for ages*, she added, even though that was not strictly true but it had the desired effect and was all that mattered in this game, set, match.

The neighborhood trattoria where they ate emptied out, darkened, the proprietor ready to close but he remained patient, recognizing this son of the man who had once given him a loan—oh, many years ago long paid up now—when banks were less generous to young Italian immigrants who spoke English with an accent and had few connections or talents other than hubris and an ability to re-create sauces, piquant and delicious, the way these *should* be made, the way food tasted back home where the sun coaxed the curl into the vines.

They left eventually, and this time he took her home willingly, only too glad to walk her to her door and this time, she could tell it was right to ask him in, which she did and after a coffee, they talked some more, messed around a little, she resisting just enough, he displaying the requisite eagerness and even though they both knew she was hardly a virgin and she knew enough about his womanizing, though she would never know just how many, they played the game as they knew they ought and waited for that fourth date, three weeks later, by which time Anna was well on her way to cutting out Gordie from her life and was showing it in ways he chose, only partially, to ignore.

So in the new year, at another of his mother's at-home Republican fundraisers, Gordie drove Sammi to Greenline early, before the other guests had arrived.

"Welcome to the elf boot," he said, leading her through the foyer under the stairs straight into the vast drawing room which overlooked the Atlantic.

"Elf boot? Why do you call your home that?"

"You'll see. C'mon, I'll show you around."

They exited the drawing room, turned left, and headed down a long hallway that ended in the tip of a triangle which was the atrium dining area. He gestured at the glass enclosed extension which led off the dining area. "Mother likes the greenhouse effect for dining."

Sammi smiled. "Where's the kitchen?"

"Way on the other end."

She peered down the long hallway. "That's inconvenient."

"Mother favors buffets."

"So why the elf boot?"

He took her palm and began tracing shapes as he spoke. "The basic shape is a perfect trapezium—two parallel sides and the other two sides form matching right angle triangles—plus there's a triangular section that extends on the southern end, here in this dining room so *voila*, an elf shoe, if you ignore the kitchen on the other end, which is almost a parallelogram, by the way, except that the edge at the front of the house is awkward the way it turns back to face the drive, and the greenhouse at the other end is this annoying trapezoid. If it were up to me, I'd make the two ends parallelograms."

She stopped his finger and looked into his eyes. "Gordie, that tickles."

"But did you get it?"

Sammi considered the question and the intensity in his voice. His excited description made little sense. But the way she felt at the moment, he could have been speaking Chinese and she would have nodded in comprehension.

He persisted. "You knew what I meant, didn't you?"

"Sure," she said, and kissed his palm lightly. "Take me up in your plane sometime. I'd like to see it from the air."

They went upstairs, and he showed her his bedroom. The bare walls surprised. The rest of the house was filled with art belonging to the Haddon estate, mostly French impressionists, and somehow, she had expected a myriad of images here as well.

She said. "Why so stark?"

"Helps me relax." He was silent and then suddenly said. "When I was fourteen, Mother made me promise that I wouldn't ever bring a girl here who wasn't my wife. To sleep I mean."

She gazed at him. "Oh Gordie, that's so, so . . . sweetly romantic."

He smiled. "I know."

8

The waste, Harold thinks, as he recalls Sammi, Anna, all those forgotten days, triggered by the memory of his first Chinese banquet. Gord and Sammi made a nice couple, and Isobel was content back then, pleased at her hand in the match. *We could have had a double wedding, it was what Isobel wanted.*

Now Harold stares at the large manila package marked "private & confidential"—divorce papers—the other unopened envelope. Why is he, or anyone, justified in counseling the prospect of marital joy? There is no bliss worthy of this present pain. It is all a ridiculous dance—*Mrs. Haddon Ashberry requests the pleasure of your company at dinner to celebrate the engagement of her son, Gordon M. Ashberry, to Melinda S. Nelson.*

"Oh Sammi, it's a *gorgeous* ring," Isobel had said, her eyes overly wide at her first view of the Haddon estate, as well as at the family diamond surrounded by pink sapphires.

Harold, strangled in his monkey suit, *ridiculous such formalities for an engagement,* heard the envy in his girlfriend's voice and was pained. He couldn't compete, shouldn't even try. Goddamned Gord had to go show him up, proposing to Sammi with an alacrity that startled everyone, *especially* Isobel who of course heard before he did.

Isobel disappeared up the stairs with Sammi to look at pictures of bridal gowns. Harold saw Larry standing alone. "Hey," he said. "Where's Anita?"

"Babysitter bailed at the last minute, and my aunt wasn't well otherwise she would do it, so Anita had to stay home. Pity," he added. "She wanted to meet Sammi."

"Great house, huh?" Harold said.

"Sure is."

"We had great times here, didn't we? Back in the good old days?" Larry grinned. "The old days, they're always good, aren't they? So when are you tying the knot?"

He shrugged. "Who knows? I'd like to make partner first, or something."

"Yup."

They gazed at the ocean in silence. Harold was uncomfortable around Larry, who made him feel like he was back in school and still knew nothing. *My best friend's good friend*, although lately he wondered at the "best" in their friendship because Gord went *invisible* since Sammi and hadn't said a thing about his being best man. Naturally, he *assumed* he would be, given Isobel and all. But this thing with Sammi, *so goddamned quick.*

Larry said. "All rather sudden, didn't you think?"

"It was," and then, throwing off caution because on some level, he and Larry were intimate, or at least had history, and the Woos had even invited him and Isobel to that Chinese banquet, *that was a nice thing and hell we all got drunk back in those early days when Gord was completely wild and really needed* both *of us to look after him*, said. "Especially given Anna."

"Oh, you know about her?"

"They broke up." He waited, hoping Larry would offer some confirmation, and when he remained silent, added, "didn't they?"

"Don't you know?"

"I thought you did."

"Okay, I'm not sure, because you know how *he* is, but I'm pretty certain they did. She's not at the club anymore and isn't performing anywhere in town that I'm aware of. Someone mentioned Paris."

"That's good to know. What was she like? You met her, right?"

"Not exactly. It's not like I got to know her. She's a knockout though."

"Oh." Harold was relieved. If Larry didn't know either then no one did. "So do you think this one's the right one?"

"Probably." He paused. "Mrs. A. approves so I guess that makes her perfect, wouldn't you say?"

The cynicism Harold heard did not sit well, but he ignored it. "Still, better than the last one ..." He stopped short, embarrassed.

Larry reassured. "Relax, race has nothing to do with this. Stella Shih's married to her career."

A waiter came by with champagne. Each man took a glass off the tray. Harold raised his. "Let's drink to the man."

Larry raised his as well. "To his not screwing up this one too?"

Both men smiled. Harold said. "Couldn't agree more."

At least he called it off with Sammi before *they hit the altar,* Harold reflects, certain now that one disastrous almost-marriage among friends is enough. After Sammi came crying, Isobel held out on sex for *three whole weeks* that time, for which he could have throttled Gord. *Friends are friends despite,* as he had said to Isobel but fair enough, she had her loyalties too since she and Sammi *were* friends after all. *Not anymore though,* not since Sammi married even further up the ladder, landing European monarchy which *really doesn't sit well* with his wife. Ex-wife. In fairness, Gord would actually have made a good father, all things being equal. He has seen him over the years with Larry's girls, with his own sons, especially Pete—*wasn't Isobel pissed over the godfather thing but hey, for a non-Catholic Gord's been a better godfather than that cousin of hers who hasn't done a thing for Junior and I'm not just talking money.* Harold, he corrects himself, hearing Harold Jr. say, "it was just a question of time, Dad. You should have seen it coming," when he and his oldest "talked" about the split up. How easily Junior took things, as if all those years of parenting hadn't meant a thing! Even Pete, Pete who is *still* in pain *the boy can't hide a thing from me I knew how devastated he was that first time I missed Christmas,* had refused to engage on the subject, only shrugging things off with that annoying "whatever," adding, "I'll just be as pedestrian and predictable as everyone else now, won't I?" as if divorce, not marriage, were the norm. Pete is at Yale and Harold is relieved as well as pleased because he's anchored now, a full-fledged adult. The separate living situation had been hardest on Pete who was *shredded,* spending weekends at Harold's that first summer before college but hating the profound and permanent disturbance to his sense of home, unlike the time in Hong Kong which was glorious but temporary.

Now, as Harold RSVP's "yes" to *this* wedding, he wonders if Isobel only wanted him for his constancy, his willingness to surrender all to wife and family (*what's mine is yours* was bottom line at the Haights, nothing like Patti who keeps a separate bank account from her husband) for the sake of everything he once—*does he still now?*— believed in. Otherwise how else can he explain the persistence of Trevor, who heaps illusions of romance on his wife, this girl who did not *really* care that he forgot Valentine's Day despite her protests, this girl who had said, *Trevor? He'd fall out of love the minute some hotter number flashed her pussy.* Why is she now willing to believe Trevor's lies? Is it only the money, all that jewelry and constant floral tributes after he moved out (*Dad, no kidding, it's like every week, isn't that sick,* Pete had confided)? Or is it the promise of something deeper, something that allows her complete surrender, something that has eluded him all these years of loving, honoring, obeying?

Another work day over, another home-alone dinner. Tim is readying a pile of word processing for a document that must exit by FedEx tonight. He switches on his radio, keeping the volume low, permitted now that office hours are officially over at six thirty.

Every morning, every evening,
Didn't we have fun?

Harold hears the music as he bids Tim good night. *Gord used to sing that,* all the time, back in the day. Back when we all were strangers in Paradise.

At the Fortune Luck Gardens, Harold says to Laura after introductions. "Silverstein? Not by chance related to a Trevor Silverstein? Lawyer?" He wants to kick himself as soon as he asks *of course he knows it's a common name . . .* this, this *stupid* wallowing in Isobel's defection.

Laura winces. "Brother-in-law. Ex."

"Sorry to hear," Harold says, glad that Lady Coincidence is fortuitously on his side. "Recent?"

"Relatively."

"Me too." And then, because wounds need air more than cover, adds. "Trevor and my ex are getting married. Probably this year."

Relief courses through Laura that *she* isn't the only one. "Mine ducked out with one of his students. Poets do that."

Harold feels a similar relief. "You shouldn't have changed your name. My sister never did and she's the happiest married woman I know." He pauses. "Names," he says. "They brand you, don't they?"

"You're right about that."

He proffers his hand. "So why don't you introduce yourself again?"

"Laura Polk," she says, shaking his hand. "Pleased to meet you Harold Haight."

"Charmed, I'm sure Ms. Polk."

She flashes flirtation, and he feels it, *the first time since* ... and now he is *really* pleased at the invitation to this wedding.

What he is also thinking, what he has only recently become aware of, is that it never occurred to him that his wife *shouldn't* have changed her name. He is forced to confront it these days because Isobel is going to become Silverstein, as she makes a point of telling him.

He and Laura are seated together at Anita's design, because she thinks they might get along. Anita's friendship with Laura dates back to when her name was still Polk, before she'd begun writing novels. At their round table of mostly non-Chinese friends of the Woo's, the seat directly opposite Harold remains vacant. The platter of appetizers arrives. Gordie is now certifiably late.

"I love these banquets," Harold says. He serves Laura a slice of crackling, and begins to tell of his time in Hong Kong, explaining that men served women at a dinner of this nature, that it was considered good manners. "Amazing what you learn when you live abroad," he concludes.

"I've never lived out of the States," she says, and tells of her long friendship with Anita, but that because her ex and Larry didn't get along, this was the first family dinner she'd come to. "It's remarkable what happens when you get divorced," she says. "Your life immediately improves."

Harold glances at her. Attractive, engaging, not exactly his type, but for the first time, "type" isn't the issue. "I guess I'll find out," he says. "Mine came through yesterday."

Laura gives him a *I'm sorry* look followed by a two-handed victory sign under the table, and they both laugh.

Harold asks. "So what is it you do?"

Gordie arrives in time for the shark's fin soup, late, but not unfashionably so. After apologizing to his hosts, he slips into his seat just as the waiter brings the tureen. He does a quick, silent salute to the table and nods at Harold who gives him a *where were you* look.

Gordie shrugs, mimes sleep, and Harold does not for a moment believe that his wired and insomniac friend would nap before an important occasion like this.

Laura says, *sotto voce.* "That's Gordon Ashberry, isn't it?"

"Do you two know each other?" wondering if she is yet another of Gord's long-ago conquests but somehow doesn't think so.

"I know *of* him."

"Oh, you mean because of that book?"

"Actually, no. I hadn't heard until I was told." She hesitates, then plunges ahead. "Larry's writing a book about him, and I read an early draft."

It takes a second to register and Harold, his surprise conveniently masked by the waiter's arm setting down his soup, asks. "What's Larry's book about?"

She pauses. "I'm not exactly sure, but I suppose at heart it's a defense of Gordon."

"Gordie," Harold says, automatically. "That's what he calls himself," he adds.

"Gordie," she repeats. "Yes," and continues to study the figure across the table as she eats the absolutely delicious, flavorful, politically incorrect soup in the bowl before her.

The dinner brings Harold back to happier times in Hong Kong, when he and Gord hung out. His friend's demeanor tonight is evasive, and Harold decides he *will* pin him down, later if possible. But Laura is more distracting than he expects, and he likes their conversation enough so that before the night is over—*why the hell not you have to start sometime Harold porn only lasts so long,* Tim White a voiceover in his head—he hands her his card and asks to exchange numbers, saying, "we could see a movie or something," even though it's been years, *decades* since he's stepped foot inside a cinema, and she laughs her silvery song, "just like in high school, huh?" as she scribbles him her cell phone number and email on a torn off section of the menu.

Gordie, meanwhile, has escaped before Harold can pin him down, before the arrival of the dessert, red bean soup, something Harold never quite developed a taste for, but which Pete ultimately loved, after making a face at his first Chinese banquet in Hong Kong. Harold takes a spoonful to be polite, secretly relieved that Pete has to be at his friend's birthday party, since he's the only other Haight who would have been here tonight. His son's presence would have cramped his style.

So now Harold holds two unexpected, secret shards, and he doesn't know what to do with this information. Seeing Gord briefly last night excavates their past. It's Marc Aden all over again, back before he knew his friend well. Friend. *Isn't* the man still a friend? In the chill of his apartment as Sunday morning light streams across his face, Harold curses aloud that he's forgotten to draw the blinds. The apartment is a mess, because Tim and the cleaning lady got into an argument and a new one has yet to be found. A one-bedroom, somewhere on the upper East side, in a building inhabited by sex and the city, where all his neighbors could almost be his children and Harold feels ridiculously . . . *Jurassic.*

In the kitchen, the coffee machine sits, unused, as it's done for two years since the day of purchase. There is juice and some fruit in the fridge—added to his diet since his regular return to the gym—but little else. He needs coffee.

Back in his college dorm, and later in the apartment he had shared with Gord, his buddy provided the comforts of domesticity. They were labeled "odd couple," naturally. The first time their friends so dubbed them, Gord told him his half brother was gay. It was one of the rare times Harold heard him speak of Marc.

What Harold knew of Gordie was what Harold asked. And he had asked over the years, because that was the way he was. *How do you know he's gay,* Harold had demanded, because Marc was still alive then although he and Gordie never met. *I met his lover,* Gordie replied, and Harold puzzled over that, wondering if it were true, afraid to ask more in case, *just in case* it meant Gordie frequented gay life which meant perhaps his friend too might be gay or bi, something Harold had not wanted to think about then, or ever, if he had a choice.

What Harold never told Gord, however, what he thought about telling him as the years passed but he couldn't find the words for, was that he had once met Marc Aden.

In the post-war era of Harold's childhood, that was less a coincidence than it might seem. Harold was ten and a boy scout. Marc Aden was a fighter pilot in peace time, doing his civic duty for the U.S. military, talking to boys to entice them into the world he inhabited. It wasn't what the propaganda said ("education" and "history" being the lingo) but it was what happened. Not that Harold needed enticing. An avid reader of *Terry and the Pirates*, the boy Harold dreamt, like Snoopy, of heroic exploits against the Red Baron or the kamikaze Japs. Korea, the first war Marc served in at the age of twenty, was something Harold only vaguely understood, the way much of the nation only vaguely understood it then, and even now it remains a mystery to most, and Harold had been a baby when the Chinese nationalists fled to Taiwan, where CAT and that world existed.

So in 1958, when Harold was ten, he eagerly went along to meet a real-life fighter pilot in person.

Marc Aden had dressed for the part in a leather bomber jacket and aviator goggles, a white silk scarf around his neck. Except for his youth, he was the romantic image of "Colonel" Claire Lee Chennault under whose command his father had flown in the American Volunteer Group, the original Flying Tiger himself, a Chinese and American patriot, the man who now lay in a hospital bed in New Orleans, dying of cancer, tough till the end. Marc Aden spoke of their training, of flying in formation and pairs, the fighters escorting bombers, of landings engineered in Burmese or Chinese fields when the fuel gauge read empty, of ace pilots in both world wars and the "kills" they scored, whose methods Chennault studied and refined. None of what he spoke of was from actual experience, since he was too young for WW II and Vietnam was still some time away (he flew in 'Nam, old at thirty four but scored his five kills for ace status but was shot down just before being pulled from combat), and most of his time in Korea had been waiting, hovering around the 38th parallel, under Mark Sr.'s sidelined wing which seldom saw combat. War in his experience to date was a boring proposition, but the excitement of legend told and re-told gave it power and glory and a reason to be.

Harold listened, rapt, to this dark haired, blue-eyed, bronzed young aviator who made him feel tough, like a man with the real possibility of bravery, who mitigated the shame he felt at having the father he had, the pacifist, the one who could not serve flag and country because of a club foot—childhood polio—but regardless of the medical condition, the father who, unlike his friends' dads, did not speak of war with pleasure, and voted Democrat. He converged around Marc with the other boys afterwards, got his autograph, asked in hushed tones whether or not Marc had ever killed an enemy, and the young man smiled mysteriously, did not say either yes or no, but who was thinking about his own father, the man he rarely saw, wishing Mark Ashberry could see him here, now, being a big brother to these boys the way he hadn't been allowed to be a real brother to his own half sibling.

That night, Harold declared at dinner that he was going to become a fighter pilot.

"Over my dead body," his father had replied.

"Now dear," his mother said. "He's just a boy."

"What's wrong with that?" Harold demanded because at ten, he had learned the value of making demands.

"You'll end up in an early grave." His own brother had been a casualty of the second war in an accidental plane crash.

"I'm too smart for that."

Eight-year-old Patti gazed at her big brother whom she still had reason to adore. "Oh goody, you can take me flying."

Their mother stared the table down. "That's enough." She glared at her husband but her voice softened. "You too, dear."

Two months later, Claire Chennault died on July 27. Harold clipped all the news stories about his latest hero, then dated, labeled and sorted them into manila envelopes. By the time he got to Yale, those clips had been replaced by first the *True Men Stories* and later by *Penthouse* centerfolds. But he kept Marc Aden's autograph, a memento, perhaps, of a time when life still yielded heroes.

9

Where's that autograph now? Probably still in the attic at home, surrounded by dust bunnies.

Harold frowns through his leaden consciousness. After the dinner, a nightcap was all he intended, but that became another and another. *No more booze.* Lately, he makes the resolution more often than he wishes he has to. It was easy staying sober when married, when parenting was a daily thing.

Perhaps he should have told Gordie about meeting Marc, even though it was only that one brief encounter. They had known each other half a year before Gordie ever mentioned a brother. Shame? Not Gord. Anger perhaps? Jealousy? Harold hadn't been sure, but what he knew was that this was his friend's pain, inchoate, and he had left it alone because why speak the unspeakable? In time, Marc Aden became just another memory.

He opens the fridge. The juice is barely enough for a small glass. Harold groans. He does not want to go out for coffee, in the cold, *again*. It's time to make a few changes in his domestic arrangements as Tim constantly prompts him to do. Giving into reality, he gets dressed. It is only eight because booze, despite its assault on his system, cannot entirely disrupt routine. Eight is acceptably late for Harold on a Sunday morning.

A few days later, he rings Larry. "So Laura says you're writing a book about Gord," he says, without preliminaries.

Larry's mind goes blank. The intersection of Laura and Harold does not compute.

"So are you?" Harold persists.

"Kind of."

"Does he know?"

"No."

"And this is okay with you?"

"I intend to tell him, but he hasn't exactly been around, as you know. Besides, it isn't exactly a book about him anymore."

"So what is it?"

He hesitates. "It's not clear yet."

"I don't get it," Harold says. "How can you write a book if you don't know what it's about?'

"Because by writing it, you find out."

Tim sticks his head in, points at his watch, reminding Harold of the next appointment. Harold nods. "Look Larry, I may as well be honest. This pisses me off."

Larry replies. "I can tell."

"You're *supposed* to be his friend."

"Friendship takes many forms."

"Don't pull that Chinese doubletalk on me," he says.

"Relax. Listen, we can talk about this, okay?"

Your best friend's close friend, but the three of you don't fit together. The idea roots around Harold's consciousness. Nothing makes sense. He likes Larry, and when he was in Hong Kong, Larry's family there went out of their way to be nice even though they and his family had nothing in common. Plus Pete likes the Woos, especially the younger girl, and sees them regularly. The thought counts, and he wishes now he wasn't quite so short with Larry, but he realizes that he simply doesn't know how to talk to the man, this academic, but with Gord being the way he's been, what choice is there?

Over the past year, longer, since the appearance of *Honey Money*, he and Larry have articulated concern for their friend to each other. Now, as he heads towards the next appointment, a meeting he suspects will be a waste of time, he thinks that the change in Gordie began earlier, dating back to when he said he wanted to give away his money, and perhaps, even earlier than that.

The irony, of course, is that much of the wealth is still intact, mostly because Harold has ensured this. There have been the odd checks sent to charities, a lot of fuss about real estate that still isn't sold, but all the stocks, bonds and funds, which comprise a significant percentage of the liquid portfolio, will not be sold until he, Harold, says so. And he hasn't said so and is not about to until Gord is willing to talk reasonably.

Laura Silverstein's phone number, logged into his cell phone, hovers. He asked for it with a vague idea that this is what divorced men do, even in their fifties. She seemed friendly enough, but Harold is unsure if that was just polite, dinner table conversation. The last time he'd asked for a woman's phone number, it was Isobel's.

The meeting slides by, *truly* pointless, about a tax fraud case that is nothing more than his client's sheer incompetence at keeping accounts. Harold is impatient with law these days and wonders how much money is enough to stop working as he does, now that Isobel doesn't harp on about alimony anymore, now that Junior is finally an adult (at least Harold hopes he is and that he'll get into law school), now that Pete seems set and likely to be okay.

Now, what he wants is to call Laura and talk about Larry's book. Somehow this does not seem like the right social behavior.

Back at the office, Tim hands him his messages. "A Ms. Silverstein called." He looks quizzically, almost maternally, at Harold. "Didn't leave a number, said you had it. She made a point about the 'Ms'," and adds, "And a Kathleen O'Mara. She said Gordon told her it was time she saw you again?"

Harold takes the message slips with a pleased, sheepish grin, goes into his office and closes the door. Tim looks triumphantly at the young woman across from him. "I *told* you these weren't business calls," and the other had to acknowledge to the older and wiser personal assistant who knew about the lives of partners, *when you're right, you're right.*

He calls Kathleen first, even though they haven't spoken in, oh, at least three years, maybe longer, and is surprised to learn of *her* divorce which it appears, Gord knows about. She says she meant to call when she first heard about him and Isobel, but time, *you know how it is.* It is easy talking to her, but he's glad she's dating someone already because her marriage was over awhile back. It's too late for Kath and too long ago now for her to be anything more than a former flame. Afterwards, he wonders when Gord and Kath talked, but forgot to ask.

Laura sounds relieved when he calls. "I'm sorry to disturb you at work, but I thought I needed to say this."

"You're not disturbing me." He waits, curious.

"The other night, I shouldn't have said anything about Larry's book. It was a violation of authorial privacy."

"There's such a thing?"

"Well, sort of. I was acting as a confidential reader, or editor, if you like, and it wasn't my place to say anything."

"Then why did you?"

She is a little put off by his inquisition, but *she did start this after all.* "Well, I suppose, well you see, from reading the manuscript, I knew you were Gordon, I mean, Gordie's best friend and in a way, I felt I knew you, not that I do, of course," she adds quickly, "it's just that it felt natural telling you."

"Then you have an advantage over me, because I don't know you," he says, and startles himself by adding, "not that I wouldn't like to."

Afterwards, after he's made a date with Laura (dinner, *not* a movie), he feels his heartbeat quicken again, the way it did on hearing Kath's voice, and can't imagine how he found the nerve. Laura asked, of course, that he not say anything to Larry and he admitted that he already had, that very afternoon, and she sighed, *it's my own fault, I should have called earlier instead of vacillating,* and he reflects, *refreshing, a woman who accepts responsibility for her actions,* something Isobel never did, and is surprised at how critical he feels towards his ex-wife on this score. It's about the harshest judgment he's ever leveled at her, a general wishy-washiness Harry displays that makes his kid sister impatient, who tells him so all the time, *wise up, Isobel betrayed you, took you for a long ride and it's okay to call her a bitch.* Patti the sweet one who calls him every week to make sure he's okay, who regularly invites him out on weekends with her family so that Harold is able to partially fill that enormous hole his life has become, this sister who isn't a kid anymore now that Harold is cut loose, dangling, a kid again who isn't.

In the gym that evening—he can do an hour's workout these days—he weighs himself and stares at his less-heavy form in the mirror (amazing how poundage disappears with exercise), grateful at least his hair's intact, *unlike Trevor's,* and almost says aloud, *you're being Gord, aren't you? Lady killer.* And then he does laugh aloud, catches himself, looks around, embarrassed, but no one pays him much mind since the whole world in a gym is gazing at its navel, or abs, most of the time.

Nothing for months, and suddenly, Gord calls and says he's going to Hong Kong with Larry in a couple of weeks or so. *Unaccountable.*

Now, a week later on a Friday afternoon in February, it is already four. He wonders whether or not to call Gord, to remind him of their "date" to walk the dog. *Ridiculous* that he should wonder. *Years* of friendship. What does it mean if you don't know as simple a thing as whether or not to call to remind? Okay, he won't. Gord never misses an appointment. Besides, he was the one who made it in the first place.

Half an hour later, he buzzes Tim, whose cubicle is around the corner, out of his line of sight. "I'm gone."

"Hot date with Laura?"

"None of your business."

"Touchy, touchy Harold. You have yourself a nice weekend with *whomever* you're seeing. Toodle-oo, darling."

Unaccountable as well, Harold thinks, that Tim has become so familiar, so . . . *fresh*, but Harold knows he doesn't mind, has become increasingly relaxed since Laura. She takes him to *poetry* readings, for cryin' out loud, and concerts and ballets, things he would never in a million years have dreamt of doing with Isobel, and truthfully, he quite enjoys this new person he's becoming. He takes her to Mets games, something Isobel had no interest in, and the time she caught that fly ball, she looked so startled and beautiful but what Harold liked most was that she turned around to the nearest kid and gave the ball to her. *So grand at the game* . . . didn't Gord used to sing some old chestnut with those words?

Harold is too early, because he arrives at the house a little after five and Gordie isn't due till five thirty. He took the train from the city and realized, too late, that the schedule changed and must now kill time. The "for sale" sign on the lawn stands like an empty guardhouse to an abandoned fort, a reminder of its former function.

It feels strange, letting himself into the space that used to be home. Terror, elated at Harold's presence after an unaccountably long absence, bounds around his master, his nostrils soothed by the familiar scent. For a few minutes, man and dog revel.

He picks up the mail from the mat, mail which piles up, wondering why Isobel still hasn't stopped all the mail here. She and Trevor have postponed their wedding a second time, which amuses him. What doesn't amuse him is that Isobel drags her feet over selling their home, always finding some excuse, the latest being *Trevor's allergic to dogs we didn't realize so I'm bringing Terror back home it's no bother I can swing by daily, feed and walk him*, although this sounds like an excuse to Harold because she lives in the city, at least a forty-five minute drive away. He puts up with it, partly because he's enjoying Laura, partly because it doesn't make that much difference—*what's an extra few months or so*, Laura said when he told her, having gone through something similar over her and her ex's home. The mortgage is long paid. Besides, he doesn't mind coming to see Terror, which he first did on the weekends, which then extended to a weekday, or two, and last week even more, although how this has come to be such a regular thing he can't quite figure out.

There is something different about the interior. It takes a moment before he sees that the drapes are new. Why has his wife bothered?

A car pulls into the driveway.

"You're early," Harold says from the doorway.

Gordie replies. "It's cold out here, certifiably."

"Nine goddamned months of silence, and that's all you have to say?" Harold stretches an arm out to hug him but Gordie tenses, backs away, leaving Harold holding empty air. "What's with you?" His voice hurt.

"Sorry, what the hell," and Gordie leans into the hug.

"That's more like it."

Terror, impatient, implores with leash between his teeth. Harold says. "We better take him out before he bursts," and they head right towards the dog park down the road.

"So what brought you out, *finally*?"

"Figured it was time you had the pleasure of my company again."

The dog drags them at a rapid clip. Gordie is grateful for the movement, both to ward off the chill and for the silence that ensues.

Terror pauses at the edge of the Schwartz's lawn, seduced by activity around a flowerbed. "No, boy," Harold cautions, as the dog begins to lift a hind leg. "Scoot.

Harold glances at the Schwartz's picture window, and catches

Gordie's eyes trained on the same spot. "Isobel says you and Gina?"

"Ancient history. Besides, do you really care what Isobel says anymore?"

"Absent *working* husbands are convenient." Harold glares at his friend, the sarcasm unmistakable.

"Listen, leave me out of this. I didn't break up anyone's marriage. What do you want? Wives get lonely. Besides, you shouldn't believe Isobel. There was nothing between Gina and me."

Reassured by what he's always believed, Harold stares at the ground, his hand firmly on the leash. "Twenty years, down the toilet. And for what? A college sweetheart who got her pregnant, promised to marry her and didn't? The dickhead made her get an abortion, *an abortion*, Gord. Some Catholic she was, huh? Then he comes sniffing around again when I'm seriously dating her. Twenty years later, she decides she's *still* in love with him. Go figure."

Gordie keeps quiet.

Harold continues the rant. "You were right about Trevor coming round when I was still out in Hong Kong with Merryweather, although Isobel *swears* nothing happened till after I got back to the States. Says I was even *less* around then. What am I supposed to believe anymore? Going abroad was a mistake, I admit, but I made up for it, came back with a better financial package, the way I promised. That's worth something, isn't it, when a man keeps his word. Isn't it? Besides, how could I be *less* around back home?"

Gordie says. "So what're you up to now? Lost weight, haven't you? Looks good."

"So have you," Harold says, "only on you it *doesn't* look good."

They arrive at the park. Harold unleashes Terror who races around the perimeter. "I miss the goddamned dog, would you believe? The boys there are times I can take or leave. And Isobel, well."

"Then take the dog."

"And where will I keep him? My shoebox apartment? Besides, dogs don't belong in Manhattan."

"Keep him at Greenline. Reg will take care of him."

Harold shoots him a quizzical look. Gordie continues. "Well, for the time being. It isn't sold yet."

"But you have to, right?"

"Eventually." What Gordie hasn't told Harold, what only Reg

and Annabel know, and which Harold only learns later after Gordie disappears, was Rosemarie's little joke in her will. If her son marries within twelve years of her death and produces a *legitimate* child, the house will remain his. It had been a concession to her lawyer who said—*but just supposing there were grandchildren, you'd want them there, wouldn't you?*—and because she was fairly certain he'd never marry, never mind produce offspring, Rosemarie agreed. All Harold knows is that a sale has to take place within twelve years of her death and the proceeds go to a charitable foundation managed by Jack Hwang.

"In fact," he continues, "you can take the boys up there, well Pete I guess, whenever you want. There's still some furniture. Just ring Reg."

Harold frowns, and his eyebrows became a single, continuous dark line. "Generous of you. But I don't know Gord."

"It's been three years, Harold. Let her go. And the home."

Harold leans against the fence by the entrance. "She doesn't have to *marry* him, Gord, does she?"

Gordie looks straight ahead at Terror who is obliviously, loyally joyful, scrambling around the park. "She hasn't yet. You want her back?"

And to his own surprise, because he has yet to hear himself say it, Harold replies. "No. Not on your life."

The air turns colder as daylight slips away. "Bring the dog home and let's get out of Jersey," Gordie says. "It's time for a beverage."

It is past midnight. Gordie is drunker than Harold. The two men are reminiscing, or, as Harold decides in the chill of the next morning's light, shoveling salt onto a gangrenous limb that would be better amputated.

"Sammi," Harold says.

"That blue-blooded bitch? Fuck her."

"Was she?"

"What?"

"A good fuck?"

"Yeah."

"Well then it wasn't a complete waste, right?'

Gordie orders another round. "Marriage, my friend, is a horse-and-carriage institution in an era of space travel. I'd be signing divorce papers today if Sammi and I married."

"You gave her your mother's ring."

"Which she flung back in my face a fortnight later. Look, I still have the scar." He touches the edge of his right jaw line. It had been an extraordinarily deep cut, because the diamond had loosened from its setting, and the edge caught his cheek as he tripped and fell against a wall, and the rock lodged in flesh just long enough.

"So why did you take things so far, with her, *and* Stella? You *like* getting beat up, is that it?"

Gordie, these days, remembers rather than forgets when inebriated, and the mention of Stella sobers him up momentarily. He squints at his glass and then at Harold. "You never did like that, did you? My whole Chinese thing."

"Give it up. You're as American as me."

"As I." Gordie tosses back the double scotch and sets the glass back on the bar. "I'm going home."

"No, you're not," because Harold knows exactly what this means, that he'll try to drive to Greenline, a suicidal endeavor. "Go to Gramercy."

"As usual, you're right." He walks straight out of the bar and into a taxi, leaving his car to be ticketed in the morning because it is opposite side of the street parking where it sits. To anyone else except Harold who knows better, Gordie doesn't look the slightest bit drunk.

It's not till morning that he remembers he never mentioned Minnie's visit to Gord last night, and wonders why he didn't. By the time he wants to call and tell him, it is too late, because Gord is gone, vanished, although many more months, even years must pass before Harold will believe this to be true, Harold being the last holdout of all Gordie's friends, telling Pete that this is just a temporary thing, because *Gord's disappeared before, that's just the way he is, trust me on this one.*

John Haight's Interlude

"And what about you?" I ask. "Will you settle down, ever?"

John's eyes dart first left, then right, refusing to meet mine. He unfolds his napkin, fusses with its placement on his lap, focuses on the still-empty wine glass. Without looking at me he says. "I am settled."

"You're not. You're restless."

He does the shoulder roll, signals a waiter who hurries over. "The Barolo," he says, and points to the most expensive one on the list. "And we'll have the Osso Bucco?" This, without raising his eyes from the menu, is really a statement.

"Whatever you wish."

Only after the waiter vanishes does he finally look at me. "You know that's not true. It's never been my wish to be so far away."

The day before yesterday, the Haight matriarch expired, after a long and painful lingering. The cancer in her liver had spread to the bone. Mrs. Aileen (*née* Donoghue) Haight is the reason Patti is the independent monkey she is and Harold toes the line so well. Yet here is John, her baby, in Hong Kong now on business, refusing to fly home for the funeral. Pete and Tempest are already in the air, en route. Harold and Patti are undoubtedly furious and their children and cousins are all gossiping like crazy.

Instead John called me, said we had to talk.

"So talk," I tell him now that he seems almost ready.

"They all had a thing for Ashberry, even my old man."

"And that's the reason you're not going to your mother's funeral?"

"No. Yes. Well, not exactly."

"You surprise me. The Haights have always been about family."

The wine arrives along with all its performative distraction. John engages the sommelier in a longer than necessary conversation. In Putonghua. I am struck by his fluency, by his ability to converse about wine entirely in Chinese. Even some of my most doggedly Chinese friends sprinkle English into such *yang fa* exchanges. John, though, sounds effortlessly Chinese. Gordie would be impressed.

"It needs to breathe," he says in English.

The wine rests on its stand besides our table. We're at Joia Ristorante Italiano in West Kowloon, on the concourse above Elements, the newest live-eat-shop behemoth to front another stretch of reclaimed waterfront, the area that was *supposed* to be the city's 21st century cultural hub. A never-to-be-realized supposition perhaps. John favors these new districts. I think it's the lack of history he likes, this absence of memory in all its post modern, urbane newness.

"Ashberry's an unforgivable prick."

"What did he ever do to you?"

"He fucked up the only girl who ever mattered to me."

He had been twenty six, in love in Tokyo. Yuki was a few years older, a jazz singer with perfect pitch. It was 1987. She didn't tell him about Gordie and her until a year later when she broke up with him.

"I didn't know you liked jazz."

"Not anymore."

"And that's why you left Japan for Hong Kong?"

"More or less."

"Why are you telling me this now?"

He doesn't answer and in the silence, I think about all that is Gordie's world, his strange daisy chain of friends and lovers, his life freed from the ordinary bonds of family the rest of the world embraces. I don't know John nearly as well as I know Patti or Harold, but he has been in my orbit for a long time, this pleasant younger man whom we all said was nice despite his being a lawyer. Which doesn't speak to character, because here is John, being not so nice, harboring a grudge against Gordie about something our man did so long ago he probably no longer remembers, and turning his back on family.

John signals for the wine to be poured and spends more time in that distraction of swishing, tasting, presenting this vintage choice to me, his guest. I am always John's guest because he will never let a woman pay, even though he has known and dated women far wealthier than he'll ever be. It is odd that this leftover graciousness—admirably chivalric or merely Jurassic, as Pete would say?—should exist in our time but there we are, many things do not change, just as grudges will be harbored, unreasonably, by even the nicest among us.

The Barolo has breathed sufficiently and is round and full on my tongue. John is the penultimate sophisticate. Exquisite gourmet palate. Sharp dresser, never flashy, his natural understatement has made him a success in Asia. How he tolerates the new China is beyond me.

"I'm telling you," he begins, "because you need to know. You remember '87, don't you?"

How could I forget? John is gazing at me imploringly, this Haight family baby who is now a couple of years shy of fifty. Gordie was just a year shy of forty back in '87, watching his one and only attempt at a real job crashing around him as his business collapsed. Harold rescued him from the IRS with John's help.

"But you helped him."

"I know. I couldn't not. Dunderdick insisted and you know how he can be."

"I wouldn't have thought you one to repress rage."

"You didn't know Yuki."

That is when I know, when I hear the violins and heart strings and recognize, at last, what is behind the niceness of this man, this seducer of women who normally never makes anyone mad. He is a romantic who cherishes forever and true love and performs for each subsequent woman as if she is his first and only love. Which is why they let him string them along. Which is why a few hold onto the hope that she will be the one. Which is why he despises Gordie, because he is almost just like him. Almost. There's no one quite like that man in our lives.

But it doesn't explain why he won't go home for the funeral. That's another story.

V

EARLIER FOR GORDIE, WE'RE NOT QUITE SURE EXACTLY WHEN, BUT BEGINNING FROM A COLD, CLEAR TIME BEFORE VIOLETTE'S WEDDING

The same night that whitens the same trees.
We, we who were, we are the same no longer.

from **"Tonight I Can Write The Saddest Lines"**
by **Pablo Neruda,**
translated by **W.S. Merwin**

December, 2001 to January, 2002

The last person Gordie expected to see again was Colin Kenton. He showed up unannounced, at Greenline, because he couldn't find Gordie in the city.

Reg stared at the once-familiar figure on the doorstep. "Mr. Kenton. We thought you were dead." Kenton looked as if he had dug himself out of the grave, his clothes disheveled, face sun-burnt, almost unrecognizable. Pockets of loose flesh hung where his cheeks had been. The curvature of his shoulders, that slump of age, made him look even older than he was. There was hardly a trace of the former authoritative air of this pilot turned maverick entrepreneur.

Kenton said. "Ashberry's here, isn't he?"

"Surely you don't expect to be let in?"

"Just do your job and announce me. Is Mrs. Ashberry here? She'll see me."

"She *is* dead. Wait a moment, please," and Reg shut the door in his face.

Reg told Master Gordon that for a man in his seventies, Kenton was still commanding. "Shall I ring the police?"

"No," Gordie said. "Don't. Let him in."

"But Master Gordon, you can't..."

"Reg, please don't cross me."

The butler tipped his head in a slight bow, struck by how much the boy sounded like his mother saying that. He brought Kenton through the dining room at the southern end and into the extension that turned back towards the front of the house, where Gordie was seated at the piano, and left the two men in there.

Gordie remained seated. He stared at his former business partner, the man who had, fifteen years earlier, drained their company's resources and disappeared, the man who left him to face the Feds alone, the man for whom he had once regularly procured Manhattan working girls of every shade and shape. "If you want money, I don't have any left. It's gone."

Kenton smiled. "Money's like the Yangtze. Follows the rise and fall of tides." He sank into a comfortable armchair. "Ashberry, give a man a drink first."

Gordie poured him a double scotch, neat, which Kenton downed and then held up the empty glass. He refilled it. "What do you want?"

Kenton glanced around the trapezoid shaped extension, the second drawing room in which Mrs. Ashberry had entertained, meaning that parties could get a little out of hand here, sealed off from the rest of the house. "So, did you ever nail Rose?" He meant Jimmy Kho's daughter who had worked in New York for Gordie.

"Screw you, Kenton."

"Touchy, touchy. Gordie, when will you grow up? You can't let women walk all over you forever."

"What do you want?"

Kenton rose, went towards the light. The far end of the glassed-in enclosure faced west towards the road in the distance, the house being set back at the end of a long driveway. The late afternoon sun suffused the room, warming it above the outdoor temperature of a chilly day. With his back to Gordie, he said. "I'm finished. Just let me stay a week or so, could you? For old time's sake?"

It was not, as Reg would later say, that Mr. Ashberry owed Colin Kenton anything. Hardly. But Gordie was the last refuge for a broken man whose only means of survival was the counterfeit identity trade he perfected as a young hustler, first in Australia and later around Asia, before his long and quasi-respectable life in business (arms trading, engaged in under cover of Gordie's legal airline leasing business, had been the company's undoing, Gordie not realizing until it was much, much too late that Rose, who had previously worked for Kenton at a small, private Asian air carrier, *must* have been helping his partner all along, or so Gordie suspected although he never found any proof). Kenton carried no luggage except his case of tools, his "doctor's bag." He stayed a month, the untreated cancer raging through him, and expired one night with only Gordie at his bedside, at least, that was how Annabel recalled it. Kenton, the man who reminded both Reg and Annabel, too much, of Mark Ashberry.

No deathbed apologies or remorse—that only happens in operas where dying is prolonged for song—but in some conversation during the month, Kenton said. "Gordie, you can fool most of the people all of the time. You just have to find the right marks."

A few days after Kenton's death, Annabel brought a shoebox of photographs to Gordie. "These were stuck away in the back of a closet in your mother's room. I must have missed it when I cleared things out. I didn't want to disturb you sooner because of Mr. Kenton. Would you like to look through them now?"

"Annabel, you know I hate photographs." It was true, because he had evaded even the college yearbook, having substituted a shot of George Harrison in his stead. How Gordie managed that Harold never got out of him, not even in their most inebriated camaraderie.

"But these might be memorable. I can't just throw them out without your going through them." She held out the box. "Go on, Gordie," she urged, stubbornly refusing to move until he told her to leave it. She told Reg later, confessing that she had looked through them—*it's his box, not hers*—and Reg frowned, but only a little, because they both felt it wouldn't hurt to make him smile, which he so seldom did now, and the familiar faces might bring back *some* happy memories, or so they hoped.

The box sat untouched for over a week. The weekend Reg and Annabel took off—a visit to Annabel's nephew who lived just across the Massachusetts border—Gordie finally opened it. He did not immediately realize this was his collection, a handful of photos that had been given him by friends. Several of Harold and family and Larry and family, a few of the Townsends, and Mimi at eighteen, a torn one, the missing half had been of the mad man (although he had seemed sane enough to everyone) who strangled, *murdered* her, the older man she'd thrown Gordie over for (*not* that she and Gordie had been going *steady* or anything as Mimi was quick to point out— *darling, who else would I surrender the maidenhead to if not Bugs Bunny*, and at sixteen, the two of them felt this was *without question*, since he was also a virgin, *not* that he would admit it to Mimi but she guessed— so when Gordie, jealous and hurt, raged at her "betrayal," what she said was, *you'll get over it, doc*). He turned over the picture of Mimi, not wanting to remember, even though he often did these days, since he spent much of his time at Greenline and passed her house each morning when he ran his daily six miles, the deserted mansion crumbling into disrepair, like Miss Haversham and her bridal feast, that the Townsends abandoned after Mimi's horrible death.

Other photos. Anna in the one he'd stolen from her. Rose as a girl, the one Uncle Jimmy had given him as a joke, saying, *here, she can be your picture bride*, when Gordie was a boy and was still thrilled by the romance of all things Chinese. He searched for one of Stella but there weren't any. Had he destroyed them all? He vaguely remembered having some. But why all these shots of Sammi, a dozen, more, even one of him with Sammi against a nondescript daytime urban background, probably New York, taken when? By whom? He flipped it over. Scrawled on the back in her loopy handwriting was the date, October 15, 1977, a date he couldn't help but remember, because after dropping off Sammi that night, Anna had ended things between them early the next morning in his car, simply announced after she'd climbed off his lap—*By the way, I'm leaving for Paris next week. Been nice, white boy*—and left without a forwarding address or number.

The photos, they were enough to make a grown man . . . he *did* weep, worn out by his isolation, inexplicable even to himself and certainly to everyone else. Fatigued by death and its stain, everywhere in his vicinity. For whom and what did he weep? Mimi perhaps? And Anna? Even Stella, the woman of whom his father strongly, *vigorously* approved. All the love he couldn't tend to or nurture, seeds merely, young shoots bursting through which never blossomed into maturity. Infatuations over the likes of Rose, a bestial beauty. The force of Sammi's presence.

In short, Gordie suffered from a surplus of "goils," a word that made him laugh when he was eight and first read it in the score for "Manhattan," among the seldom-sung lyrics of the third stanza, a rhyme for "spoil." The music belonged to Mimi's Uncle Arthur, and Gordie pulled it out of the giant piles of sheet music in their home. The Townsends loved Broadway glitter and the magic of moving images. Mimi's dad *might or might not have been Rosemarie's lover* Mimi whispered when they were seven, but Gordie never dared ask his mother who gazed longingly at James Townsend at social affairs— back in the days when the better homes of Greenline still threw parties—something which did not escape Gordie's notice.

When Mimi fell in love with her mad, murderous paramour—a painter he said he was—Gordie went on a rampage. He had been seventeen. Girls from Greenline's public high school, only too glad to succumb to the rich boy from the coast. Girls from private high schools, in their competitive bid for boys. College girls who thought he was older. Young wives who knew he wasn't. The older Mrs. Robinsons in all the tony suburbs to which he had entry as well as the chicks at the clubs in Manhattan where velvet cords proved no barrier to wealth.

Within two years, his list read as follows: Amy, Barbara, Cathy (there were at least two named Cathy with a C as well as one with a K), Deidre (she was older), Freida (Scandinavian), Harriet (too heavy but with an astonishingly succulent mouth), Iris, Janet (English with Emma Peel legs), Moira (the bad Irish girl, from Catholic school of course who lived up to the image), Nora, Olga (Greek and perpetually angst ridden), Patricia (not Patti but one who didn't shorten her name, only her skirts), Rita, Sue (like Cathy, there were multiple Sue's), Terry (tomboy virgin, who wrestled), Ursula, Vera (the one over forty who predated *The Sensuous Woman*), Wendy, Yvonne (*everyone* should know Yvonne even though he never read Dubus' story), Zelda. As morbid as his list making was—he kept track with dates and the alphabet, looking for the Q (there was a Queenie but she didn't count because it was only her nickname) and X, which he didn't find many of till after '79, as Chinese migrants of all stripes trickled into America with their "alphabet" that provided names with Q's, X's, Z's as well as G's and E's—he felt that morbidity even when he could have been excused for wild young oats, it became the pattern to which he succumbed in between the girls and women he professed to love. He ceased and desisted the list making, especially when he met Stella, but on their wedding day he disappeared into some woman's bed and crawled out too late to make it on time, and after that the list making continued, quadrupling at least, until Sammi.

The idea. What *was* the idea? Was there an idea? Not to ever pay for sex the way Harold occasionally did before meeting Isobel, the way Kenton would, especially in Asia as if it were his right as the great white hunter? The way he suspected Mark had to for years, because his parents slept together only as long as it took to have him and no longer, or so it seemed to Gordie when he was old enough to wonder about these things. As jealous as he was of Jack Hwang making eyes at Rosemarie, which Jack did until she died, Gordie was certain their "affair" remained entirely platonic.

Sammi! The *force* of that woman's presence! It all came back to him now as he flipped through the stack of photos. Had he believed her then? And all those other times when she seemed to fit so absolutely into his inner life? That day, the first time she came to Greenline, that moment when they stood by his bedroom door and kissed, he did not doubt her sincerity. How different from Mimi who, upon being told of the promise, made a face and said *that's the sickest thing I've ever heard,* and insisted on making love to him there just to "break the spell" as she called it, and at sixteen, he wasn't about to say no. He hadn't dared tell any woman after that until Sammi, not even Stella, although Stella wouldn't have laughed, would have just taken it in stride because in her family, such a promise would never need to be extracted, because in her very Chinese family, the idea of what was proper was a principle that required no further discussion.

He began to tear all the photos of Sammi into strips. It was stupidity, telling her he wasn't sure he could go through with the marriage. It would have been easy enough to let her catch him in some compromising situation, to let her dump him publicly and hang on to dignity, of a sort. Instead, she had gone to see his mother, told her that Gordie was every bit as bad a two-timing cad as her husband whom *everyone* knew slept around quite publicly (this was not strictly true, but Sammi had a talent for fiction when required) and *everyone* knew she was doing it with Jack Hwang, and Rosemarie was cowed by the force of this young woman's anger and lies, the same fury she could not herself articulate because it had always been easier to pretend Mark simply, didn't, really, exist, (since he was gone half the time anyway) and to be reminded, to be *humiliated* by this snip of a girl who went around *slandering* her and Jack (or so she believed) was more than Rosemarie could bear, being by then quite a bit more frail and insecure as age and drinking and the loss of beautiful youth caught up with her, and she slid into a long depression for well over a year, there was only Jack Hwang, the faithful, to comfort her, upset as she was at her son towards whom she remained cool for quite a time.

Later, much later, after everyone either believed that Gordie had deliberately vanished or was the victim of foul play, Reg and Annabel recalled the charred remains of the photos in the fireplace. Even the box was burnt. As for Colin Kenton's counterfeit identity kit, which Reg had trashed without ever opening, the police didn't know that there was anything to ask. When Reg discarded it after Kenton's death, Annabel had cautioned her husband, *what if a next of kin,* but Reg was determined, declaring, *who'd claim him?* Wanting to rid their home of the detritus that was the man, and since no one had called in the month before Kenton's demise, let alone shown up or sent condolences for the funeral, despite notices in American, Asian and Australian papers the young master insisted on placing, that ended that discussion.

Interlude

So maybe Bino's wrong about Gordie and me. If I really were in love with this man in my world, his life should have turned out better, sweeter. Or at least easier.

March, 2003

Before he left on the Northwest flight with Larry Woo, Gordie told Reg and Annabel that he was going on a journey. His bags were packed and the garage door opened.

Reg surveyed the scenario. "And will you return, Master Gordon?"

"Quit being droll, Reg. You know how to reach me."

"That we do. Have a safe trip."

After his departure, Annabel said. "Something doesn't feel right. I'm worried. Perhaps we should call . . ." she stopped abruptly.

"Who? Mrs. A's lawyers? Hardly."

"Harold Haight?" she ventured.

"Let's wait and see if he calls."

"Fair enough. Where do you suppose he's going this time?"

It had become Gordie's practice, in the last fifteen or so years, to call Reg with a local number whenever he arrived at his destination. Reg expected to hear anywhere from within twenty-four to forty-eight hours after he left. Even when Gordie departed from the city, rather than from Greenline, he would usually call Reg from his last domestic airport of embarkation, at which time he might, if he remembered to do so, tell Reg where he was headed. The arrival of the cellphone simplified matters in this regard, although since Gordie only traveled internationally, reaching him still required at least a local cellphone number to avoid the absurdly high incoming charges to his U.S. based number. At least, this had been Gordie's practice while Rosemarie was alive. Since her death, this was only his second trip anywhere; the first had been to Beijing, shortly after he had told Harold he wanted to give away his money. It was, as far as Reg knew, the only time the young master had visited the Chinese capital. So he was surprised when Gordie said nothing about the trip. Of course, Gordie could be strangely morose whenever he didn't drink, which he hadn't after returning that time.

Annabel wrote all Gordie's country codes on a map. Most of these were in Asia.

Fifty hours later, Gordie still hadn't called.

"Do we worry yet?" Annabel asked at breakfast.

Her husband did not reply. Annabel did not like that because it meant he was flummoxed, a state abhorrent to butlers. "If you don't ring his cell phone I will."

"That raises two questions."

"Which are?"

"If he's removed the SIM card, will we be able to tell? And if he hasn't left the country, why would he call?"

"Ah," she said. "I hadn't thought of the second."

Seventy-two hours later, Gordie rang to say he was in Detroit.

"Master Gordon, we were worried. You didn't call us." Reg thought there was something slightly different about his voice but couldn't decide what.

"No news is good news."

Reg said, "And will you be returning this evening?"

"I will. Can you manage a steak tonight?"

"I'm sure Annabel can."

The steak sat on the grill, uncooked all evening because Gordie never came home. His cell phone rang into voicemail until the battery died. It was never found.

January, 2008

That winter, the chimney at the Haddon estate came alive most nights. It was unseasonably warm, and had anyone been watching, they might have wondered at so many fires in such balmy weather. But Greenline along the coast was deserted; the few remaining residents were elsewhere for the winter and in all the abandoned, shuttered mansions, what creatures that stirred did not pay heed to these signs of life at their neighbor's.

Reg's excuse to Annabel was that this would save fuel, the price of which had risen since last winter. She did not question this. The stockpile of logs might as well be used up before they left. *In the spring, we'll leave in the spring* he had promised her, because it would allow them sufficient time to get both the grounds and house in order, after which the estate lawyers could contract maintenance. It was not that they were being kicked out. The estate could not be sold as long as Harold continued his staying tactics in Gordie's favor. No matter how quickly Rosemarie's lawyers wanted the sale, as long as Gordie could not be declared legally dead, there remained the possibility that he could turn up married with child and reclaim his home. And as long as it still was his home, it was theirs too, because Rosemarie's will made that much clear and Harold, Annabel knew, would defend their rights as long as he could since he, like Reg, would never believe Gordie had died and left them.

But Annabel wanted to leave. Annabel had had enough of the deserted, cavernous Haddon mansion where *only the ghosts of misery live now,* as she said to her favorite nephew. Their own home, one she had decorated herself over time, patiently, longingly, awaited them on the other side of Haddon Way. The colors were warm, earth tones, with lovely floral accents, not like this empty, white mansion. Even the paintings on the walls felt dead and would be better off in a museum. It would be a blessing to retire, to have her various nephews and nieces and family come to stay with them, so that she could feed them and look after them, because they couldn't visit at the estate. *Let's face it,* as she once told her favorite niece, *it's the Ashberry home and has been as long as I've lived there even though Reg persists in calling it the Haddon home and still gets so upset about Rosemarie that I don't say anything about that anymore. We're old anyway so what does it matter now? I just want to live out our last years in peace.*

As January threatened to merge into May, it was all Annabel could do not to shriek at her husband that it was time, please, to leave, please leave.

She remained patient though, this one last time, holding herself in check as Reg kept finding more and more to take care of in this prolonged shutting down of the estate, as he methodically cleared and stored Gordie's things. Besides, she knew how much it pained Reg to say goodbye, even if he didn't let on, and felt it best to leave him be. The Greenline mansion was his only American home which, after all the years he'd lived there, was the only home he really had.

Half a year before Master Gordon disappeared Reginald had told him he and Annabel wished to retire and leave the estate. Probably in another year or so. It had been early afternoon and Reg went to the sun room to find him. He was, as usual, at the piano.

Gordie stopped playing and looked up at Reg. "Retire?" he said, surprised. "But you're still young."

"That's kind of you to say, sir, but I am over seventy and Annabel's not exactly a vernal hen."

"But what will you do?"

"Entertain, sir."

Gordie smiled and his amusement comforted Reginald. It had not been easy, working up to saying this. The specter of Rosemarie Haddon, accusatory, hovered around him and he knew it was best to leave, as much as he hated the idea of severance.

He continued. "We won't be far away, sir, and if you ever needed us, you'd only have to call, or email. Annabel's quite good on the computer."

"That she is."

"You know we'd never abandon you if you needed us."

"I know that, Reg. Thank you."

Master Gordon had been almost perfunctory. It puzzled Reg at first, but later that afternoon, Gordie came to him and asked for a cup of tea. He could have been a boy again, sneaking into the servant's quarters where his parents did not allow him to go. He looked serious, even a little sad, and Reg was thrust back to yet another of those *moments of our wounded child,* as Annabel named them, those times the boy retreated in hiding from parental wrath, despair and life without reason blowing up in his face again.

"Ceylon or Earl Grey, sir?"

He reflected longer than he usually did while Reg waited. "Do we have any of that Chinese gunpowder green?"

"Very good choice, sir."

Gordie laughed. "Don't, Reg. You sound too much like a Merchant-Ivory film."

"I do what I can to amuse, sir."

When the tea was ready, they sat together at the small, round table which had once graced a tea shop in an English village and which Annabel had found in a thrift shop, or so its story went.

"It is good," Gordie said.

Reg waited. The young Master would eventually speak; it was his pattern.

A long moment of companionable tea sipping followed.

Then. "I'll miss you both."

"And we you, sir."

"But I do understand."

"Thank you, sir."

"Will Harold...?"

"We'll be more than taken care of. I'll make all our arrangements with Mr. Haight. He's always very easy to discuss financial matters with."

"You'll let me know if there's any problem?"

"Of course, sir, but I don't anticipate any."

They could hear Annabel in the kitchen next door whipping egg whites for the meringue.

"Reg, why do you suppose Mother...?"

The look in his eyes was painful to Reginald. He knew exactly what he meant—*why does Mother love a stranger more than me?*—although Master Gordon would never say that. Instead, what Gordie said after a long pause was *oh never mind.* It was just like the very first time the boy had come to him, after Mark had argued with Rosemarie, slammed the door and left. The engine roar was a rapid exit down the driveway and he did not return for a month. The morning Mark returned, Gordie had come to him. *Reg, doesn't Father like it here?* What he had told the young master was that *people didn't always know what they wanted* and Gordie had replied *okay, never mind.*

Reg said. "You mean, about her will?"

"Yes. You were there, right, when she had it drawn up?"

"I was, sir."

"Imagine wanting to sell our home. Why would she even think that? Do you know why?"

He paused, struggling to find something for the master that would provide solace and perhaps a little peace. "Perhaps she thought you might find it too much to care for."

"Really Reg? Do you really believe that? And what was that silly clause all about? Me having a child?"

"I think." He stopped. The face of the teenage Rosemarie flashed— pretty, bright, happy—long before life killed her spirit. That girl had never been mean. Never.

"Yes?" Gordie's face was expectant.

Reginald wished he could find a way out. He knew it wasn't what really troubled the master, but they both knew better than to raise the subject of Jack Hwang. Finally. "I think," he said slowly, "she just wanted you to have someone to make you happy, sir. A family, I mean."

Gordie glanced at his tea, took another sip. "Thank you, Reg." A few minutes later, he left. It was the only time he had ever broached the subject of his mother's will.

The will, the one she had made in 1988 with its mocking clause, about her son producing a legitimate heir within twelve years after her death, was because Rosemarie's believed she would never live beyond eighty. Gordie would be in his mid-fifties by the time the clause kicked in, still young enough to father a child but wholly unlikely to do so. But Reginald knew it was the second clause that pained Gordie, that the house would go to Jack Hwang's charity if he did not marry and produce a child within that time.

Afterwards, Reg made up his mind to cross Rosemarie for sure, the one and only time he ever would. He would never tell the young master or anyone else. Not even Annabel.

Reginald chose his most important incendiary night with care. He had secreted Rosemarie's second will in his safe box down in the wine cellar. Annabel almost never went there, but the young master did so with some regularity. However, Gordon would never touch anything in the box, of that Reginald was fairly certain, and besides, the Master had been gone for a long while now.

A slight sensation of guilt twigged. He did not normally keep secrets from his wife, at least not about anything significant. Annabel was away, having left the day before to visit her favorite niece up in Montpelier, Vermont. He was completely alone.

Now, in the wine cellar, he read the will one last time.

The earlier will, the one that Rosemarie's lawyers still thought was their client's latest, was superseded in her own hand and witnessed only by Reginald at the end of '96, a few months before her death. She had summoned him to her bedside, because she seldom left her room anymore by then.

You need two witnesses, don't you, madam? Reginald had asked when she handed it to him to witness.

Rosemarie Haddon glared at her faithful servant. *Just get Annabel to sign it when she comes back later. She'll do it if you tell her too, you know that. Now please just sign this Reginald, and arrange to have it sent to my lawyers.*

She's drunk, he told himself, because she was a little tipsy. She isn't in her right mind. Yet here she was, almost eighty-four, still alive, and Gordie showing no inclination to marry, never mind bear a child. *My lawyers were the ones who wanted that clause. I know my son well enough to know he doesn't give a rat's ass about anyone except himself.*

It wasn't true, Reginald wanted to say. Gordon has a big heart, so big it takes in too much for his own good. But he remained silent.

Anyway, Jack Hwang will make good use of the estate, and it'll all be for a good cause.

She sat up in bed and poured another martini out of the shaker on her bedside table. *Why are you still standing there?*

I'm sorry madam. Will there be anything else?

No. And Reginald, don't you cross me on this.

His mistress' voice came back to him as he took stock of the cellar. That morning, he had awakened from a dream of Gordie, aged around fourteen. As dreamscape eroded, what Reginald heard the boy say was, *it has to be white, all white,* and then he saw the image of an empty, white wall.

Over breakfast, he tried to puzzle out the meaning of his dream. Annabel would have worked it out. She always could. Reginald rarely remembered his dreams but when he did, they struck him as significant, since the need to do so must be instinctive. It was the white room, of course, but what he was trying to recall was whether or not Gordie really had ever said that to him (he could reasonably assume that he had but Reginald knew being reasonable did not always suffice in matters to do with the young master).

After breakfast, he removed the spare skeleton key from his butler's cabinet, went upstairs and unlocked Gordie's room. Late morning light flooded the bare white walls in this east-facing sanctuary. There were no curtains or blinds. Reginald often wondered how the master ever slept. The undisturbed room, which Annabel cleaned weekly, seemed as empty and bare now as it had for years, going way back to well before his disappearance, to Gordie's childhood. These same walls had once burst with imagination—Tin Soldier, Pooh Bear, Mad Hatter, Peter Pan, Water Babies, Pied Piper, Jack on a Beanstalk, the Twelve Wild Swans and Seven Dwarfs—all the images Rosemarie had had painted on the nursery walls in richly muted colors when she, finally pregnant again at thirty-five, dreamt of a boy. Reginald had been little more than a boy himself then, barely eighteen but already assistant to his uncle, the Haddons' long-time butler, a confirmed bachelor, the man who had taken him in when he had been orphaned at age eight, the year Rosemarie miscarried. Gazing at the blank walls, he could almost see those colorful pictures of childhood, the ones that Gordie had, one night without warning, painted over white. Gordie had been around thirteen and Rosemarie did not realize her masterpiece was gone until several months later.

What was Gordie trying to tell him?

He did one last check because this room had secret hiding places everywhere. Once they had decided to leave and close up the estate, he and Annabel had ferreted out what they could, but some missing clue might explain the Master's disappearance. He opened the closet, emptied of all the clothes that once hung there. Annabel had found what they thought was the last hiding space, the top section of the side panel which proved to be a false one that opened to a shelf where Gordie had stored two photos. One was of his parents, smiling at a party, *circa* the late fifties. The other was of Stella Shih in her wedding dress. Annabel cried when she saw these. Reg comforted her, said Gordon probably forgot they were there and was unlikely to have looked at them again, and that perhaps this was better after all.

The built in drawers were all empty, as he opened one after another in sequence. When he reached the bottom drawer, he felt around its base. He had done so previously, as it seemed an obvious place for a secret space, but found nothing. Something made him try again, and he tapped and pressed all over the smooth white surface and heard the boy's voice saying, *white, white* and then he recalled the last thing of his dream, Gordon saying, *listen to me, listen,* and just at that moment his finger found the point along the edge that gave way and there it was, the last hiding hole, from which he removed a cassette tape.

Closing up the room for the last time, he locked the door and headed to the cellar.

He spent a peaceful afternoon taking inventory. Little had changed since the last check some four years earlier; five bottles gone, but Reginald could account for every one of those consumed at dinners by the master, alone, no guests.

Before dinner that evening, he lit a fire and burned the second will. He suspected Jack Hwang never knew, because he hadn't said anything after her death. He would have done if he thought he could get the estate right away as Rosemarie had wanted. Besides, Reg was certain Rosemarie didn't see Jack again after she made that second will, since he controlled all visitors to her bedside and had turned Jack away the one time he had come because Rosemarie was asleep. And then she was dead and gone.

Over dinner, he played the tape which looked to be relatively new. His master's voice spoke.

"A Chinese scholar's greatest sanctuary is his room. There is a table on which to spread the scrolls of rice paper, the container for the ink stone which is ground into a foul smelling liquid, and the depression to hold the brushes. Behind him on the bookshelf are the paperback classics, printed on lightweight rice paper with a sewn binding, all of which adds to the weightlessness of his endeavors. In college, I used to visit a certain history professor's home, with its huge library of books, mostly hardbacks, and marvel at the weighty aura of that room. It was overpowering. In Chinese studies, there is a handful of classics to master that suffice to make you sound schooled (since how many Americans could contradict or challenge that knowledge anyway?). I looked at the syllabus

in my freshman year and decided that yes, this I could do, this tonal language that was best acquired by repetitive rote memorization, because I sing, and repetition is how you remember melodies and lyrics.

It was that or Vietnam.

I burnt my draft card, I'm sorry to say. Sorry, not because the war was right, which it wasn't, but because it disappointed Dad and estranged us. He died without ever quite forgiving me.

Dad had become part of the 375th Squadron of the 14th Air Force Group under Claire Chennault, the Flying Tigers, and they went to China in June of 1942. Mark was old by standards, but, as he frequently pointed out, guys over thirty made it to "ace" status, something that eluded him. In '48, he left Pacific American to start a flying school, and then Korea happened, and Mark went because he was that kind of man.

Rabbits don't fight. They copulate and look cute, at least, that's what I told Mother. Rosemarie Haddon Ashberry glared at me, but the tremor of a smile gave her away.

What I didn't tell her then, or ever, was that I had registered myself as a citizen abroad, using Jimmy Kho's address in Hong Kong. I did this during my trip there in '65. Dad didn't know of course. He would have grasped the implications of Draft Board 100, based in Washington D.C. for Americans overseas, and from which hardly anyone got called. Also, I had drawn a high number.

So I am sorry I burnt my draft card because it was an irrelevant act.

There were times in my childhood I tried to make myself dream about Dad as a great war hero with Mother as his adoring bride. If I could dream them into a unit, they might become one for real. There was a unit, after a fashion, but not from the pages of any guide to parenting. Or marriage. Their marriage was a compass to steer clear of the institution.

Gordon, boy, you're not one of those goddamned ho-mo-sexuals, now, are you? Mark shouted at me outside Sterling Library. He had driven to New Haven when Mother told him I was planning to switch my major to music. I did not sing at Yale or in high school or anywhere Mark could hear, and for years what I did was tape myself singing jazz, accompanied by recordings of Monk or Coltrane or Evans or just about anyone. It was my own private karaoke.

Mother loathed jazz. Mother loathed, despised, reviled; the verb dislike never sufficed.

I gave away my wealth and became famous for a moment. Fame was not the point. Rather, I desired a future because the present did not hold. The future is exemplary."

Here the tape ended. We're not certain what Reginald did with it.

. . . A KISS

The last time I saw Gordie, it was a little over a year later, just before the ox year dawned. He was sitting at the far end of the bar at Morton's in Hong Kong when I walked in at Happy Hour. Sitting in *my* seat, I thought, annoyed. The one by the lamp against the wall where I read. I plunked down way at the other end.

"Hey," I said. "Why aren't you in New York?"

He raised his scotch in a toast. "老朋友 *Lao peng you*. Long time no see."

I signaled Joseph for my usual. "It's almost autumn 'old friend,' don't you know?"

He didn't speak. My usual drink arrived. Vodka martini, up, slice of lime. "Well," I offered, raising my glass. "To you." I sipped, then added, "and dreamers with empty hands?" He would know those lines from *Autumn in New York*.

"I quit singing," he said, "especially that one."

"Why?"

"Richard Gere wrecked it for me." He gazed at the rain pelting the city. "Of course, everyone's wrecking everything for me these days."

"Melodrama does not become you, my friend."

"You should talk. What hope have I left?"

"There's always," and here I sang, "*tomorrow, tomorrow . . .*"

"Not the O'Hara aria. Not from you."

We have always sung-bantered like this, about the possibilities of our existence, famished for reality as we are. It gets *me* through my fractured life. What his excuse is I'm still figuring out. Maybe I'll never really know.

We were the only two in the place. Betty Carter was belting out her rendition of *Isn't It Romantic* over the P.A. *He'll kiss me every hour / Or he'll get the sack!*

I invariably end up here, at this bar in the Sheraton, whenever Hong Kong rains. Joseph the chief bartender calls me his rain date. I let Gordie be at his-my end because he seemed to want the solitude. It doesn't matter how long you've known someone, if he doesn't want to talk, there's no point insisting.

We drank in silence for another ten minutes or so. Then he stood, knocked back his drink and dropped three red bills on the bar. "Gotta go," he said. "Good seeing you."

He came over, took my right hand, leaned down and licked my lower lip, the way he likes to, with a quick flick of his tongue. "Blueberries," he said, "hint of orange. X-woman, your diet's improved."

I rested my left hand on his arm a brief moment. "Thanks to you, my man. Now, scat. It's time."

He gave me this long, wistful smile I know only too well and raised my hand to his lips. His kiss was softer than rabbit fur. "Don't be a stranger."

"I'll think about it."

"I mean it." He wasn't grinning. "Cross the heart, if you have one that is, and hope to die?"

The shadow of his rabbit hole darkened the doorway, cutting off the last ray of daylight that glimmered through the west-facing glass walls.

I loosened his grip. The back of my hand caressed his chin. "Time to go," I said gently. "Party's over."

The rabbit hole swallowed him slowly and he slid into its inky dark. Our fingertips brushed lightly. He did not struggle but there was panic in his voice. "Don't be a stranger, okay? *Zai jian?*"

In our last mind fuck, Teresa Teng Laih-gwan 鄧麗君 sang.
Goodbye my love Wo di ai ren, zai jian 我的愛人再見。

This plaintive tune could almost make a woman weep. I blew an air kiss at his vanishing form. As the last of him disappeared, he sang. 總有一天能再見 *There'll be a day we'll meet again.* 那醉人的歌聲... 醉人 *zui ren*, literally, this "drunken person's" song but a *zui ren* is the one who intoxicates, bewitches, captivates and perhaps owns you in the end.

The last of him vanished into the hole from which he came.

Bye Doc, I started to say. But didn't.

END

ACKNOWLEDGEMENTS

Gratitude to all those real-life characters who inform and even people my fiction, without whom I would not understand this world I've tried to create. There are many more than I can name, but specifically, the following deserve special recognition:

Alvin (Bino) Realuyo, Filipino poet, novelist, activist and change agent. Author of The Umbrella Country and *The Gods We Worship* for the years of friendship and literary inspiration.

Christopher Phillips, who studied Chinese at Yale around the same time Gordie did, for his generosity in assisting my early research for this novel.

Chuck Jones (1912 – 2000), creator and animator of Bugs Bunny, who knew that the line between illusion and life was, at best, imaginary.

Cliff Deeds who hired me into Federal Express and was a great boss, and by extension Fred Smith, pilot, CEO and founder of the company that has informed my fiction in ways both strange and profound.

Consuelo de Saint Exupéry (1901-1979, b. Consuelo Suncin Sandoval Zeceña), author of *The Tale of the Rose* and wife of the fighter pilot author of *The Little Prince*.

Dennis Engbarth, journalist, long-time resident of and advocate for the state of Taiwan, for Chinese tea and sympathy over the years.

Greg Chako, jazz guitarist, arranger and composer, for teaching me all about jazz.

Jack Tchen, historian and director of the Asia/Pacific/Americas Studies program at New York University for our conversations.

James Salter, American fiction writer *extraordinaire*, especially for his novel *The Hunters*.

John Adams, composer, for *Nixon in China* and *The Chairman Dances*, the music that was the catalyst to begin this book.

Lau Kin Wai, art curator, gourmet, essayist who, among many other achievements, gave the graffiti street artist known as "The King of Kowloon" an art space in our city, and to whom I will always raise a glass of red wine.

Lieutenant General Claire Lee Chennault (1893 – 1958) founder of the Flying Tigers.

Maryann (Mimi) Barker, the best boss ever who remains a friend long after our stint at the law firm we both toiled at, a work world that exposed me to everything I didn't yet know about class and inequity in America.

Mike Ingham, Hong Kong resident and professor of English at Lingnan University, Hong Kong, for continuing to believe in and inspire the young minds of our city, even in a subject as "irrelevant" as literature.

Nigel Collett, historian, author of *The Butcher of Amristar*, and founder of the Tongzhi Literary Group of Hong Kong for his friendship and literary gaydar.

Tim Woo, librarian at the University of Otago, Dunedin, New Zealand, for his assistance in providing me a comparative guide to Chinese transliterations which was invaluable in my early work on the novel.

And to the entire gang at Morton's of Kowloon, for the fabulous bar (and restaurant) they run, my refuge through typhoons both fictional and real. Especially **Joseph, Tek, Rochan** and **Steve.**

Thanks also owed to the **Chateau de Lavigny**, Lausanne, Switzerland, for my time there as a resident writer where several important discoveries were made about this novel.

I have borrowed and quoted from the lyrics of numerous jazz standards and other songs from the Great American Songbook as well as from other musical numbers. The following compositions & renditions have been particularly informative or meaningful for this book:

1932: "Isn't It Romantic" Music by Richard Rodgers • Lyrics by Lorenz Hart

1935: "My Romance" Music by Richard Rodgers • Lyrics by Lorenz Hart

1936: "Easy to Love" Music & Lyrics by Cole Porter

1937: "I'll Take Romance" Music by Ben Oakland • Lyrics by Oscar Hammerstein II

1938: "Prelude to a Kiss" Music by Duke Ellington & Irving Mills • Lyrics by Irving Gordon

1940: "I Could Write a Book" Music by Richard Rodgers • Lyrics by Lorenz Hart

1961: "My Romance" live recording by Bill Evans on his album *Waltz for Debby*

1976: "再 見我的 愛 人" a.k.a "Goodbye My Love" famously recorded by 鄧 麗 君 a.k.a. Teresa Teng

March 27, 1976 Live Recording, Lee Theatre, Hong Kong:
http://www.youtube.com/watch?v=VcyUueeccBk

作曲：平尾昌晃 Music by Hirao Masaaki • 作詞：文采/文君 Lyrics by Wen Cai

1993: "Isn't It Romantic" recorded by Betty Carter from her album *Inside Betty Carter*

CPSIA information can be obtained
at www.ICGtesting.com
Printed in the USA
LVOW08s1205190217
524728LV00001B/221/P